I0002274

Evolving Legacy Systems
Transitioning to Microservices and Cloud-Native Architectures

Copyright © 2024 by NOB TREX L.L.C.

All rights reserved. No part of this publication may be reproduced, distributed, or transmitted in any form or by any means, including photocopying, recording, or other electronic or mechanical methods, without the prior written permission of the publisher, except in the case of brief quotations embodied in critical reviews and certain other noncommercial uses permitted by copyright law.

Contents

4

Preface

Welcome to *Evolving Legacy Systems: Transitioning to Microservices and Cloud-Native Architectures*, a comprehensive guide written to support technologists in modernizing their technological infrastructures. The aim of this book is to offer detailed, structured insights into the process of transitioning from traditional, often monolithic systems to the more dynamic, scalable, and maintainable realms of microservices and cloud-native architectures.

In today's rapidly evolving technological landscape, businesses face mounting pressure to upgrade their IT infrastructure to remain competitive. Legacy systems, although stable and sometimes aligned with certain business needs, often fall short in areas such as efficiency, scalability, and integration with modern technologies. This book directly tackles these challenges, focusing on practical strategies, architectural considerations, and essential practices needed for a successful migration.

This book covers a diverse range of topics, including:

- An in-depth exploration of legacy systems, examining the factors that drive the need for replacement or upgrade.

- A comprehensive analysis of microservices architecture, delving into its principles, benefits, and implementation strategies.

- Insights into cloud-native environments, with an emphasis on how these architectures enhance and support microservices.

- Practical steps and considerations for assessing current systems, planning migrations, managing data, and ensuring seamless transitions.

- Discussions on the ongoing maintenance and security considerations required in new architectures, ensuring systems remain not only updated but sustainable and secure.

Our target audience for this book is broad, encompassing IT professionals, software developers, system architects, project managers, and C-level executives who are contemplating or actively engaging in the migration from legacy systems to modern technological paradigms. Additionally, academic professionals and students in the fields of computer science and software engineering may find the discussions and methodologies presented here valuable for both theoretical and practical learning contexts.

Ultimately, our goal is to equip readers with the knowledge and tools necessary for making informed decisions and implementing migration strategies that align with business objectives and technological advancements. We strive to present our content in a clear and direct manner, ensuring that even complex concepts are both accessible and actionable.

We hope that this book will serve as an essential resource in your journey to evolve legacy systems into more future-ready solutions, facilitating innovation, efficiency, and competitive advantage in your respective fields. Happy reading and successful migrating!

Chapter 1

Introduction to Legacy Systems and the Need for Migration

Legacy systems, characterized by outdated technology that often impedes growth and innovation, remain prevalent in many organizations. These systems, while potentially stable and well-understood, generally lack the flexibility, scalability, and efficiency required by modern business demands. This chapter discusses the critical nature of these systems, their common challenges, and the imperative of migrating to more advanced architectures such as microservices and cloud-native solutions to stay competitive and agile in today's fast-paced market.

1.1 What are Legacy Systems?

Legacy systems refer to software applications, hardware technologies, or entire IT systems that have been in use within an organization for a significant amount of time and continue to serve critical business processes despite possible inflexibility and outdated technological foundations. These systems are generally based on earlier computing paradigies and might use software or hardware components that are no longer supported by vendors. Such systems pose unique challenges yet

11

are indispensable due to their deep integration into crucial operational workflows.

Primarily, legacy systems utilize technology stacks that have not kept pace with contemporary advancements in IT infrastructure and software architecture. The backbone technologies are often those that preceded the emergence of cloud computing, big data technologies, or widespread mobile integration. Typical characteristics include an extensive use of monolithic architectures, reliance on physical servers as opposed to virtualized environments, and the use of older programming languages and databases that may no longer be efficient or secure by today's standards.

For instance, many banking and insurance companies continue to utilize mainframe computers running applications in COBOL—a programming language that saw its peak usage decades ago. These applications are mission-critical yet consistently resist modification, integration, or scaling attempts. The disconnect between the functional requirements of such systems and the capabilities provided by modern IT solutions exemplifies the foundational definition of legacy systems.

Operationally, legacy systems may also exhibit performance inefficiencies or growth-related limitations that arise from age-related degradation or from architectures not designed to scale with increased loads or network demands that modern user bases require. The associated hardware often requires a specific operational environment and skilled technicians familiar with their maintenance and operations, which may lead to increased costs and logistical challenges.

Financially, while legacy systems are often seen as fully depreciated capital expenses with minimal direct costs, they introduce indirect costs in terms of operational inefficiencies, increased downtime, and the high cost of specialized personnel. Application-specific challenges also occur, particularly in terms of integrating these older systems with new applications or data streams necessary for modern business analytics and decision-making processes.

However, despite these challenges, legacy systems remain entrenched in many sectors due to the significant capital, effort, and time required to replace or upgrade them. These systems often continue to provide a particularly reliable processing functionality that newer technologies have not yet adequately replicated. Moreover, the data contained within and processed by legacy systems can represent decades of accumulated knowledge indispensable for current business operations or compliance requirements.

12

Thus, understanding legacy systems in the context of both their technological and operational characteristics is crucial for any planning related to upgrading or migrating to more contemporary technology solutions like microservices or cloud-native architectures. This understanding ensures cognizance of the risks and requirements that will inform subsequent strategies and decisions in a migration or modernization project.

1.2 Characteristics of Legacy Systems

Legacy systems, by their very definition, refer to software applications, platforms, or technologies that, while once cutting-edge, are now significantly outdated. These systems are still in use today, not because they provide the best functionality or user experience but due to their deep integration into the organizational infrastructure and the significant resources required to replace or upgrade them.

Firstly, legacy systems are often marked by their monolithic architecture. In a monolithic design, various components and functionalities are tightly interwoven into a single, indivisible unit. This architecture complicates updates or modifications as changes in one area can inadvertently affect other areas, leading to a higher risk of system disruption during maintenance or feature updates.

- A core characteristic is the lack of modularization, which limits the ability to make isolated improvements without risking the stability of the entire system.

- Such systems frequently operate on outdated code that few developers are proficient in, complicating maintenance and update efforts.

Secondly, these systems often utilize obsolete technologies which may no longer be supported by vendors. This discontinuation of support not only poses significant security risks, as security patches and updates are no longer available but also leads to compatibility issues with newer technologies and systems.

Example: A legacy system running on Windows XP might face numerous security vulnerabilities as Microsoft ceased providing regular security updates for Windows XP since April 2014.

The reliance on older hardware is another characteristic trait of legacy systems. Aging hardware, which is often essential for the operation of the software, poses a risk in terms of availability and reliability. Replacement parts for such hardware are scarce and expensive, and a hardware failure could result in extended downtime and data loss.

```
1   // Example of outdated hardware dependency
2   // This pseudocode represents a system check for hardware compatibility, typical in
        a legacy system.
3   if (system_hardware.date < 2005) {
4       alert("Hardware upgrade required. System may not perform optimally.");
5   }
```

Interoperability is a further obstacle. Legacy systems typically have poor support for integration with modern systems and software, which hampers data exchange and workflow automation across the business landscape. This isolation affects operational agility and can inhibit the adoption of new technologies that enhance business processes.

- Legacy systems often feature bespoke, proprietary interfaces that are not compliant with modern API standards, making them rigid and isolated.

From a financial perspective, legacy systems represent a significant operational expense mostly attributed to maintenance costs and the labor-intensiveness required to keep them running. Operations on such platforms require specialized skill sets that are becoming increasingly rare in the labor market, further inflating these costs.

```
1   // Example of a function designed for a legacy system that requires specialized
        knowledge to maintain.
2   void ProcessLegacyData(SystemData data) {
3       // Complex and outdated processing logic
4       process_data(data);
5       if (data.requiresSpecialHandling) {
6           handle_special_case(data);
7       }
8       // Ongoing maintenance requires in-depth knowledge of the system's
            idiosyncrasies
9   }
```

Finally, these systems frequently operate beneath optimal performance levels. They struggle to handle increased workloads or scale up effectively to meet growing business needs, often resulting in longer processing times and reduced responsiveness. This diminished performance can negatively impact customer satisfaction and business operations.

The characteristics highlighted above collectively illustrate why legacy systems, despite their stability and the critical functions they serve, form a barrier to business innovation and growth. They encapsulate the urgent need for architectural evolution to align with contemporary demands and technological progress. By understanding these defining attributes, organizations can better strategize their modernization efforts to minimize risks and maximize the effectiveness of their IT investments.

1.3 Challenges and Limitations of Legacy Systems

The challenges presented by legacy systems impede organizational agility and innovation, reflecting a significant barrier to business growth and efficiency. This section delineates these challenges and spotlights their limitations in detail.

Technical Debt and Compatibility Issues

Legacy systems accumulate technical debt, a metaphorical representation of shortcuts and compromises in software development that necessitate future refactoring. High levels of technical debt lead to increased maintenance costs and reduced system reliability. A prevailing compatibility issue arises when these systems struggle to integrate with modern technologies or platforms, thereby hindering seamless data exchange and process automation. Consider a banking software developed in COBOL; integrating this with modern Java-based APIs for real-time data analytics can be cumbersome and error-prone.

```
1  // Example of integrating COBOL with Java (conceptual only)
2  CALL 'EXTERNAL_API' USING DATA-EXCHANGE-AREA.
3      MOVE RETURNED-DATA TO JAVA-BASED-STORAGE.
```

Error: DATA TYPE MISMATCH BETWEEN COBOL AND JAVA API.

Scalability and Flexibility Limitations

Legacy systems were often designed with fixed hardware and user limitations, making scalability a major issue. As user demand increases, these systems become unable to handle the load efficiently due to their monolithic architecture. Moreover, modifying a legacy system to add or alter functionality carries substantial risks due to their tightly coupled components; making small changes can inadvertently affect other

15

non-related areas, complicating updates and improvements. Mentions of scalability often conjure up images of server crashes during critical business hours, a tangible consequence of these limitations.

```
1   // Pseudocode to illustrate system crash due to high load
2   IF userConnections > maxCapacity THEN
3       SHUTDOWN server
4   ENDIF
```

Increased Operational Costs

Maintaining legacy systems often requires senior engineers with specific expertise in out-of-date technologies, whose salaries are statistically higher than those proficient in newer technologies due to rarity. The operating costs are further escalated by the inefficient use of resources such as energy consumption by obsolete hardware which does not meet contemporary energy standards.

- Salaries for expert COBOL programmers

- Costs for running mainframe systems

- Budget allocation for emergency repairs and downtime mitigation

Security Vulnerabilities

Older software does not receive frequent updates or patches, making it susceptible to new forms of cyber attacks. Legacy systems, by their nature, lack modern security features like multi-factor authentication or encrypted data storage, making them easy targets for security breaches.

```
1   // Illustration of an insecure data handling in a legacy system
2   READ FILENAME FROM DATA-ENTRY.
3   OPEN FILE RECORD(FILENAME).
4       DISPLAY "SENSITIVE DATA: ", DATA-ENTRY.
5   END FILE.
```

- Lack of data encryption

- Absence of regular security patches

- Inadequate monitoring tools

Given these challenges, organizations must assess the critical need to modernize or entirely replace their legacy systems to mitigate risks, reduce costs, and enhance operational efficiency and security. The decision to migrate encompasses not only technological considerations but strategic business alignment to ensure competitiveness in the market.

1.4 Reasons to Migrate Legacy Systems

Legacy systems, while often stable and reliable, pose several long-term strategic, technical, and financial challenges that directly impact an organization's agility and efficiency. Migrating these systems to modern architectures like microservices and embracing cloud-native technologies has become essential for several compelling reasons.

- **Technological Obsolescence:** Legacy systems frequently rely on older technologies that are no longer supported, posing significant risks of failure and security vulnerabilities. Upgrading to current technologies mitigates these risks and leverages improvements in hardware and software efficiency.

- **Evolving Business Needs:** Modern businesses require flexibility to adapt to market changes and innovations. Legacy architectures typically lack this adaptability, inhibiting the ability to introduce new functionalities efficiently or scale operations dynamically.

- **High Maintenance Costs:** The cost of maintaining outdated systems can be prohibitively high. Moving to modern architectures can reduce operational costs through improved process automation, better integration capabilities, and reduced reliance on specialized skill sets tied to outdated technologies.

- **Integration Challenges:** Legacy systems often exist as isolated silos making integration with other modern systems cumbersome. A modernized architecture facilitates easier integration with other business processes, tools, and applications, leading to enhanced productivity and streamlined operations.

- **Improved Customer Experience:** The expectations of customers evolve rapidly, necessitating systems that can support seamless user experiences across multiple platforms. Microservices and

17

cloud-native architectures provide the agility to update and deploy new features more swiftly and reliably, enhancing customer satisfaction.

- **Data and Analytics:** Old systems typically do not support modern data analytics tools, which hampers decision-making processes. By updating systems, organizations can harness the power of big data analytics to gain actionable insights and drive business intelligence.

- **Risk Management:** The risks associated with legacy systems not only stem from technical failures but also from regulatory non-compliance. Modern systems are designed with compliance in mind, ensuring that the organization adheres to industry standards and regulations, thus mitigating potential legal and financial penalties.

The migration from a legacy system involves the transformation of both the technological base and the operational philosophy to a more contemporary framework that supports ongoing and future business objectives. This strategic decision often necessitalizes restructuring of the legacy codebase, architecture, and deployment methodologies, transitioning towards a service-oriented or microservices architecture that better aligns with current and future enterprise needs. This transition allows businesses to be more responsive to market changes, enhancing their competitive edge, and fostering innovation. Such benefits extended by upgraded systems justify the efforts and investments involved in the migration process, portraying it not just as an operational necessity but as a strategic business move.

1.5   Benefits of Modernizing Legacy Systems

The decision to modernize legacy systems brings a multitude of benefits that can significantly alter the operational dynamics of an organization. These benefits span various dimensions including performance enhancements, cost reduction, improved flexibility, and compliance with modern standards. We will now explore these benefits in depth.

Performance Enhancements

Modernizing legacy systems often results in improved performance. This includes faster processing times, reduced latency, and higher throughput. A critical element in achieving this is the optimization of code and the integration of more efficient, state-of-the-art technologies. Consider an example of a legacy system relying on synchronous processing methods. By transitioning to an asynchronous model, the system can handle more requests simultaneously, thus speeding up overall execution times.

```
1   // Example of synchronous code in a legacy system
2   public void processRequests(List<Request> requests) {
3       for(Request req : requests) {
4           process(req); // Each request is processed one at a time
5       }
6   }
7
8   // Example after modernization to asynchronous processing
9   public void processRequests(List<Request> requests) {
10      CompletableFuture<?>[] futures = requests.stream()
11          .map(req -> CompletableFuture.runAsync(() -> process(req)))
12          .toArray(CompletableFuture[]::new);
13      CompletableFuture.allOf(futures).join(); // Processes requests concurrently
14  }
```

The difference in execution time can be marked as shown in the simulated output below.

```
Execution Time Before Modernization: 500ms
Execution Time After Modernization: 130ms
```

Cost Reduction

Modernizing legacy systems can lead to substantial cost savings. These savings are realized through more efficient resource utilization, reduction in maintenance costs, and the elimination of expensive legacy hardware or software licenses. For instance, migrating to cloud-based services often reduces the need for physical infrastructure and the associated maintenance costs.

- Reduced hardware cost due to optimization of server usage.

- Lower software licensing fees by transitioning to open-source solutions where feasible.

- Decreased maintenance costs as new code bases are more maintainable and require fewer resources.

Improved Flexibility

Legacy systems are frequently criticized for their rigidity and inflexibility, making it difficult to implement new features or integrate with modern systems. Modern architectures, such as microservices, allow organizations to develop and deploy services independently. This modularity supports a more agile development environment, which can adapt more quickly to market or regulatory changes.

```
1    // Legacy monolithic architecture
2    public class Monolith {
3        void processOrder() {
4            validateUser();
5            computePayment();
6            scheduleDelivery();
7        }
8        // Other methods
9    }
10
11   // Example of a microservice architecture
12   public class OrderService {
13       @Autowired
14       UserService userService;
15
16       @Autowired
17       PaymentService paymentService;
18
19       @Autowired
20       DeliveryService deliveryService;
21
22       public void processOrder() {
23           userService.validateUser();
24           paymentService.computePayment();
25           deliveryService.scheduleDelivery();
26       }
27   }
```

Compliance with Modern Standards

Legacy systems often fall short of current security, data protection, and accessibility standards, which can expose the organization to risks and legal liabilities. Modernization projects provide an opportunity to address these compliance issues by incorporating current best practices and technologies that meet or exceed these standards.

Modernizing legacy systems not only aligns with strategic business goals but also addresses technological and market demands. As technology and business practices evolve, the pressure to remain relevant and competitive necessitates these upgrades. The return on investment from modernizing is measurable not only in direct financial gains but also in enhanced operational capabilities and strategic positioning in the marketplace.

1.6 Impact of Digital Transformation on Legacy Systems

Digital transformation involves the integration of digital technology into all areas of a business, fundamentally changing how organizations operate and deliver value to customers. It is not merely about upgrading old software or adopting new technologies, but about revolutionizing business processes and models. For legacy systems, this transformation can have profound impacts, reshuffling the traditional perspectives on IT investments and service delivery.

Firstly, digital transformation compels companies to reassess the roles their legacy systems play in current operations. These systems, often built on outdated architectures, are typically ill-equipped to handle the agility and scalability demands of modern digital business practices. This mismatch can lead to various operational inefficiencies. For instance, legacy systems often require manual processes or rely on batch-oriented operations, which are inherently slower compared to the real-time processing capabilities of modern systems. The latency in processing can lead to delayed insights into market conditions, impacting decision-making processes.

With digital transformation, there is a substantial emphasis on data analytics and real-time data processing. Legacy systems usually suffer from compatibility issues with newer technologies that are designed to leverage data more effectively. For example, integrating a legacy system with modern data analytics tools often requires extensive middleware or custom adapters, which can be both costly and resource-intensive to maintain.

```
1   // Example of a middleware integration code snippet
2   public class DataAdapter {
3       LegacySystem legacySystem;
4
5       public DataAdapter(LegacySystem legacySystem){
6           this.legacySystem = legacySystem;
7       }
8
9       public DataModel adaptData(){
10          LegacyData legacyData = legacySystem.retrieveData();
11          return new DataModel(legacyData);
12      }
13  }
```

Moreover, as organizations drive towards more customer-centric business models under digital transformation, the customer experience becomes paramount. Legacy systems, not originally designed to support high levels of customer interaction or digital touchpoints, often struggle to offer the seamless, personalized experiences expected by today's consumers. This can lead to increased customer churn and missed opportunities in customer retention and acquisition.

The security aspect of legacy systems under digital transformation is also critically important. As the threat landscape evolves with advances in technology, legacy systems become more vulnerable. These systems may not support newer security protocols or integrate well with modern security tools, leading to potential breaches and compliance issues.

- Enhanced risk of data breaches due to outdated security measures.

- Incompatibilities with modern authentication protocols.

- Difficulties in achieving compliance with current data protection regulations.

To address these challenges and to harness the benefits of digital transformation effectively, many organizations opt to either completely replace their legacy systems or incrementally integrate them with newer technologies. This strategic decision typically involves considerations of cost, potential disruptions, and the expected benefits of upgraded systems.

In the context of migrating or integrating legacy systems within digitally transformed infrastructures, it is imperative to undertake a thorough assessment of both the technical debt and the strategic value of existing systems. Organizations must evaluate whether upgrading these systems will indeed lead to improved operational efficiency, better customer experiences, and enhanced decision-making capabilities.

As companies evolve in the digital era, the impact on legacy systems is undeniable. Embracing this change is essential not only for maintaining competitive advantage but also for ensuring operational resilience and scalability in the face of ever-changing market dynamics. Ensuring that legacy systems do not become a bottleneck in this transformation journey is crucial for the continued success and growth of any organization.

1.7 Overview of Microservices and Cloud-Native as Upgrade Pathways

Microservices architecture represents a fundamental deviation from the traditional monolithic design, where all functionalities are tightly integrated into a single service or application. In contrast, microservices design embraces a suite of small, independent services that communicate over a well-defined API to serve a single business capability. This architecture inherently promotes scalability, flexibility, and the continuous deployment of complex applications.

Each microservice in this architecture is developed, deployed, and managed independently. This autonomy allows development teams to adopt the DevOps culture effectively, enhancing both development and operational capabilities. For instance, consider the deployment process; in a microservices architecture, it's possible to deploy services independently without needing to redeploy the entire application. This granular control significantly reduces downtime and improves system resilience. Below is an example code snippet demonstrating a simple microservice in a typical Flask Python application:

```
1  from flask import Flask, jsonify
2  app = Flask(__name__)
3
4  @app.route('/api/service')
5  def my_microservice():
6      return jsonify({'message': 'Hello from Microservice'})
7
8  if __name__ == '__main__':
9      app.run(port=5000)
```

Communication between microservices is typically managed using lightweight protocols such as HTTP / REST or asynchronous messaging systems like Apache Kafka or RabbitMQ. Each microservice remains a black box to others in terms of its internal operations, ensuring that the system's various components remain loosely coupled.

On the other hand, cloud-native architectures are designed to exploit the scalable capabilities of modern cloud environments. These systems are built from inception to reside in cloud ecosystems, benefiting from cloud services and infrastructure. Cloud-native applications harness the potential of on-demand resource provisioning and scalability provided by cloud platforms such as AWS, Google Cloud Platform, and Microsoft Azure.

23

Building applications in a cloud-native environment involves practices such as containerization, orchestration, microservices, immutable infrastructure, and declarative APIs. Specifically, containerization with tools like Docker encapsulates an application and its environment to facilitate consistent operation across different computing environments. The orchestration of these containers is often managed by Kubernetes, which automates application deployment, scaling, and management. The following Python code snippet illustrates a simple deployment scenario using Kubernetes API in Python:

```
1   from kubernetes import client, config
2
3   config.load_kube_config()
4
5   v1 = client.CoreV1Api()
6   print("Listing pods with their IPs:")
7   ret = v1.list_pod_for_all_namespaces(watch=False)
8   for i in ret.items:
9       print("%s\t%s\t%s" % (i.status.pod_ip, i.metadata.namespace, i.metadata.name))
```

Migrating to a microservices architecture or a cloud-native framework from a legacy system requires careful strategic planning and execution. This migration involves decomposing the legacy monolithic applications into individual components that can be managed and scaled independently. Transition strategies might include the Strangler Fig Pattern, where new features are built as microservices and old features are gradually replaced.

Moreover, the adaptability and resilience provided by these modern architectural approaches enable organizations to respond swiftly to market changes and customer needs, significantly reducing the time-to-market for new features and enhancements. Effective use of DevOps strategies and CI/CD (Continuous Integration/Continuous Deployment) pipelines ensures rapid, reliable, and repeatable deployments. This integrated approach to development, testing, and deployment accelerates innovation and improves product quality by catching defects early in the lifecycle through automated testing.

The decision to adopt microservices and cloud-native technologies thus reflects an organization's commitment to leveraging technological advances to enhance operational efficiency, foster innovation, and deliver superior value to customers. As these technologies continue to evolve, they redefine the landscape of application development and deployment, offering robust solutions that address the complexities and challenges of modern business environments.

24

1.8 Case Studies: Success Stories of Legacy Migrations

Case studies of successful legacy migrations provide valuable insights into practical strategies and methodologies for transitioning from traditional monolithic architectures to microservices and cloud-native solutions. This section presents detailed descriptions of several enterprises that successfully executed legacy system migrations, highlighting the initial challenges, strategic decisions, and final outcomes of these endeavors.

Case Study 1: Financial Services Company

A prominent financial services company faced significant scalability and agility problems with its legacy banking system based on mainframe technology. This system, though stable, was extremely expensive to maintain and cumbersome to update with new features.

- **Implementation Approach:** The firm opted to incrementally migrate its services to a series of interlinked microservices. This modular approach allowed for minimal disruption during the migration process.

- **Technologies Used:** The new architecture was built using Docker containers orchestrated with Kubernetes, and the services were mostly developed in Java leveraging Spring Boot, which was chosen for its robust ecosystem and compatibility with legacy systems.

The transition process employed a `Strangler Fig` pattern, wherein new features were gradually built as microservices and old functionalities were simultaneously deprecated. The financial firm encountered the following primary benefits:

```
- Reduction in operational costs by 40% within the first two years.
- Increased new feature release speed by threefold.
- Enhanced ability to scale services during high-demand periods.
```

25

Case Study 2: Retail Giant

A leading global retailer was constrained by an outdated inventory management system which made real-time stock updates nearly impossible, leading to significant losses in sales opportunities and customer dissatisfaction.

- **Implementation Approach:** The retailer decided to completely overhaul its system with a cloud-native approach directly, deciding against a gradual migration due to pressing competitive and operational pressures.

- **Technologies Used:** AWS Cloud services were employed, including AWS Lambda for serverless functions, Amazon S3 for storage, and Amazon DynamoDB for a high-performance NoSQL database system.

To ensure a smooth transition, the company conducted extensive planning and testing phases focused on achieving minimum downtime. This was supported by heavy use of blue-green deployment techniques.

```
- Enhanced system performance and response times by up to 50%.
- Reduction in downtime during system upgrades from hours to minutes.
- Enabled real-time data processing leading to a 30% boost in customer satisfaction ratings.
```

Case Study 3: Healthcare Provider

A national healthcare provider used a legacy system that was inefficient in handling the increasing amount of patient data and did not comply with new regulatory standards. The migration objective was not only to enhance technological capabilities but also to improve compliance and data security.

- **Implementation Approach:** The migration plan involved adopting a microservices architecture tailored to the specific needs of healthcare delivery and regulatory compliance.

- **Technologies Used:** The project utilized HIPAA-compliant services from Microsoft Azure, focusing heavily on Azure Kubernetes Service (AKS) and Azure DevOps for continuous integration and delivery.

The healthcare provider applied a phased approach, starting with less critical services to reduce risks and gather insights before full-scale implementation.

```
- Met new regulatory standards within the first migration year.
- Enhanced data security and patient privacy measures significantly.
- Increased the efficiency of patient data processing by over 40%.
```

These case studies exemplify the transformative potential of legacy migrations when approached with careful planning and appropriate technology utilization. Each scenario underscores the importance of a strategy tailored to specific organizational needs and the considerable benefits that modernizing legacy systems can bring to a business. The experiences detailed here serve as robust examples for other enterprises considering similar modernization initiatives.

1.9 Common Myths and Realities about Legacy System Migration

Migrating legacy systems is replete with misconceptions that can skew stakeholders' expectations and impede rational decision-making. An informed perspective on these myths, contrasted against documented realities, is essential for the systematic planning and successful execution of migration projects.

Myth 1: Legacy System Migration is merely a technology refresh.

Many perceive legacy system migration as simply updating the technology stack or installing the latest software versions. However, the reality is far more complex.

- Migration involves rethinking how applications interact with each other. It usually requires significant changes in architecture, such as moving from monolithic to microservices-based architectures, which necessitates a fundamental redesign of the application.

- Realignment of business processes often accompanies a migration project, with the aim to exploit new technical capabilities to increase business efficiency and effectiveness.

Myth 2: Migration should always result in cost reductions.

Expectations often lean towards significant cost savings as a direct result of migrating from a legacy to a modern system. While cost efficiency is a potential outcome, it should not overshadow the main goals of migration.

- Initial costs of migration can be substantial, accounting for new software, infrastructure, training, and downtime during the transition.

- Savings and ROI typically materialize over time through enhanced efficiency, flexibility, and scalability rather than immediate cost reduction.

Myth 3: The existing functionality will be replicated exactly in the modern system.

A common misunderstanding among stakeholders is that the new system will function exactly like the old one but simply perform faster or on a modern platform.

- Migration offers an opportunity to refine or remove outdated functionalities that may no longer be necessary, aiming for not just replication but improvement and optimization.

- Due to the differences in technology capabilities, certain legacy features may not be directly replicable or may be irrelevant in the context of modern operational practices and user expectations.

Myth 4: Legacy System Migration is predominantly an IT Department project.

Migration projects must not be visualized as solely IT-driven initiatives. They have broad organizational impacts and require cross-departmental collaboration.

- Beyond the IT department, engagement from departments like Finance, HR, Sales, and Operations is crucial. Their insights can influence the design and functionality of the migrated system based on practical daily-use scenarios.

- Procuring buy-in and fostering an understanding across the organization about the migration's benefits ensure smoother transitions and operational coherence post-migration.

28

Myth 5: Once migration is completed, the process ends.

Assuming that the end of the physical migration marks the completion of the process is a simplistic and potentially risky outlook.

- Post-migration phases often involve significant periods of adjustments, optimizations, and training.

- Continuous support and iterative enhancements are necessary to adapt more effectively to the new system and to address emerging business needs and technological developments.

Understanding the distinction between myths and realities in legacy system migration is pivotal. This awareness ensures realistic planning, fosters stakeholder alignment, and enhances the likelihood of achieving strategic objectives through the migration effort. Addressing these myths systematically can liberate decision-makers to approach this complex transition with accurate expectations and grounded strategies, thereby enabling more measured and effective project execution.

1.10 Preparing for a Legacy Migration Project

Migration from legacy systems to modernized architectures involves several pivotal and systematic preparations to ensure success and minimize disruptions. This section delineates these essential steps, focusing on strategies to design and execute a legacy migration with precision.

Firstly, conducting a comprehensive assessment of the existing legacy system is crucial. This involves cataloging the technologies currently in use, understanding the data flow and dependencies, and identifying all integration points both internally and with third-party services. Tools like static code analyzers and dependency mapping software can automate aspects of this process, providing detailed insights into the complex web of interactions within the legacy systems.

```
Output example of a dependency mapping tool:
- ModuleA
   -> ModuleB (database dependency)
   -> ModuleC (service dependency)
- ModuleD
   -> ModuleE (API dependency)
```

Following the system assessment, the next step is to prioritize components based on various criteria such as business value, complexity of migration, and risk of service disruption. This prioritization helps in planning the migration sequence that aligns with business objectives while considering technical challenges.

- Critical business features that generate the most revenue should be prioritized for early migration to quickly benefit from modern infrastructure capabilities.

- Components with the least number of dependencies might be migrated earlier to reduce initial complexities and gain momentum.

- High-risk components, such as those handling sensitive data or requiring high availability, should be meticulously planned to ensure security and compliance are maintained throughout the transition.

Defining the target architecture is also essential. Decision-makers should align on whether a microservices architecture or another form of cloud-native solution is suitable. This involves determining the scaling needs, resilience requirements, and preferred technology stack. Collaborations with architecture experts and using domain-driven design can help in scoping out the required changes and envision the end state effectively.

Once the architecture is scoped out, setting up a pilot project can serve as a proof of concept to validate the migration strategy, tools, and processes. The pilot should ideally represent a microcosm of the larger system but have limited scope so as to contain potential impacts. Critical factors to monitor in the pilot include performance metrics, fault tolerance, and system behavior under load.

Stakeholder communication is integral throughout the migration project. Regular updates, adjusted timelines, and shared learnings help

---

```
1  foreach module in Legacy System do
2      if module is independent then
3          Migrate module to new architecture;
4          Test module functionality in new environment;
5      else
6          Identify and document dependencies;
7          Plan sequential migration with dependent modules;
```

---

maintain alignment and manage expectations across the organization. Additionally, establishing a feedback loop with end-users can provide insights that might influence adjustments in the migration approach.

Finally, preparing for continuous improvement post-migration by setting up mechanisms for ongoing monitoring and optimization assures that the system remains robust and adaptable. Leveraging A/B testing, performance monitoring tools, and user feedback channels will be instrumental in this context.

This systematic approach to preparing for a legacy migration project lays a solid foundation for modernizing legacy systems, facilitating a transition that not only updates technology but also enhances overall business competitiveness and agility.

Chapter 2

Fundamentals of Microservices Architecture

Microservices architecture is a method of developing software systems that focuses on building single-function modules with well-defined interfaces and operations. This approach offers enhanced modularity, making applications easier to develop, test, deploy, and, more importantly, scale. The chapter delves into the basic principles of microservices, their core advantages over traditional monolithic architectures, and essential strategies for effective implementation.

2.1 Introduction to Microservices

Microservices architecture is a software design approach that structures an application as a collection of loosely coupled services, which implement business capabilities. Each service is a self-contained unit and operates independently; this modular nature enables better scalability, ease of deployment, and technological diversity.

Key to understanding the microservices architecture is its contrast with the traditional monolithic software design. In a monolithic architecture, all components of the software are interconnected and interdependent. While this can simplify initial development, it complicates later adjustments and scalability because any small change affects the entire system. Furthermore, scaling necessitates duplicating the entire application, using more resources than typically required. The microservices approach seeks to address these inefficiencies by dividing functionalities into separate, autonomous services, each running its process and communicating with lightweight mechanisms, often an HTTP resource API.

The independence of services allows individual deployment, scaling, and development of each microservice without affecting the operations of others. This is made possible through the use of containers that encapsulate a microservice with all its dependencies in a lightweight runtime environment. Containers can be deployed on any system without the need for additional configuration, thus enhancing the portability of the application.

- Each microservice is designed around a business domain, adhering to the principle of Domain-Driven Design (DDD). This design principle ensures that the development teams can understand and develop the application in alignment with business goals.

- Microservices are decentralized by nature. This decentralization applies to both data management and the governance of the services themselves. Services typically manage their own database, either different instances of the same database system or entirely different database systems.

- Continuous delivery and deployment are integral to microservices architecture. With services that are independently deployable, it becomes possible to implement continuous deployment pipelines where each service is developed, tested, and deployed without waiting for a full application release.

The architecture supports polyglot programming and persistence, which allows teams to choose the best programming language, data storage, and tools that are optimal for each service's functionality. Such diversity is practical because the complexity of each microservice is limited and clearly defined by its boundaries.

In terms of design, a core practice within microservices architecture is the adherence to APIs for service communication. These APIs are meticulously designed to allow minimal coupling and clear contracts between services. The API gateway pattern often plays a central role; it acts as a single entry point that routes requests to the appropriate services. This setup not only eases the development and operational

34

processes but also provides a layer of abstraction that can enhance security by preventing direct access to back-end services.

Despite the multitude of technical advantages, adopting a microservices architecture is not without challenges. Microservices introduce complexity in the deployment and operation stages, requiring robust automation, and monitoring practices. Nevertheless, when implemented with careful planning and suitable tools, the microservices architecture can significantly enhance application scalability, resilience, and agility. Organizing an application as a suite of small services enables more rapid, reliable, and frequent delivery of large, complex applications.

2.2 Key Principles of Microservices Architecture

Microservices architecture advocates a suite of small, autonomous services that work together. Each service executes a unique process and communicates through well-defined APIs. Understanding the core principles guiding microservices architecture is critical to successfully implementing and maintaining systems based on this model.

Decomposition

Decomposition is the act of breaking down a complex application into smaller, independent parts. In the context of microservices, the application is typically decomposed by business capability. Each service should represent a single business function and possess the necessary data to perform that function effectively.

- Identify distinct features within the application that can operate as standalone services.

- Ensure that each microservice is small enough to be managed by a single team, promoting agility and faster cycles of development.

- Services must own their domain data and logic ensuring loose coupling and high cohesion.

Independence

Microservices must be developed, deployed, and scaled independently. This independence is key to enhancing the agility of the development process and improving the resilience of the overall application.

- Use modular programming techniques to create services that do not share data structures with other services.

- Deploy services in isolated environments to prevent changes in one service from affecting others.

- Each microservice should have its own database to ensure full autonomy.

Do One Thing Well

Following Unix's philosophy, each microservice should focus on one capability and perform it well, without being distracted by other functionalities. This principle simplifies development, testing, and maintenance of each service.

- Services should be designed to solve a specific problem or perform a singular function effectively.

- Avoid the temptation to add multiple functionalities into a single service which can lead back to a monolithic design.

Black-Box Design

Microservices should be designed as black boxes, where the internal implementation details are hidden from other services. Interfaces, in the form of APIs, provide the only communication bridge between services.

- Define APIs that abstract the internal workings of the service and present a clear, simple interface to its consumers.

- Use API versioning to manage changes without breaking service consumers.

Decentralized Data Management

Microservices architecture recommends decentralized data management, allowing each service to manage its database. This reduces database management complexity and eliminates any single point of failure.

- Employ different data storage technologies that best fit the service's needs.

- Ensure transaction consistency through distributed transactions or eventual consistency as per the service requirement.

Automate Everything

Automated testing and deployment are crucial to managing the complexities of multiple services evolving in their life-cycles independently. Automation ensures consistency, reliability, and speed in both deployment and operation phases.

- Use continuous integration and continuous deployment (CI/CD) pipelines to automate testing and deployment processes.

- Implement monitoring and logging across all services to quickly detect and resolve issues.

The principles of microservices architecture require thoughtful application of design paradigms tailored to specific business needs. Implementing these principles encourages the development of scalable, flexible, and resilient software architectures. As microservices continue to evolve, adherence to these core principles serves as a foundational guide for both developing new applications and decomposing existing monolithic systems.

2.3 Advantages of Microservices over Monolithic Architectures

The transition from monolithic architectures to microservices architectures defines a shift from a unified, single application development model to a more fragmented approach where each function of an application operates as an independent service. This architectural style brings numerous benefits that cater to the dynamic nature of modern digital demands.

Improved Scalability

One of the primary advantages of microservices is improved scalability. In monolithic architectures, scaling can become problematic as the entire system must be scaled even if only one aspect of the application experiences higher demand. Conversely, microservices allow for selective scalability. Individual components can be scaled independently without the need to scale the entire application. This targeted scalability not only makes the system more resource-efficient but also provides agility in resource management during variable loads.

- Scalability of high-demand services without affecting the entire system.

- Efficient utilization of resources corresponding to the need of individual components.

- Enhanced agility in managing service availability during peak loads.

Faster Deployment Cycles

Microservices accelerate deployment cycles, enabling organizations to bring services to market more quickly than with monolithic structures. Each microservice is developed, tested, and deployed independently which considerably reduces the complexity and duration of these processes. This independent deployment capability allows for frequent updates and quicker introduction of features or fixes enhancing responsiveness to market or regulatory requirements.

- Incremental changes are easier and faster to manage.

- Reduces the risk associated with deployment by isolating change impacts.

- Continuous integration and continuous deployment (CI/CD) practices are easier to enforce, accelerating overall release processes.

Enhanced Fault Isolation

Fault isolation is more straightforward in a microservices architecture because services are independent. If an error occurs in a single microservice, it does not necessitate taking down the entire system. Each service can also implement its specific fault-tolerance and failure management mechanism, tailored to its operational peculiarities and risks. This containment limits the scope of any given failure and minimizes disruption to the overall operation of the application.

- Independently managed services mean less downtime and higher availability.

- Bugs or failures in one service do not impact others, maintaining the system's operational integrity.

- Service-specific fault tolerance strategies can be developed and applied.

Technological Heterogeneity

Microservices provide the flexibility to use different technology stacks tailored to the particular needs of each service. This allows developers to utilize the best tools for specific tasks without committing to one technology or language throughout the entire application. This heterogeneous approach not only optimizes performance but also facilitates innovation and adoption of new technologies without disrupting existing services.

- Freedom to choose the right tool for each service's needs.

- Facilitates the adaptation of emerging technologies.

- Promotes innovation through diversity in technology choices.

Improved Maintainability and Understanding

Monolithic applications can grow to be large and complex, making them difficult to understand and maintain. Microservices split the application into smaller, manageable pieces, each handling a specific aspect of the application's functionality. This modularization simplifies understanding the codebase and maintaining the system over time.

Developers can focus on specific areas without needing to comprehend the full scope of the application, which also reduces the learning curve for new team members.

- Smaller, focused code bases are easier to manage and understand.

- Modularization helps new developers onboard more quickly as they need to understand smaller, discrete components.

- Enhances long-term maintainability through improved modularity.

This section has elucidated how the decomposition of applications into microservices not only enhances technological flexibility and operational efficiency but also scales more adeptly in accordance with the demands of modern software environments. Each microservice operates autonomously, yet coherently, ensuring that technological updates and service enhancements can be executed swiftly and more securely. This architecture not only facilitates robust, scalable applications but also aligns with progressive business strategies optimizing for quick adaptation and resilience.

2.4 Components of a Microservices Architecture

The successful implementation of a microservices architecture requires several foundational components that work together to create a robust, scalable, and flexible system. Each component plays a critical role in ensuring that the system functions as intended, and therefore must be carefully designed and implemented. These components include individual microservices, service discovery mechanisms, API gateway, centralized configuration, and logging and monitoring systems.

Individual Microservices: The core unit of a microservices architecture is the microservice itself, which is a small, autonomously deployable service that performs a single business function. Each microservice runs in its own process and communicates with other services via a well-defined interface using lightweight mechanisms such as HTTP/REST, gRPC, or message queues.

```
1   // Sample microservice interface in HTTP/REST
2   @GetMapping("/api/user/{userId}")
```

```
3  public ResponseEntity<User> getUserById(@PathVariable String userId) {
4      User user = userService.getUserById(userId);
5      return ResponseEntity.ok(user);
6  }
```

Service Discovery and Registry Mechanisms: In a dynamic environment where microservices can be frequently scaled up or down, and instantiated on different servers, a robust service discovery mechanism is essential. This component allows services to register themselves and to discover the locations of other services automatically.

```
Service A available at 192.168.1.5:8080
Service B available at 192.168.1.9:8090
```

API Gateway: The API Gateway is a critical component acting as a single entry point for all client requests to the backend services. It handles request routing, composition, and protocol translation, and can also implement security policies such as authentication and rate limiting.

```
1  // Sample API Gateway routing configuration
2  routes:
3    - id: user-service
4      uri: lb://USER-SERVICE
5      predicates:
6        - Path=/api/users/**
7      filters:
8        - StripPrefix=1
```

Centralized Configuration: Managing configurations across multiple services can be challenging; hence, centralized configuration services are used. These services provide a central place to manage external properties for applications across all environments.

```
User-service configuration:
    database-url: "jdbc:mysql://localhost:3306/userdb"
    database-user: "admin"
    database-password: "admin123"
```

Logging and Monitoring Systems: As microservices are distributed in nature, centralized logging and monitoring become crucial for troubleshooting and ensuring system health. These systems collect logs and metrics from all microservices and provide tools for querying and visualizing this data.

```
1  // Sample log message structure
2  {
3      "timestamp": "2023-03-01T12:00:00Z",
4      "serviceId": "user-service",
5      "level": "INFO",
6      "message": "User retrieved successfully"
7  }
```

In addition, a typical microservices architecture might also incorporate other key components such as distributed caching, message brokers for asynchronous communication, and externalized state management services. Together, these components contribute to the resilience, agility, and scalability of a microservices-based system, allowing organizations to better handle their growing and evolving software landscapes. Each component must be carefully orchestrated to work seamless synergy, thus supporting the overarching goals of modern software applications - agility, scalability, resilience, and fast deployments.

2.5 Communication Patterns in Microservices

Communication patterns in microservices are crucial as they determine how independently deployed services interact with each other to form a complete system. Each microservice is designed to perform a specific business function and it communicates over a network, necessitating effective and robust communication strategies to ensure system reliability, latency, and throughput. The complexity of communication increases with the number of services, making it vital to choose the right communication pattern. Here, we explore several common communication patterns used in microservices architectures, namely Synchronous RESTful API communication, Asynchronous messaging, and Event-driven communication.

Synchronous RESTful API Communication: In this pattern, a client sends a request to a service and waits for the response. Communication happens in real time and the client blocks the progress until the response is received. The REST architectural style is predominantly used with HTTP/HTTPS protocols and typically leverages standard methods such as GET, POST, PUT, and DELETE.

Consider a practical scenario involving a user attempting to place an order in an e-commerce system. The user service needs to communicate with the inventory service to check item availability and then with the order service to place the order. Here is an example of how synchronous RESTful communication might look in a typical application:

```
1  import requests # Pre-requisite: pip install requests
2
3  def check_inventory(product_id):
4      response = requests.get(f"http://inventory-service/check?product_id={product_id}
       ")
5      return response.json()
6
7  def create_order(user_id, product_id):
```

```
 8    order_data = {'user_id': user_id, 'product_id': product_id}
 9    response = requests.post("http://order-service/create", json=order_data)
10    return response.json()
11
12    # Example usage
13    inventory = check_inventory(101)
14    if inventory['available']:
15        order_response = create_order(user_id=1, product_id=101)
16        print(order_response)
```

In the above example, all calls are blocking; the client performing the REST calls waits for the server's response before proceeding.

Asynchronous Messaging: Asynchronous communication decouples client and server interactions by introducing a message broker or queue. Services send messages without waiting for an immediate response, making this pattern highly suitable for operations that require background processing or where immediate consistency is not critical.

For implementing asynchronous communication, technologies like Apache Kafka, RabbitMQ, or AWS SQS are commonly used. Here is a pseudocode illustrating how an order service might interact with an inventory service asynchronously:

Algorithm 1: Asynchronous communication using message queues

---

1 **Function** CreateOrder(*userID, productID*):
2   SendMessage("order_queue", "CreateOrder", {userID, productID})
3   **return** "Order creation command sent."

Event-driven Communication: This pattern is a form of asynchronous communication where services produce and consume events. An event (e.g., 'item added to cart', 'order placed') is a significant change in state broadcasted through an event stream. Services react to these events and process them accordingly. This pattern encourages designing systems based on loosely coupled event-driven components, which improves modularity and scalability.

For instance, when a new order is placed, an 'OrderPlaced' event is published to an event bus. Other services such as the billing service and the delivery service subscribe to these events and react when they occur. This model is especially favoured in systems where state changes need to be propagated across multiple services efficiently and where each

43

service must only know about the events, not the internal workings of other services.

Each of these communication patterns has its place in microservices architectures, and the choice of pattern depends largely on the specific requirements and context of the application. As systems scale, a combination of these patterns often emerges. Through careful selection and implementation of communication patterns, developers can build resilient, flexible, and scalable microservices systems. While the initial complexity of managing these patterns can be high, the long-term benefits for maintenance and scalability justify the effort.

2.6   Service Discovery and Registry Mechanisms

Service discovery and registry are fundamental components in the microservices architecture that address the challenge of locating and communicating with various services within a distributed system. In environments where microservices are dynamically located across multiple hosts and can scale in and out independently, hard-coding service endpoints can lead to brittle configurations and failures. Therefore, effective service discovery mechanisms are crucial for operational robustness and agility.

At its core, service discovery involves two main processes: registering services and discovering services. During registration, a service instance provides its contact information to a service registry, which acts as a database of active service instances. The discovery process then allows any service in the system to query the registry to find other services' endpoints dynamically.

Service Registry: The service registry must be robust, up-to-date, and easily accessible. High availability and consistency of the service registry are paramount, as any failure or stale data can lead to incorrect service communication and potential system failure. These are typically implemented using either a client-side discovery pattern or a server-side discovery pattern.

Client-side Discovery Pattern: In the client-side discovery pattern, the client service is responsible for querying the service registry, resolving the necessary service endpoints, and handling the load balancing of requests. Here is an example of how service registration and lookup might be coded:

```
1   class ServiceRegistry {
2       private Map<String, List<String>> services = new HashMap<>();
3
4       public void registerService(String serviceName, String serviceUrl) {
5           services.computeIfAbsent(serviceName, k -> new ArrayList<>()).add(serviceUrl
            );
6       }
7
8       public List<String> getServiceUrls(String serviceName) {
9           return services.getOrDefault(serviceName, Collections.emptyList());
10      }
11  }
```

Server-side Discovery Pattern: The server-side discovery delegates the service discovery responsibility to a dedicated router or a load balancer. The client makes a request to the router, which then queries the service registry and directs the client's request to the available service instances. This pattern can reduce complexity on the client side and centralize discovery logic.

Each of these patterns has its advantages and limitations. Client-side discovery allows clients to respond more agilely to changes in service availability without waiting for an intermediary. Conversely, server-side discovery simplifies client logic by abstracting the discovery process, but it introduces a new critical component that must be highly available and scalable.

Implementation Tools and Technologies: Several tools and technologies facilitate the implementation of service discovery mechanisms. Popular options include:

- **Eureka**: Originally developed by Netflix, Eureka is an AWS-compatible service registry that provides predominantly client-side service discovery.

- **Consul**: HashiCorp's Consul offers a more comprehensive toolset by providing a service registry with integrated health checking, key/value storage, and support for both client-side and server-side discovery.

- **Zookeeper**: Apache Zookeeper is often used in conjunction with Kafka for message synchronization across services but can also support basic service registration and discovery.

- **Kubernetes**: While Kubernetes is generally known for container orchestration, it also provides robust service discovery capabilities built into its platform.

Critically, when selecting a service discovery mechanism, one should consider factors such as the deployment environment (e.g., cloud vs. on-premise), integration complexity, team familiarity with the tool, and specific use case requirements.

In ensuring seamless interactions between microservices, the choice and implementation of service discovery and registry mechanisms require careful planning and consideration. By abstracting the details of service locations and enabling dynamic response to changes in the environment, these components play a critical role in enhancing the flexibility and resilience of microservices architecture.

2.7 Inter-Service Communication: Synchronous vs. Asynchronous

Inter-service communication (ISC) is a foundational aspect of microservices architecture that determines how independently deployed services interact with each other to form a cohesive application. Two dominant forms of ISC in microservices are synchronous and asynchronous communication. Each method has its implications on the system's performance, resilience, and scalability.

Synchronous Communication: In synchronous communication, the client sends a request to the server and waits for the response before continuing its execution. This method is characterized by its straightforward implementation and direct style of communication.

- **HTTP REST:** One common protocol for synchronous communication is HTTP/REST. It is widely used due to its statelessness and compatibility with the web technologies. Here is an example of a synchronous HTTP GET request implemented in a microservices architecture:

```
1   import requests
2
3   def get_order_details(order_id):
4       response = requests.get(f"http://order-service/orders/{order_id}")
5       order_details = response.json()
6       return order_details
```

```
{
    "orderId": 1234,
    "productIds": [101, 102],
    "status": "Shipped"
}
```

- **Blocking nature:** The major drawback of synchronous communication, such as the HTTP REST example provided, is its blocking nature. The service requesting data is blocked until it receives the response from the provider service. This can lead to increased latency and vulnerability to failures in the provider service.

Asynchronous Communication: Contrastingly, asynchronous communication allows a service to issue a request and then proceed with other processing without waiting for the response. This non-blocking approach can significantly improve the system's efficiency and fault tolerance.

- **Message Queuing:** One effective implementation of asynchronous ISC is the use of message queues. Services communicate by sending messages to a queue, which are then processed by the receiving service at its own pace.

```
1   import pika
2
3   connection = pika.BlockingConnection(
4       pika.ConnectionParameters('localhost')
5   )
6   channel = connection.channel()
7
8   channel.queue_declare(queue='order_queue')
9
10  def publish_order(order_id):
11      channel.basic_publish(
12          exchange='',
13          routing_key='order_queue',
14          body=str(order_id)
15      )
16      print(" [x] Sent order id %r" % order_id)
```

```
[x] Sent order id 1234
```

- **Decoupling:** Asynchronous methods like message queuing help in decoupling services, allowing them to operate independently. This decoupling reduces the interdependencies among services, enhancing the resilience and scalability of the application.

Choosing between synchronous and asynchronous communication requires examining the specific requirements of each service interaction

47

within the application, such as response time and fault tolerance needs. While synchronous communication may be favoured for its simplicity and direct interactions, asynchronous approaches offer superior flexibility and resilience under high loads or in distributed systems where services are loosely coupled.

Ultimately, ISC in a microservices setup should aim at achieving an optimal balance between system responsiveness and robustness, making informed choices about when to use each communication style based on the contextual needs of the application. As we move further into microservices adoption, these patterns will continue to evolve, influenced by emerging technologies and architectural innovations.

2.8 Database Management in Microservices: Database per Service

The "Database per Service" model is fundamental in microservices architectures, advocating for the segregation of databases across the different services. This approach ensures that each microservice manages its database, thereby adhering to the principles of high cohesion and loose coupling. Effective implementation requires understanding the interaction between independent data stores and the microservices they support.

Each microservice in this model owns a private database that other services cannot access directly. The delineation of database responsibilities addresses several challenges posed by the monolithic database architecture, including cumbersome migration tasks and data model conflicts among various modules of the application.

Core Concepts of the Database per Service Model

The core concept of the Database per Service model hinges on the encapsulation of the database schema and the data access logic within the microservice itself. This encapsulation ensures that the microservice's persistence mechanisms are shielded from other services, thereby fostering autonomy and enabling teams to develop, deploy, and scale their services independently of others.

Key design considerations include:

- **Schema Ownership:** Each microservice owns its schema, which can evolve without coordination with other services.

- **Service API Exposure:** Interaction with the stored data must happen through well-defined APIs rather than direct database queries.

- **Data Duplication:** Common information required by multiple services should be handled through API calls to the respective service owning that data, thereby minimizing data duplication.

Implementing Database per Service

Implementation of this model typically requires selecting the type of database best aligned with the service's needs—whether relational, NoSQL, or even a more specialized database like time-series or graph databases. Here is a practical example illustrating how a microservice might manage its database.

```
1  CREATE TABLE Order (
2      OrderID int,
3      OrderDetails text,
4      CustomerID int,
5      Status text
6  );
7
8  INSERT INTO Order (OrderID, OrderDetails, CustomerID, Status)
9  VALUES (1, '2x Product XYZ', 123, 'Pending');
```

This SQL script represents a simplistic approach where an 'Order' microservice manages orders in an isolated relational database, with the microservice's API serving as the only entry point for manipulating these data entries.

Benefits of Database per Service

Adopting a database per service strategy offers several advantages:

- **Scalability:** Services can scale independently, as they are not bound by database resource constraints shared with other services.

- **Resilience:** Failure in one service's database does not directly affect other microservices.

49

- **Flexibility in Technology Choices**: Teams can pick the most appropriate data storage technology based on the specific needs and characteristics of the service.

Challenges and Mitigation Strategies

While beneficial, the database per service model presents certain challenges:

Data Consistency: Maintaining consistency across different services can be complex due to the distributed nature of databases. Employing patterns like Saga for managing distributed transactions can help in addressing this challenge.

Complex Queries Over Multiple Services: Executing joins or complex queries over disparate services becomes challenging. This can be mitigated by implementing a Command Query Responsibility Segregation (CQRS) pattern that separates read data models from write data models, enabling efficient querying and data updates management.

To conclude, adopting the Database per Service model within a microservices architecture necessitates deliberate design decisions. Challenges such as data integrity and complex transaction management require advanced design patterns and continuous monitoring. Nonetheless, the independence and the scalability achieved by employing this model prove critical in environments demanding rapid adaptation and resilient performance.

2.9 Scaling Microservices

Scaling microservices is a critical aspect of managing and maintaining the robustness and efficiency of applications using this architectural style. By nature, microservices are designed to scale out rather than scale up. This approach not only enhances the application's performance but also its resilience and fault tolerance.

Types of Scaling: There are two primary types of scaling strategies applicable to microservices - horizontal scaling and vertical scaling. Horizontal scaling, also known as scaling out, involves adding more instances of the microservices to handle increased load. Conversely, vertical scaling, or scaling up, entails adding more resources such as CPU or memory to existing instances.

- Horizontal scaling is generally more aligned with the philosophies of microservices architecture because it allows each service to scale independently based on its specific demands.

- Vertical scaling may still be used in certain scenarios but could potentially lead to resource underutilization and is less flexible.

Horizontal Scaling Considerations: When scaling microservices horizontally, several factors must be considered to ensure effective scaling:

- **Statelessness:** Microservices should be designed to be stateless; state management should be delegated to a persistent storage system. Stateless services are easier to scale since any instance can handle any request.

- **Load Balancing:** A load balancer is essential in distributing incoming requests across all available instances of the microservices uniformly. This ensures that no single instance becomes a bottleneck.

- **Service Discovery:** As services scale out, the system must dynamically detect and route requests to new instances. This requires an efficient service discovery mechanism.

Implementing Load Balancers: The configuration and implementation of load balancers greatly affect the scalability and responsiveness of microservices. Load balancers can operate at various levels:

- Level 4 (L4): Operates at the Transport Layer, directing traffic based on TCP or UDP sockets.

- Level 7 (L7): Functions at the Application Layer, providing the capability to distribute requests based on HTTP header information, application data, or cookies.

Challenges of Scaling Microservices: Scaling microservices is not devoid of challenges and here are a few critical ones:

- **Complexity:** As the number of service instances increases, the system becomes more complex to manage. Automation and robust monitoring solutions are imperative to manage this complexity effectively.

51

- **Consistency:** Ensuring data consistency across services can become challenging, especially in a distributed setup where data might be partitioned.

- **Network Latency:** Increased communication between services can lead to higher network latency. Optimizing API calls and using asynchronous communication can help mitigate this issue.

Effective scaling also requires a continuous integration and delivery pipeline that supports automatic scaling based on predefined triggers and metrics. This automates the deployment of new service instances as needed, ensuring that the application can handle increased loads without manual intervention.

Besides the operational aspects of scaling, the strategic use of resources is vital. Leveraging cloud environments can offer auto-scaling capabilities which adjust resources dynamically based on the application needs. Cloud platforms typically provide tools to define scaling policies and metrics, greatly simplifying the scaling process.

Lastly, the observability of microservices during scaling operations is crucial. Monitoring tools and logging mechanisms must be configured to provide real-time insight into the health and performance of each microservice. This data is critical for optimizing scaling strategies and ensuring that the system maintains high availability and performance under varying loads.

By addressing these considerations and challenges, organizations can harness the full potential of microservices to achieve not only operational excellence but also cost efficiency and improved service delivery.

2.10 Challenges and Solutions in Microservices Deployment

Deploying microservices involves several challenges that are quite distinct from the traditional monolithic approach. Each challenge requires specific strategies and tools to ensure a smooth transition and operational stability. This section discusses major deployment challenges and outlines practical solutions.

Complexity in Managing Services: Microservices increase the complexity of the system by decomposing a monolithic application into multiple, smaller services. Each service potentially has its own lifecycle, dependencies, and scaling requirements.

- **Solution:** Employ automation tools for continuous integration and continuous deployment (CI/CD). Tools such as Jenkins, GitLab CI, and CircleCI can automate the testing, building, and deployment processes, reducing human error and improving repeatability.

- Use service orchestration platforms like Kubernetes or Docker Swarm. These platforms help in managing the lifecycle of containers, which typically encapsulate microservices, handling tasks like deployment, scaling, and networking automatically.

Service Discovery and Load Balancing: With potentially hundreds of services, each with dynamic instances, traditional static methods of service discovery and load balancing are not feasible.

- **Solution:** Implement dynamic service discovery mechanisms that allow services to query a central registry to find each other. Tools such as Consul, Eureka, or Etcd can be used as a service registry.

- Employ smart load balancers and API gateways that integrate with these service registries for dynamic routing and load distribution, such as NGINX or Traefik.

Inter-Service Communication: The choice between synchronous and asynchronous communication affects the reliability and coupling between services.

- **Solution:** For synchronous calls, use RESTful APIs or gRPC for strict consistency and validation demands.

- For asynchronous processes, adopt a message broker such as RabbitMQ, Kafka, or ActiveMQ, which allows decoupling of services and ensures reliability even in high-load scenarios.

Data Management: Breaking a monolithic database into a distributed microservice model leads to challenges in data consistency and integrity.

- **Solution:** Adopt the Database per Service pattern, where each microservice manages its own database. This approach reduces dependency conflicts but requires careful handling of transactions and data integrity across services.

- Implement transaction strategies like the Saga pattern, which manage distributed transactions without tight coupling by using a series of local transactions orchestrated by an event-driven process.

Monitoring and Debugging: Microservices can be deployed on different environments and might scale differently, making traditional monitoring and logging inadequate.

- **Solution:** Use centralized logging and performance monitoring tools that can aggregate logs and metrics across services. Tools like Elasticsearch, Logstash, Kibana (ELK stack), Prometheus, and Grafana provide powerful ways to visualize and analyze logs and metrics in real-time.

- Implement distributed tracing tools such as Jaeger or Zipkin to trace the request flow across multiple services and diagnose latency issues or failures accurately.

Configuration Management: Managing configuration across hundreds of services can be daunting, especially with services having varying configuration needs based on the environment.

- **Solution:** Use centralized configuration services like Spring Cloud Config or HashiCorp Vault, which offer secure, centralized management of service configurations and sensitive data across all environments.

- Ensure that configurations can be dynamically refreshed so that services do not need to be restarted when configuration changes.

These challenges, though non-trivial, can be effectively handled by leveraging modern tools and designing systems with best practices in mind. The inherent benefits of microservices, such as enhanced scalability, flexibility, and resilience, make these challenges worth addressing.

2.11 Using Containers and Orchestration in Microservices

The adoption of containers and orchestration platforms in microservices architectures plays a crucial role in the efficient management, deployment, and scalability of services. Containers offer a lightweight, executable package of software that includes everything needed to run a piece of software, including the code, a runtime, libraries, environment variables, and configuration files. This section elaborates on how containers are used within microservices frameworks and the role of orchestration systems in managing clusters of containers.

Containers in Microservices

One of the fundamental benefits of using containers in a microservices architecture is the isolation they provide. Each container operates independently of others and can be executed on any platform that supports the container's runtime environment, thereby enhancing the portability across different systems and infrastructures.

The use of containers begins with containerization of individual microservices. This process involves encapsulating a microservice in a container with its own dependencies. The following listing exemplifies a basic Dockerfile configuration for a simple Python-based microservice:

```
1   # Use an official Python runtime as a parent image
2   FROM python:3.8-slim
3
4   # Set the working directory in the container
5   WORKDIR /usr/src/app
6
7   # Copy the current directory contents into the container at /usr/src/app
8   COPY . .
9
10  # Install any needed packages specified in requirements.txt
11  RUN pip install --no-cache-dir -r requirements.txt
12
13  # Make port 4000 available to the world outside this container
14  EXPOSE 4000
15
16  # Define environment variable
17  ENV NAME World
18
19  # Run app.py when the container launches
20  CMD ["python", "app.py"]
```

This Dockerfile outlines several key steps in container setup: selecting a base image, setting a working directory, copying source code into the

55

container, installing dependencies, exposing a port, and specifying a command to run at startup.

Orchestration Systems

Container orchestration is essential when dealing with multiple containers across different development, testing, and production environments. Orchestration platforms, such as Kubernetes, Docker Swarm, and Apache Mesos, manage the lifecycle of containers. These platforms aid in deploying, scaling, and networking of containers automatically across a cluster of servers.

Kubernetes, in particular, has emerged as a de facto standard for container orchestration in microservices architectures. It offers robust features that support both declarative configuration and automation. The following are key features of a Kubernetes-based orchestration for microservices:

- **Automated Scheduling**: Kubernetes automatically schedules containers based on resource availability and constraints without manual interventions.

- **Self-Healing Capabilities**: It replaces and reschedules containers from failed nodes to healthy ones and can automatically restart containers that fail or do not respond to user-defined health checks.

- **Automatic Scaling**: Kubernetes can horizontally scale container replicas automatically based on CPU or memory usage thresholds.

- **Load Balancing**: It can distribute network traffic among container instances to improve overall application performance and availability.

To deploy a cluster of microservices, a YAML configuration file is typically used in Kubernetes to describe the desired service state. Below is an example of a Kubernetes deployment YAML file for a microservice configured with replicas and resource requests:

```
1   apiVersion: apps/v1
2   kind: Deployment
3   metadata:
4     name: example-microservice
5   spec:
6     replicas: 3
7     selector:
```

```
 8    matchLabels:
 9      app: example
10    template:
11      metadata:
12        labels:
13          app: example
14      spec:
15        containers:
16        - name: example
17          image: example/microservice:v1
18          ports:
19          - containerPort: 4000
20          resources:
21            requests:
22              memory: "64Mi"
23              cpu: "250m"
```

Each microservice deployed through Kubernetes can be monitored and managed independently, offering significant advantages for large-scale systems where hundreds of services interact.

The integration of containers with orchestration tools significantly simplifies the process of managing microservices life cycles and scaling operations. This approach not only improves operational efficiencies but also enhances the robustness and resilience of microservices architectures. As technology and tools evolve, these practices are likely to gain further enhancements, leading to more streamlined development workflows and greater scalability for large-scale applications.

2.12   Success Metrics for Microservices Implementations

The success of microservices implementations can be significantly influenced by defining and monitoring appropriate performance indicators. Effective metrics not only guide the development and operation phases but also provide stakeholders with insights into the impact of microservices architectures on business objectives. This section delineates critical success metrics that are essential for evaluating the health and efficacy of a microservices deployment.

- **Deployment Frequency:** The regularity with which new releases are successfully deployed to production is an essential indicator of the agility and responsiveness of the microservices architecture. High deployment frequencies are typically indicative of

effective CI/CD (Continuous Integration/Continuous Deployment) processes, which are vital in microservices environments
for promoting rapid iterations and improvements.

```
1  # Example: Script snippet to measure deployment frequency.
2  # This script could track deployment attempts and successes.
3  deployments_log = get_deployment_logs(start_date, end_date)
4  successful_deployments = filter_successful(deployments_log)
5  deployment_frequency = len(successful_deployments) / total_days
6  print("Deployment Frequency: ", deployment_frequency)
```

- **Change Failure Rate (CFR):** This metric reflects the percentage
  of changes leading to degraded service or subsequently requiring
  remediation (e.g., hotfixes, rollbacks). A lower CFR is indicative
  of more stable and reliable microservices systems. Monitoring
  CFR provides insights into the robustness of the codebase and the
  efficacy of the existing testing and deployment infrastructure.

```
1  # Example: Python function to calculate Change Failure Rate.
2  def calculate_CFR(total_changes, failures):
3      return (failures / total_changes) * 100
```

- **Service Availability:** Defined as the percentage of time the service is functional and accessible, service availability is crucial
  in customer-facing applications where reliability may directly
  impact user satisfaction and revenue. Microservices should be
  designed with fault tolerance in mind to ensure high availability.

```
Service Availability: 99.9%
```

- **Mean Time to Recovery (MTTR):** This metric measures the average time taken to recover from a failure. A shorter MTTR is
  often a reflection of a system's resilience and the effectiveness of
  its incident response practices. Microservices architectures can
  leverage patterns like service fallbacks and circuit breakers to
  reduce MTTR.

```
MTTR: 30 minutes
```

- **Scalability Efficiency:** Scalability efficiency measures how effectively a system can scale in response to varying loads. This is
  particularly important in microservices architectures due to their
  distributed nature and the dynamic scale of operations.

```
1  # Example: Tracking Scalability Efficiency
2  initial_load_response_time = measure_response_time(initial_load)
3  increased_load_response_time = measure_response_time(increased_load)
4  scalability_efficiency = calculate_efficiency(initial_load_response_time,
       increased_load_response_time)
5  print("Scalability Efficiency:", scalability_efficiency)
```

58

- **End-to-End Latency:** The total time taken for a request to traverse through multiple services before getting the response. Lower latency contributes to better user experiences and more efficient operations. This metric is essential to monitor in microservices due to the multiple network calls that can introduce delays.

```
End-to-End Latency: 150 ms
```

Monitoring these metrics requires tools and systems capable of gathering and reporting data across services and infrastructures. Popular choices include Prometheus for monitoring and Grafana for visualization, which together can provide comprehensive insights into microservices performance and trends.

By incorporating these key performance indicators into regular monitoring routines, organizations can address potential issues proactively, adjust strategies in a timely manner, and ultimately drive successful outcomes in their microservices implementations.

Chapter 3

Understanding Cloud-Native Architecture

Cloud-native architecture is designed to exploit the scalable, flexible infrastructure of modern cloud computing. By leveraging various cloud services, it supports building and running applications that are resilient, manageable, and observable. This chapter breaks down the components of cloud-native systems, highlights their benefits, and explains how businesses can fully utilize cloud capabilities to enhance their operational continuity and innovation.

3.1   Definition of Cloud-Native Architecture

Cloud-native architecture is explicitly engineered to exploit the advantages of a cloud computing delivery model. It encompasses a broad array of practices and technologies supporting scalable, elastic, and self-managing applications that operate on dynamic cloud environments. This architecture promotes rapid, frequent, and reliable delivery of large, complex applications.

A cloud-native system promotes resilience by structuring services as small, independently deployable units orchestrated in a system of microservices. Each of these microservices is focused on accomplishing one business function and utilizes automated, containerized platforms

61

to ensure responsiveness and continuity across various computational and storage resources of cloud infrastructure.

- **Microservices:** Each component service functions autonomously and communicates with other services through well-defined APIs. This enhances the overall elasticity and resilience of applications.

- **Containers:** Containers facilitate consistent deployment regardless of the environment, since each container operates independently of the others and includes its own libraries and configurations.

- **Dynamic Orchestration:** Systems use automated management to maintain service health and scale based on demand. This dynamic nature allows for optimal resource utilization and can reduce costs associated with manual operations and over-provisioning.

To effectively address the challenges of running and managing distributed applications, cloud-native architecture leverages a range of supporting technologies such as containers, service meshes, microservices, immutable infrastructure, and declarative APIs. By abstracting away many underlying infrastructural complexities, developers can focus on functionality and innovation.

```
1   # Example of a basic microservice-based application structure in Python leveraging
        Flask
2
3   from flask import Flask, jsonify
4
5   app = Flask(__name__)
6
7   @app.route('/api/service')
8   def my_microservice():
9       return jsonify({"message": "Hello from a microservice!"})
10
11  if __name__ == '__main__':
12      app.run(port=5000)
```

The above example highlights a straightforward implementation of a microservice in a cloud-native architecture where each microservice can be containerized and scaled independently.

```
Output:
{
  "message": "Hello from a microservice!"
}
```

From a design perspective, cloud-native architectures utilize declarative formats for setup automation, minimizing manual interference. This setup ensures that the applications are agile, maintainable, and observable - not only during development but also across their operational life cycle. Sustained observability in cloud-native systems is achieved through advanced monitoring services that dynamically collect logs, metrics, and traces to keep the system performance transparent and under continuous assessment.

The adoption of this architecture involves a change in the traditional software development approach, focusing instead on a more granular composition of services, which significantly increases the complexity of managing each individual component. However, this complexity is balanced by the robustness provided by a distributed system environment where service failures are contained and addressed without affecting the uptime of the entire application. Service mesh technologies can be especially helpful here, managing communication and service discovery between the microservices. This leads to a resilient design where services can rapidly adapt to changes in demand or failures within the ecosystem.

This architectural style not only supports the operational aspect of modern applications but also profoundly impacts the strategic agility of the organization, allowing it to respond to market changes more quickly and with more flexibility than traditional, monolithic architectures.

3.2 Core Principles of Cloud-Native Design

Cloud-native design is fundamentally centered around enhancing the flexibility, scalability, and resilience of applications by leveraging the intrinsic strengths of the cloud computing model. The key principles guiding the architecture of cloud-native applications include automation, microservices, containers, orchestration, and observability. Each of these components plays a pivotal role in ensuring that applications are both robust and agile.

Automation is the cornerstone of cloud-native environments. It significantly reduces human error, enhances consistency, and accelerates the delivery of new features and updates. Automation in cloud-native systems spans several dimensions:

- **Infrastructure as Code (IaC):** This practice involves managing and provisioning computing infrastructure through machine-readable definition files, rather than physical hardware configuration or interactive configuration tools.

- **Continuous Integration and Continuous Deployment (CI/CD):** CI/CD automates the integration of code changes from multiple contributors into a single software project, and the automated deployment of this software into live production environments.

The deployment of **microservices** is another defining principle. Microservices architecture breaks down applications into their core functions, each of which runs as a separate service. This separation allows for:

```
1   - Independent deployment cycles for different services, facilitating quicker
        updates and bug fixes.
2   - Enhanced scalability as services can be scaled independently based on demand.
3   - Improved fault isolation, where the failure of a single service does not impact
        the availability of others.
```

Containerization supports the microservices structure by encapsulating services in containers, which include all necessary binaries and libraries. This ensures consistency across different environments and simplifies deployments. Containerization technologies such as Docker have become synonymous with cloud-native strategies because they provide:

- A lightweight alternative to traditional virtualization that requires less overhead.

- Strong isolation for process and environment, improving the security and consistency of deployments.

Orchestration is essential in managing the lifecycle of containers, especially when operating at scale. Kubernetes, a leader in this space, automates the deployment, scaling, and operation of application containers across clusters of hosts. Orchestration capabilities include:

```
1   - Automated rollouts and rollbacks.
2   - Load balancing and traffic routing.
3   - Self-healing mechanisms, restarting failed containers and replacing and
        rescheduling containers when nodes die.
```

Lastly, **observability** in cloud-native systems comprises logging, monitoring, and tracing. Proper implementation helps in understanding the behavior of applications and troubleshooting issues swiftly. Tools and practices related to observability ensure:

```
1   - Real-time logging and monitoring.
2   - Distributed tracing, to follow the path of requests through various microservices
        .
```

By adhering to these core principles, businesses can create a robust architecture that takes full advantage of the cloud's potential for providing flexible, scalable, and resilient IT infrastructure. Moreover, as the adoption of cloud-native technologies grows, continual innovation within each of these domains is likely, promising to extend the capabilities of what cloud-native systems can accomplish. Thus, enterprises must stay informed and agile, ready to integrate new advancements to maintain and enhance their competitiveness in a rapidly evolving digital landscape.

3.3 Benefits of Adopting Cloud-Native Architectures

Adopting cloud-native architectures provides a multitude of benefits which are pivotal for organizations aiming to enhance their scalability, resilience, and efficiency in software development and operational management. This section explores these advantages, emphasizing how they contribute to transforming traditional IT infrastructure into more dynamic and adaptive systems.

Enhanced Scalability

One of the core attributes of cloud-native architectures is enhanced scalability. Scalability is the capability of a system to handle a growing amount of work by adding resources to the system. In a cloud-native environment, services are designed to scale out automatically based on the demand. This means that an application can handle increases in load without manual intervention, thus providing a seamless user experience regardless of the load.

```
Output Example: Auto-Scaling Activity Log
Timestamp: 2021-07-12 12:00:01
Action: Scale Out
Service: User Authentication Service
New Instance Count: 10
Reason: CPU Utilization > 75% for 10 minutes
```

This scaling is predominantly managed through the orchestration layer, such as Kubernetes, which monitors the performance indicators of the services and adjusts their resources accordingly.

Improved Resilience

Cloud-native architectures are inherently designed to improve system resilience. Resilience in cloud-native terms refers to the ability of the system to provide and maintain an acceptable level of service in the face of faults and challenges to normal operation.

- Fault Isolation: In microservices architecture, each service is decoupled and isolated from others. This ensures that a failure in one service doesn't cascade and disrupt other services.

- Redundancy: Cloud-native systems implement redundancy by running multiple instances of the same service across different servers or even data centers. This provides failover capabilities, ensuring high availability and disaster recovery.

Operational Agility

Cloud-native architecture supports operational agility, which refers to the ability of an organization to respond quickly to market changes with minimal impact on the current operations. This agility is achieved by adopting practices such as continuous integration and continuous deployment (CI/CD), which automate the software delivery process.

The decoupling of services further enhances agility by allowing teams to develop, test, and deploy updates to individual components without impacting the operation of other services.

Cost Efficiency

Cloud-native architectures also bring forth significant cost efficiencies, primarily through resource optimization and consumption-based pricing. Since services scale automatically, resources are used optimally, with no idle capacity costing the organization unnecessarily. Moreover, the pay-as-you-go pricing model of public clouds ensures that organizations only pay for the resources they actually use. This eliminates

---

Algorithm 2: CI/CD Pipeline Process

Input: Source code update
Output: Deployment in production environment

1 sourceCode ← receive update;
2 execute unitTests();
3 **if** *unitTests pass* **then**
4   build artifact();
5   deploy to staging environment();
6   execute integrationTests();
7   **if** *integrationTests pass* **then**
8   deploy to production();

9 **else**
10   report failure();

---

the need for significant upfront capital investment in hardware and reduces ongoing operational costs.

Easier Maintenance and Update Cycles

Maintaining and updating software in cloud-native architectures is streamlined due to the use of containers and microservices. Containers package software with all its dependencies, ensuring consistency across different environments and simplifying the deployment process. Combined with microservices, containers enable teams to update or replace parts of the system independently, without affecting other components of the application.

```
1  # Example: Containerization using Docker
2  FROM python:3.8-slim
3  WORKDIR /app
4  COPY requirements.txt requirements.txt
5  RUN pip install -r requirements.txt
6  COPY . .
7  CMD ["python", "application.py"]
```

The benefits detailed in this section underscore the transformative impact of adopting cloud-native architectures, positioning organizations to leverage computational resources more effectively, enhance system reliability, and adapt more agile operational practices. This adaptability not only supports current technological needs but also equips businesses to swiftly respond to future technological advancements and market demands.

3.4 Containerization: The Building Block of Cloud-Native

Containerization is a lightweight form of virtualization that allows for the encapsulation of an application's code, configuration, and dependencies into a portable container image. These container images can be executed consistently across different computing environments, which is a fundamental requirement in cloud-native architectures. This section delves deeply into why containerization is pivotal as a building block for cloud-native systems, how it contributes to the adaptability, efficiency, and scalability of applications, and the critical role it plays in achieving the declarative management of cloud resources.

Containers are a central technology in cloud-native architectures, primarily due to their ability to provide an abstraction from the host operating system. This abstraction enables the containerized application to run isolated from other processes, ensuring that it has access to the resources it needs without interference and adheres strictly to the resource limits defined for it. Unlike traditional virtual machines (VMs), which include both an application and the necessary elements of an entire operating system, containers include only the application and its immediate dependencies, making them significantly lighter and faster to start than VMs.

The container's core is provided by a container runtime environment, which manages the life cycle of containers. Commonly used runtime environments include Docker and Kubernetes, where Docker provides the tools necessary to containerize and run applications, and Kubernetes offers more extensive orchestration capabilities, including managing multiple containers spread across multiple hosts, providing them with automated scaling, deployment, and networking functionalities.

One key aspect of containerization in cloud-native architectures is its facilitation of immutable infrastructure principles. This is achieved by standardizing the environment in which applications are developed, tested, and deployed. Given that each container is built from a fixed container image, it should operate identically regardless of the environment it runs in, which minimizes the "it works on my machine" problem. The adoption of containers thus leads to more robust, predictable deployments.

For example, assume a container is built with the following command using Docker:
docker build -t my-application:latest .
This command creates a container image named 'my-application' with the tag 'latest' based on the Dockerfile in the current directory. The resulting container can then be run on any Docker-compatible host, ensuring the same behavior across development, testing, and production environments.

Furthermore, containerization enhances the scalability of applications. Containers can be rapidly started and stopped, making it feasible to dynamically adjust the number of active containers in response to varying load, a practice often referred to as horizontal scaling. This agility is crucial in cloud-native environments where elasticity and quick responsiveness to changing demands are essential.

```
1  To illustrate, Kubernetes uses the following command to scale a deployment:
2  kubectl scale deployment my-application --replicas=10
3  This command adjusts the 'my-application' deployment to have 10 active replicas,
      allowing the system to handle increased load by distributing it across more
      instances of the application.
```

In adherence to cloud-native principles, containers also contribute to resilience and self-healing capabilities. By running multiple containers across different nodes and using health checks and self-recovery mechanisms provided by orchestration tools like Kubernetes, applications can achieve higher availability. If a container fails, the system can automatically replace it with a new one, hence maintaining the desired state with minimal interruption to service.

- Containers ensure consistent environments from development through to production, reducing the risks associated with environmental inconsistencies.

- They promote the use of microservices by making it easier to isolate, maintain, and scale individual components of larger applications.

- Container orchestration tools offer capabilities such as automated rollout and rollback, simplifying the process of updating applications and reverting to previous states if problems arise.

The strategic integration of container technology provides a robust scaffolding for constructing and managing more complex cloud-native ecosystems. This ensures operational continuity, fosters business agility, and simplifies the task of maintaining and scaling cloud-native applications. As such, containerization is not merely a feature of cloud-native environments but a fundamental building block. The adaptability it brings encapsulates much of what makes cloud-native architecture a powerful model for modern software deployments.

3.5 Service Meshes and Their Role in Cloud-Native Architectures

Service meshes are a critical component in the cloud-native architecture landscape, offering a dedicated infrastructure layer for handling inter-service communication. This layer facilitates complex service-to-service communication processes, including load balancing, service discovery, health checking, authentication and authorization, and observability. By decoupling these functionalities from the application code, service meshes enhance the modularity and maintainability of microservices.

One of the primary protocols employed by service meshes is the Envoy proxy, which was originally designed by Lyft. Envoy operates alongside the application code, usually as a sidecar proxy. This pattern allows Envoy to control all incoming and outgoing calls to a service. To manage these sidecar proxies, a control plane is required, and it is provided by solutions such as Istio, Linkerd, or Consul Connect. These tools offer configurations and policies which are pushed to the proxies dynamically.

Because service meshes manage communication across services, they naturally support some of the foundational principles of cloud-native architectures:

- **Resilience:** Service meshes can significantly bolster the resilience of cloud-native applications. They handle retries, failovers, and circuit breakers seamlessly.

- **Scalability:** Automatic load balancing and smart routing ensure that service meshes can scale within microservices environments dynamically.

- **Observability:** Integrated logging, tracing, and metrics collection capabilities that service meshes provide, improve the visibility across services.

The functionalities of a service mesh are primarily conducted through two distinct components:

70

- **Data Plane:** The data plane is constituted of sidecar proxies that manage the network communication between services. They intercept and route traffic to ensure proper policy enforcement and telemetry data collection.

- **Control Plane:** The control plane manages the mesh's overall configuration and provides policy and routing capabilities. It acts as the brain of the service mesh, guiding the sidecar proxies deployed on the data plane.

Here is a minimal example using Istio, a popular service mesh implementation. The following YAML configuration illustrates how an Istio Gateway can be defined and configured:

```
1   apiVersion: networking.istio.io/v1alpha3
2   kind: Gateway
3   metadata:
4     name: my-gateway
5   spec:
6     selector:
7       istio: ingressgateway # use Istio default gateway implementation
8     servers:
9     - port:
10        number: 80
11        name: http
12        protocol: HTTP
13      hosts:
14      - "*"
```

In this configuration, the `Gateway` resource defines a load balancer that operates at the edge of the mesh. It handles incoming HTTP traffic on port 80 and routes it appropriately based on further Istio routing configurations.

To understand how traffic is routed within the service mesh, consider this simplified view on an Istio VirtualService:

```
1   apiVersion: networking.istio.io/v1alpha3
2   kind: VirtualService
3   metadata:
4     name: my-service
5   spec:
6     hosts:
7     - "my-service.default.svc.cluster.local"
8     http:
9     - route:
10      - destination:
11          host: my-service.default.svc.cluster.local
```

This `VirtualService` specifies routes for the host `"my-service.default.svc.cluster.local"`, usually mapped internally to a Kubernetes service in the cluster.

71

Technical efficiencies aside, service meshes introduce complexity in terms of the operation and management. They typically demand a higher degree of infrastructure awareness for correctly configuring and managing the control plane and the proxies. However, adopting a service mesh brings substantial net benefits in terms of easier service management, security enhancements, and runtime flexibility, aligning effectively with the overarching goals of cloud-native systems to be resilient, manageable, and observable.

The unfolding trend towards these platforms underlines a commitment to a system where operations and maintenance strategies are as scalable and dynamic as the applications running on them. Service meshes, despite their complexity, deliver critical capabilities that allow such a mindset to be practically realized, offering a robust method to navigate the challenges of modern software development and operations.

3.6 Microservices vs. Cloud-Native: Understanding the Relationship

Microservices architecture and cloud-native are often discussed in tandem, but it is critical to delineate the distinct attributes and contributions of each to the modern software development landscape. Understanding the relationship between these two concepts is foundational for architects, developers, and strategic decision-makers looking to leverage the full potential of distributed computing environments.

Microservices architecture describes a methodological approach to developing a single application as a suite of small services, each running in its own process and communicating with lightweight mechanisms, often an HTTP resource API. These services are built around business capabilities and independently deployable by fully automated deployment machinery.

On the other hand, cloud-native architecture epitomizes a design philosophy that promotes elasticity, resilience, and agility. While microservices focus on the application's architectural layout, cloud-native is broader, encompassing the service deployments in environments that leverage the cloud's flexibility. In essence, cloud-native design ensures applications capitalize on the inherent characteristics of cloud computing frameworks, such as dynamic resource scheduling, fault tolerance, and scalability.

To illustrate the practical implementation of these concepts, consider the deployment of a microservices-based application in a cloud-native environment:

```
1   # Deployment configuration snippet using Kubernetes
2   apiVersion: apps/v1
3   kind: Deployment
4   metadata:
5     name: user-service
6   spec:
7     replicas: 3
8     selector:
9       matchLabels:
10        app: user
11    template:
12      metadata:
13        labels:
14          app: user
15      spec:
16        containers:
17        - name: user-service
18          image: username/user-service:1.2
19          ports:
20          - containerPort: 8080
```

In this Kubernetes deployment configuration, 'user-service' is isolated as one manageable, deployable component among others in a potentially larger application. Each instance of a service can be independently scaled, thus adhering to both microservices and cloud-native paradigms for resource management and fault isolation.

The synergy between microservices and cloud-native architectures becomes particularly evident when examining scalability and resilience:

- Scalability: Microservices allow components of the application to scale independently according to demand without affecting other services. Cloud-native environments enhance this by providing automatic scaling solutions, such as Kubernetes Horizontal Pod Autoscaler, which adjusts resources based on real-time metrics.

- Resilience: Error containment and recovery are simplified in a microservices architecture because independent service failures typically do not impact the availability of other services. Cloud-native platforms support this by enabling rapid provisioning of backup instances and facilitating robust service discovery and connectivity mechanisms.

Nevertheless, adopting these methodologies is not without challenges. Microservices require diligent domain analysis to prevent misalignment with business boundaries, and transitioning to a cloud-native infrastructure demands a solid understanding of cloud-specific skills and technologies. Decision-makers must consider these aspects when evaluating migration or transformation strategies, ensuring that benefits in flexibility, agility, and scalability are not overshadowed by complexity or resource overhead.

Each approach offers distinctive benefits and, when used in conjunction, can fortify an organization's software deployment strategy. By aligning microservices principles with cloud-native operational strategies, organizations can achieve better workload distribution, improved system resiliency, and higher application agility, turning the combined attributes of both paradigms into a coherent, scalable, and resilient infrastructure.

This comprehensive understanding enables organizations to harness the full scope of capabilities offered by contemporary technological advancements while preparing the architectural groundwork for future innovations in cloud computing and service deployment methodologies.

3.7 State Management in Cloud-Native Applications

State management in cloud-native applications is a fundamental concept that ensures the persistence, consistency, and availability of the application's state across its distributed components. Efficient state management is crucial for achieving the resilience and scalability that cloud-native environments promise. In distributed systems like those typical in cloud-native architectures, managing state becomes more complex due to the ephemeral nature of the components and the need for maintaining state consistency across multiple, potentially geographically dispersed, instances.

Challenges in State Management

The transition from monolithic to cloud-native architectures introduces several state management challenges:

- **Distribution of State:** As applications are decomposed into microservices, state needs to be handled in several smaller, decoupled components rather than a monolithic centralized database.

74

- **Data Consistency:** Ensuring data consistency across different services and their instances can be challenging due to the distributed nature of cloud-native applications.

- **Performance:** Accessing distributed state can introduce latency, leading to potential performance bottlenecks if not managed correctly.

- **Failure Handling:** In a distributed environment, strategies need to be devised to cope with partial failures without affecting the state's integrity.

Strategies for Effective State Management

To address these challenges, certain strategies and patterns can be adopted:

- **Stateless Services:** Where possible, designing services to be stateless so that state is maintained outside the service, either in a database or a state store, which can be a more resilient approach to failure and helps in scaling the application.

- **Database per Service:** Each microservice can have its own database in which only data relevant to that service is stored. This pattern helps in achieving loose coupling among services but requires careful handling of transactions spanning multiple services.

- **Caching:** Employing caching techniques to temporarily store data that is frequently accessed or computationally expensive to fetch can significantly improve performance.

- **Event Sourcing:** Capturing all changes to an application state as a sequence of events and storing these events can allow the application to recreate its state from these events. Moreover, it enables extensive audits and historical analysis.

- **Command Query Responsibility Segregation (CQRS):** Separating the read and update operations of a database can help manage the complexity of distributed data management by improving performance and scalability.

Technological Solutions for State Management

Several technologies and tools support effective state management in cloud-native applications:

- **Distributed Caches:** Tools like Redis or Memcached provide quick data access scattered across multiple services.

- **NoSQL Databases:** Databases such as Cassandra or MongoDB, which are designed to spread data across many nodes efficiently.

- **Message Brokers:** Systems like Apache Kafka or RabbitMQ can be used to manage asynchronous data flows and ensure data consistency across services.

- **Service Mesh:** Implementing a service mesh can help in managing service-to-service communications securely, reliably, and transparently, thereby indirectly influencing the state management strategies.

Incorporating these strategies effectively requires deep integration with the CI/CD pipeline to ensure configurations and dependencies are correctly managed across the deployment stages. Automated testing must be employed extensively to check data integrity, performance under load, and the efficacy of failover mechanisms in state management practices.

The correct choice of patterns and technologies depends largely on the specific requirements and constraints of the application and organization. However, the ultimate aim is to provide a seamless, consistent user experience and ensure robust data handling capabilities in a distributed cloud-native environment.

3.8 Building Resilience and Reliability in Cloud-Native Systems

Achieving resilience and reliability in cloud-native systems necessitates a robust strategy that encompasses multiple aspects of architecture and design. This section will elaborate on the implementation of redesign policies, fault tolerance mechanisms, health checking protocols, and resilience patterns like circuit breakers and retry algorithms, essential for maintaining system stability and ensuring system recovery from failures.

Redesigning for Failure: In cloud-native environments where systems are inherently distributed, potential points of failure must be anticipated and systematically addressed. The redesign for failure involves decomposing applications into microservices that are independently deployable, scalable, and resilient. Each service must be designed to perform its functions even when dependent services are unavailable.

```
1  // Example of a microservice handling failure of a dependent service
2  if(dependentService.isAvailable()){
3      response = dependentService.getResponse();
4  } else {
5      response = getDefaultResponse();
6  }
```

Fault Tolerance Mechanisms: To build fault-tolerant systems, engineers must incorporate specific patterns and technologies. One effective approach is the implementation of redundancy and replication across multiple geographical zones, ensuring availability even during zone-specific outages.

```
Output example when a primary zone fails:
"Fallback to secondary zone activated. Service continuity maintained."
```

Health Checking Protocols: Regular health checks are critical to detect and address issues before they escalate into failures. Kubernetes, a popular orchestration platform, implements health checks through liveness and readiness probes, which confirm if an application is running correctly and is ready to accept traffic.

```
1  // Kubernetes liveness probe example in YAML
2  livenessProbe:
3      httpGet:
4          path: /health
5          port: 8080
6      initialDelaySeconds: 15
7      timeoutSeconds: 2
```

Implementing Resilience Patterns: Patterns such as circuit breakers and retries play a pivotal role in enhancing system resilience by preventing a cascade of failures and allowing the system to recover smoothly.

- `Circuit Breaker:` Helps to cut the request flow to a failing service, allowing it time to recover and redirecting traffic to other stable services.

77

- Retry: Involves reattempting a failed operation with exponential backoff to avoid overwhelming the service and to give it time to recover.

```
1   // Retry mechanism with exponential backoff
2   for(int i = 0; i < maxRetries; i++) {
3       try {
4           // Attempt to call the service
5           return service.call();
6       } catch (ServiceUnavailableException e) {
7           // Wait exponentially longer
8           Thread.sleep((long) Math.pow(2, i) * 100L);
9       }
10  }
11  throw new MaxRetriesReachedException();
```

This method of integrating myriad resilience strategies ensures that cloud-native applications can sustain operational performance and mitigate disruptions effectively. The application of these strategies requires rigorous testing and continuous monitoring to adapt to evolving challenges in dynamic cloud environments. By fostering a culture that prioritizes resilience and reliability, businesses can leverage the full spectrum of cloud-native benefits to support sustained growth and adaptability.

3.9 Continuous Integration and Continuous Deployment (CI/CD) in Cloud-Native

The application of Continuous Integration (CI) and Continuous Deployment (CD) methodologies is fundamental in the development life cycle of cloud-native applications. These practices enhance the speed, reliability, and efficiency of deploying applications in such dynamic environments.

Continuous Integration refers to the practice of frequently integrating code changes into a central repository. This process incorporates automated tests that run with each integration to ensure compatibility and to detect errors early. In a cloud-native context, CI processes need to be designed to handle the rapid provisioning provided by cloud services and the scalable nature of containerized applications.

Given a typical CI workflow, developers commit changes to the version control system. Upon each commit, a CI server automatically fetches the latest codebase, builds the application, and runs a series of tests.

These tests include unit tests, integration tests, and security scans designed to validate the integrity and security of the code.

```
1   # Example of a Jenkinsfile to implement a CI pipeline in a cloud-native environment
2   pipeline {
3       agent any
4       stages {
5           stage('Build') {
6               steps {
7                   sh 'make build'
8               }
9           }
10          stage('Test') {
11              steps {
12                  sh 'make test'
13              }
14          }
15          stage('Deploy') {
16              steps {
17                  sh 'make deploy'
18              }
19          }
20      }
21  }
```

Continuous Deployment extends Continuous Integration by automatically deploying all code changes to the production environment after the test phase. This practice is especially beneficial in cloud-native architectures where the ability to rapidly deploy and scale services is crucial. Automation in CD minimizes human error, reduces deployment time, and ensures a consistent state of deployment.

Consider the following mechanism for CD within a Kubernetes-based environment:

```
1   # Example of a GitHub Actions workflow to implement CD in Kubernetes
2   name: CI/CD Pipeline
3
4   on:
5     push:
6       branches:
7         - master
8
9   jobs:
10    build:
11      runs-on: ubuntu-latest
12      steps:
13        - uses: actions/checkout@v3
14        - name: Build Docker image
15          run: docker build . --tag myapplication:${{ github.sha }}
16
17    deploy:
18      runs-on: ubuntu-latest
19      needs: build
20      steps:
21        - uses: actions/checkout@v3
22        - name: Deploy to Kubernetes
23          run: |
```

```
24   kubectl apply -f k8s/
25   kubectl rollout status deployment/myapplication
```

Implementing CI/CD in cloud-native architectures inherently utilizes Docker for containerization and Kubernetes for orchestration. Such infrastructure supports the decoupling of services that microservices impose, and the orchestration features of Kubernetes facilitate the management of microservices' life cycle efficiently.

- Docker containers encapsulate microservices, ensuring consistency across environments and reducing conflicts between working environments.

- Kubernetes automates the deployment, scaling, and operations of application containers across clusters of hosts.

This synergy between Docker and Kubernetes not only simplifies development workflows but also enhances operational control and monitoring. Metrics and logs are collected systematically, feeding into live dashboards that aid in real-time monitoring and troubleshooting.

```
Result of applying Kubernetes deployment:
deployment.apps/myapplication deployed
deployment.apps/myapplication successfully rolled out
```

Systems that embrace cloud-native CI/CD practices show marked improvements in deployment frequency, failure recovery times, and overall application resilience. With the dynamics of competition and innovation in modern software development, integrating these practices is no longer optional but mandatory for businesses aiming at technological leadership and operational excellence. The integration of automated CI/CD pipelines thus aligns well with both the business goals and the technical goals, maximizing resource utilization and optimizing developmental operations.

3.10 Scaling and Performance Optimization in Cloud-Native Environments

Scaling and performance optimization in cloud-native environments are critical components that leverage the scalable and flexible infrastructure of cloud computing to its fullest potential. This section discusses strategies and techniques for effective scaling and optimizing performance in cloud-native systems.

80

Horizontal vs. Vertical Scaling

Cloud-native application architectures are designed to accommodate both horizontal and vertical scaling, but they tend to favor horizontal scaling due to its alignment with the principles of cloud computing.

- **Horizontal scaling** involves increasing the number of instances of the same application to handle more load. It is well-suited for cloud environments because it allows applications to leverage the elasticity of the cloud. This method enhances fault tolerance and facilitates load balancing.

- **Vertical scaling,** on the other hand, involves adding more resources to the existing infrastructure, such as CPU or memory. This can provide a quick boost to application performance but has its limitations in scalability and does not fully utilize cloud capabilities.

The preferred approach in cloud-native environments is horizontal scaling because it supports the dynamic management of varying loads and maximizes resilience and availability.

Auto-scaling Strategies

Auto-scaling is a fundamental characteristic of cloud-native applications, enabling automated adjustment of resources based on the current demand. Cloud platforms like AWS and Azure provide auto-scaling services that dynamically increase or decrease resource allocation.

- **Reactive Scaling:** This auto-scaling strategy adjusts resources in real-time based on current traffic, using metrics such as CPU usage and memory demand. Reactive scaling can quickly adapt to changes but may lead to resource wastage if not calibrated precisely.

- **Predictive Scaling:** Utilizing machine learning algorithms to analyze historical data and predict future demands, predictive scaling plans resource allocation in advance. This approach optimizes resource usage and cost by preparing the system for expected changes in load.

By implementing a combination of both reactive and predictive scaling, organizations can optimize performance and manage resources efficiently.

Performance Optimization Techniques

To achieve optimum performance in a cloud-native environment, several strategies should be considered.

- **Caching:** Implementing caching mechanisms can significantly reduce the load on backend services by storing copies of frequently accessed data. Technologies like Redis and Memcached are commonly used for caching in cloud-native architectures.

- **Load Balancing:** Effective load balancing distributes traffic evenly across server instances. This not only prevents any single instance from being overwhelmed but can also help in minimizing response times and maximizing throughput.

- **Resource Allocation:** Fine-tuning the allocation of CPU, memory, and I/O resources based on the application's requirements and characteristics ensures that the system runs efficiently without overusing resources.

Monitoring and Analysis

Continuous monitoring and performance analysis are essential to understand the behavior of applications and their resource consumption patterns. Tools like Prometheus and Grafana are frequently used for monitoring metrics and visualizing performance data in real-time.

Benchmarking and profiling are also integral practices that help in identifying bottlenecks and inefficiencies within an application. Regular analysis of this data informs better decision-making regarding performance tuning and scaling strategies.

By meticulously implementing scaling strategies and optimizing performance through continuous monitoring and adaptive adjustments, cloud-native applications can achieve high scalability and improved performance. Embedding these practices into the CI/CD pipeline ensures that performance optimization becomes an integral part of the development lifecycle, thereby maintaining the efficiency and effectiveness of cloud-native systems.

3.11 Security Practices for Cloud-Native Applications

In cloud-native architectures, where services are dispersed across various environments, security becomes a multifaceted challenge. This section elaborates on secure practices, focusing on methodologies that ensure robust security at different levels of a cloud-native system.

One of the foremost strategies in securing cloud-native applications is the principle of least privilege. This principle should be implemented strictly across both human and non-human actors such as services and processes. Using Kubernetes, for instance, administrators can manage role-based access controls (RBAC) to enforce minimal access rights. Below is an example of how one might define RBAC in a Kubernetes deployment:

```
1  apiVersion: rbac.authorization.k8s.io/v1
2  kind: Role
3  metadata:
4    namespace: default
5    name: pod-reader
6  rules:
7  - apiGroups: [""] # "" indicates the core API group
8    resources: ["pods"]
9    verbs: ["get", "watch", "list"]
```

Another critical area is network security. In cloud-native applications, the network should be segmented using techniques such as firewalls, Virtual Private Clouds (VPCs), and network policies. These control the traffic that can flow between services, thus reducing the risk of lateral movement in case a service is compromised. Kubernetes network policies, for instance, allow administrators to control traffic at the IP address or port level, as seen in the following example:

```
1   apiVersion: networking.k8s.io/v1
2   kind: NetworkPolicy
3   metadata:
4     name: api-allow
5     namespace: backend
6   spec:
7     podSelector:
8       matchLabels:
9         role: api
10    policyTypes:
11    - Ingress
```

```
12    ingress:
13    - from:
14      - namespaceSelector:
15        matchLabels:
16          project: frontend
17      ports:
18      - protocol: TCP
19        port: 80
```

Application security is another pillar of cloud-native security that incorporates practices such as regular updates and vulnerability scanning. Tools like Clair can be integrated into CI/CD pipelines to automate the scanning of container images for known vulnerabilities. Here is an example command using Clair to scan an image:

```
clairctl report --local docker_image_name
```

Encryption is a critical security measure in cloud-native environments. Data in transit and at rest must be encrypted to protect it against breaches and unauthorized access. TLS (Transport Layer Security) should be employed to encrypt data in transit whereas encryption mechanisms provided by cloud providers can secure data at rest. It is pertinent to manage encryption keys securely, using dedicated services like AWS Key Management Service (KMS) or HashiCorp Vault.

Furthermore, observability plays a significant role in security by enabling the detection of unusual behaviors that may signify security incidents. Cloud-native observability tools like Prometheus, combined with Grafana, can provide real-time monitoring and alerting for a variety of metrics and logs. Below is an example of a Prometheus alert rule:

```
1    groups:
2    - name: example
3      rules:
4      - alert: HighErrorRate
5        expr: job:request_errors_per_second > 10
6        for: 5m
7        labels:
8          severity: page
9        annotations:
10          summary: High request error rate detected
11          description: '{{ $labels.job }} has a request error rate > 10 errors/s'
```

This monitoring can be complemented with runtime security tools like Falco, which detect anomalous activities in application behaviors by monitoring the system calls made by running containers.

Finally, ensuring security in cloud-native applications requires a systematic approach to integrating security at every phase of the application lifecycle. This approach is characterized by automation, regular

84

audits, and feedback mechanisms that promote continuous improvement in security practices alongside application development iterations.

3.12 Evolving Trends and Future of Cloud-Native Technologies

Presently, the technology landscape is dynamically evolving, increasingly leaning towards innovations that not only support scalability and flexibility but also empower enterprises to launch and adapt services swiftly in response to the market demands. The future trajectory of cloud-native technologies is influenced by several emerging trends that signify a profound shift in how systems are developed, deployed, and maintained.

Firstly, we witness an undeniable surge towards serverless architectures. Serverless computing, distinct from conventional cloud service models, abstracts the server layer entirely, offering developers a strictly platform-centric view. This paradigm shift minimizes the operational overhead of managing servers and lets developers focus solely on the business logic. In serverless architectures, applications are structured as a collection of functions that are triggered by events.

```
Example of a Serverless Function:
{
    'FunctionName' : 'DataProcessor',
    'Runtime' : 'nodejs10.x',
    'Handler' : 'process.handler',
    'Role' : 'arn:aws:iam::123456789012:role/service-role/lambda-role',
    'Description' : 'Processes data and stores results',
    'Timeout' : 5,
    'MemorySize' : 128
}
```

Secondly, Artificial Intelligence (AI) and Machine Learning (ML) integrations in cloud-native environments are becoming increasingly prevalent. By leveraging AI, cloud-native applications can offer predictive analysis, natural language processing, and intelligent decision-making capabilities. This integration is pivotal in automating complex operational tasks, including dynamic scaling and system health monitoring.

```
1  from sklearn.datasets import load_iris
2  from sklearn.linear_model import LogisticRegression
3
4  X, y = load_iris(return_X_y=True)
5  model = LogisticRegression(solver='liblinear', random_state=0).fit(X, y)
```

```
6  print(model.score(X, y)) # Output shows model accuracy
```

The emerging importance of edge computing in a cloud-native sphere
can't be overlooked. Edge computing pushes data processing to the
periphery of the network, thus near the data source. This is critical in
use cases where real-time processing and reduced latency are essential,
such as in IoT devices or mobile applications. Edge computing, when
integrated into cloud-native strategies, enhances performance by alle-
viating bandwidth issues and accelerating response times.

- Decreased latency by processing data at the edge.

- Reduced data transmission costs.

- Increased application responsiveness.

Securing these technologically advanced, distributed systems presents
new challenges, particularly in governance, compliance, and data protection. Thus, the evolution towards enforcing security policies as code
– a methodology where security practices are programmatically integrated into cloud-native applications – is notable. This shift facilitates
more robust and verifiable security standards.

```
1   # Example of implementing security policy in Kubernetes
2   apiVersion: networking.k8s.io/v1
3   kind: NetworkPolicy
4   metadata:
5     name: api-allow
6   spec:
7     podSelector:
8       matchLabels:
9         role: api
10    policyTypes:
11    - Ingress
12    ingress:
13    - from:
14      - ipBlock:
15          cidr: 192.168.5.0/24
16      ports:
17      - protocol: TCP
18        port: 8080
```

Finally, quantum computing is poised to significantly impact cloud-
native architectures. Although it is still in nascent stages, the potential
to process information exponentially faster than classical computers
can revolutionize cloud services. This would particularly enhance
cryptographic operations and complex problem-solving capabilities
within cloud-native applications.

These evolving trends highlight that cloud-native technologies are not static but are continually adapting to accommodate new technologies and methodologies. This constant evolution ensures that enterprises leverage cloud-native architectures not just for current requirements but are also well-prepared for future technological shifts. As cloud-native architectures become deeply integrated with these cutting-edge technologies, they offer more robust, scalable, and secure environments that can drive significant business innovation and efficiency.

Chapter 4

Assessment and Planning for Migration

Assessment and planning are critical initial steps in the migration from legacy systems to advanced technological frameworks like microservices and cloud-native infrastructures. This chapter outlines a systematic approach for evaluating existing systems, identifying migration objectives, and constructing a detailed road map that guides the entire migration process. These planning stages ensure that the transition supports strategic business goals while managing risks and resources effectively.

4.1 Overview of Migration Assessment and Planning

Migrating legacy systems to microservices and cloud-native architectures necessitates a well-structured framework for assessment and planning. This initial phase helps in aligning the technological upgrades with business strategy and operational goals. Accurate assessment leads to effective planning, which is crucial for minimizing risks and ensuring a smooth transition.

The migration assessment starts with a comprehensive evaluation of the current legacy systems. This involves an analysis of the software

architecture, database schema, network configuration, and other critical components. The goal is to gain a deep understanding of the
existing system's strengths and limitations. This assessment should
also include an inventory of all hardware and software assets, and
evaluation of the scalability, security, and compliance aspects of the
current system.

Following the technical assessment, the next step involves identifying
the various business processes that depend on the legacy system. This
requires close collaboration with business stakeholders to ascertain
their needs and expectations from the migration. Understanding the
business processes facilitates identifying which components are crucial
for business operations and should therefore be prioritized during the
migration.

The planning phase of the migration takes into account the insights
gained from the assessment phase. It includes defining clear and measurable goals for the migration, which might range from improving system scalability and performance to achieving better cost management
and compliance with modern standards. Mapping out these goals
helps in setting realistic expectations and provides a benchmark for the
success of the migration project.

The migration plan must also detail the technological approach for the
migration—including the choice of microservices patterns and cloud-
native solutions that align with the identified business needs and technical requirements. Decisions on whether to refactor, re-platform, or
rebuild each component are made based on detailed analyses of cost,
risk, and impact. These decisions are encapsulated within a phase-wise
rollout plan, which outlines the migration process, timelines, and the
resources required at each stage.

Effective migration from legacy systems to modern architectures also
involves meticulous risk assessment to anticipate potential challenges
that might impact business continuity. The risk management strategy
includes identifying probable risks, analyzing their potential impact,
and devising mitigation strategies.

Resource allocation is another critical component of the planning phase.
This task involves arranging the necessary financial, technical, and
human resources. Budget planning becomes essential here as it covers
not only the immediate costs of the migration but also the ongoing
operational costs post-migration.

Lastly, the planning documentation should include a detailed migration roadmap. This roadmap outlines the step-by-step process for migration, supported by timeline estimates and key milestones. Regular updates and revisions to the plan might be required as the migration progresses, to accommodate unforeseen challenges and lessons learned during the implementation.

By adhering to this detailed assessment and planning process, organizations can ensure that their migration effort is systematically aligned with broader business objectives while optimizing the use of resources and minimizing downtime and disruptions. As such, this initial stage lays a critical foundation for the success of migrating to a microservices and cloud-native infrastructure.

4.2 Identifying Goals and Objectives for Migration

The initiation of a migration from a legacy system to a microservices or cloud-native architecture requires a clear delineation of goals and objectives. These goals not only guide the migration process but also align it with the broader business strategy. Successful migration is dependent on understanding both the "why" and the "what" of the transformation. This section explores how to establish comprehensive and strategic objectives, ensuring alignment with overall corporate goals.

Firstly, aligning migration efforts with business goals is essential. Organizations need to assess how the migration will support business initiatives such as increasing market responsiveness, improving product scalability, or reducing operational costs. By forging such alignments, technology migration reinforces business objectives rather than just serving as an IT exercise.

- Identifying objectives related to business growth such as entering new markets or enhancing customer experience.

- Focusing on objectives for operational efficiency, for instance, reducing the time to market or improving system uptime.

- Establishing targets for cost management, including reducing legacy system maintenance costs or lowering overall IT spending through cloud optimization.

91

Secondly, the technical objectives of the migration need to be stated explicitly. These are typically centered around system performance, data management, scalability, and maintainability:

- Enhancing system performance to meet an increase in user demand.

- Improving data integrity and accessibility by adopting advanced data management technologies and practices available in cloud-native environments.

- Achieving scalability to handle dynamically varying workloads without compromising system performance.

- Increasing system maintainability and reducing overheads through improved service modularity offered by microservices architectures.

These technical achievements lay the groundwork for integrating new technologies while deprecating obsolete and rigid ones. Legacy systems often pose significant integration challenges due to monolithic architectures that inhibit quick adaptation to changing technologies or business needs. Therefore, the goal here takes the shape of loosely coupled services and systems that offer higher flexibility and quicker integration with other services and tools, which is a hallmark of microservices.

Moreover, the migration is also influenced by regulatory and compliance requirements. Goals include:

- Ensuring compliance with up-to-date data protection regulations, which could be a significant driver for the migration.

- Aligning with industry-specific standards and regulations to not only maintain regulatory compliance but also enhance security features and system reliability.

The establishment of clear KPIs (Key Performance Indicators) is critical to track the success of the migration in terms of meeting these objectives. For effective measurement, each objective should be associated with specific, measurable, achievable, relevant, and time-bound (SMART) criteria. An objective like 'Improving system performance'

92

might be measured by reduced response times or increased transaction throughput, quantified by specific targets to be achieved post-migration. Another example can be cost reduction, measured based on the percentage decrease in operational and maintenance costs of IT systems after moving to a cloud-native infrastructure.

Success in migration highly depends on the preciseness in the definition of these objectives. Each identified objective must be translated into specific migration steps, ensuring each step is justified with a clear business or technical requirement, which is further embodied in the broader migration strategy. The relevance of such detailed specifics ensures a focused migration effort, optimizing resource usage and minimizing disruptions during the transition phase, ultimately leading to a successful transformation.

4.3 Analyzing the Existing Legacy System

To execute a well-informed migration from a legacy system to a microservices and cloud-native architecture, it is imperative to conduct a thorough analysis of the existing system. This includes understanding the architecture, performance baselines, dependencies, and business functionalities supported by the legacy system.

Architecture Analysis

The initial step in this process is the analysis of the current architecture. This involves cataloging all hardware, software, and network resources that are currently in use. The architecture of the legacy system often dictates potential strategies for decoupling services during the migration phase.

- Identification of monolithic components: Understanding large and intertwined systems components that may need decomposition into microservices.

- Dependency mapping: Identifying and documenting dependencies between different system components to understand the interconnectivity and potential challenges in decoupling.

Performance Assessment

Establishing performance baselines is crucial for ensuring the migrated system meets or exceeds the current capabilities. This involves data collection regarding the response times, throughput, and resource utilization of the existing system.

```
Response Time: Average time taken to respond to requests during peak usage.
Throughput: Number of transactions or operations processed per unit time.
Resource Utilization: Percentage usage of CPU, memory, and I/O operations.
```

Detailed performance metrics are paramount in determining which aspects of the system are critical and the potential impact of migration on system performance.

Dependency Analysis

This step addresses the understanding of both internal and external dependencies that affect the legacy system's operations. It is crucial to identify services and systems that interact with or depend on the legacy system.

- External systems: Documenting third-party services, data feeds, and other systems that integrate with the legacy system.

- Internal dependencies: Analyzing dependencies within the system such as shared databases, common libraries or modules.

Business Functionality Mapping

A core part of the analysis is mapping out the business functionalities that the legacy system supports. This includes detailed documentation of the business processes facilitated by the system, data flow diagrams, and user interactions.

- User role definitions: Identifying different user types and their interaction with the system.

- Process flow diagrams: Graphically representing the processes that are supported by the legacy system.

Risk Identification

Identifying potential risks associated with each component of the legacy system is also integral. This entails understanding the complexities and specific challenges that may arise due to outdated technology, custom code, or operational inefficiencies.

At this juncture, a comprehensive and meticulous assessment of the existing legacy system has been conducted. The accumulated insights serve as the foundation for subsequent migration planning. They enable decision-makers to design a migration roadmap tailored to minimize risks, leverage the most suitable technological solutions, and ensure continuous alignment with business objectives.

4.4 Evaluating Technical Debt and Maintenance Costs

Evaluating technical debt and maintenance costs is an essential component of the migration planning process. Technical debt refers to the implied cost of additional rework caused by choosing an easy solution now instead of using a better approach that might take longer. Legacy systems often carry significant technical debt, which can be attributed to outdated technologies, lack of modularity, tightly coupled components, and non-compliance with current security standards.

Identification and Quantification of Technical Debt

Accurately identifying and quantifying technical debt involves a comprehensive review of the legacy system's source code, architecture, and associated documentation. Key indicators of technical debt include repeated code, large classes or methods, lack of unit tests, and reliance on outdated or unsupported libraries and platforms.

- Examination of source code to identify violations of good coding practices and the existence of "code smells" which may indicate deeper problems in the system.

- Use of static analysis tools to automate the detection of potential issues in code quality and security vulnerabilities.

95

- Review of documentation and version histories to assess the frequency of changes and the reasons for those changes, which might suggest areas of instability and high maintenance costs.

After identifying the problematic areas, it is crucial to estimate the required effort for refactoring. This estimation can be approached by the Application of complexity metrics like Cyclomatic complexity and Technical Debt Ratio, where:

- *Cyclomatic complexity* measures the complexity of a program's control flow graph and is used as a predictor of the maintainability of a component.

- *Technical Debt Ratio* is calculated by dividing the remediation cost by the development cost, expressed as a percentage. This ratio quantifies the relative cost to "pay off" the debt.

Assessing Maintenance Costs

Maintenance costs in legacy systems are influenced heavily by the technical debt they carry. Higher debt often correlates with increased expenditure on bug fixing, adapting existing features to new requirements, and ensuring the system operates on current technology platforms. Calculation of maintenance costs requires understanding the current and future states of system operation, including:

- Evaluation of the existing support contracts and the costs associated with third-party services.

- Assessment of the internal team's efforts to maintain operational stability, including time spent on debugging and implementing minor enhancements or regulatory upgrades.

- Forecasting future maintenance needs based on the growth of the organization and potential changes in regulatory requirements that impact the system.

Financial models such as Cost of Delay can be incorporated to relate maintenance costs with operational efficiency and risk to provide a monetary image of ongoing expenses versus potential gains from migration. Furthermore, this evaluation feedback should be documented elaborately for stakeholders' review, highlighting the urgency or non-urgency of the migration based purely on cost benefits.

The result of this evaluation is a critical input for the go-no-go decision of migration projects. Armed with knowledge about what parts of the system are costing the most in terms of maintenance and where the most significant chunks of technical debt lie, decision-makers can prioritize migration efforts effectively. These efforts optimize the allocation of resources, striking a balance between immediate business needs and long-term technological sustainability, presenting a holistic approach to managing legacy system challenges during migration planning.

4.5 Defining Migration Scope and Phasing

Defining the migration scope and phasing involves delineating the components of the existing system that will be moved to the new architecture, and scheduling the transition in manageable, iterative phases. This meticulous approach facilitates effective resource management, reduces potential risks, and ensures minimal disruption to business operations.

When initiating the scope definition, the first step is to categorize the services or modules of the legacy system based on their migration readiness and business value. The categorization should clearly distinguish between different system components using criteria such as:

- Usage frequency

- Dependencies on other components

- Complexity of the data environment

- Relevance to core business processes

Each service or module is mapped into one of three categories:

- High Priority: These services are critical for business operations and customer interaction. They typically handle core functionalities and are ideal candidates for early migration to leverage cloud-native benefits.

- Medium Priority: Services that are less critical but would benefit from scalability and better maintenance in the new architecture

97

fall into this category. They are migrated after the high-priority ones.

- Low Priority: These often include legacy services that are rarely used or being phased out. These services might not be migrated at all or could be maintained in a legacy wrapper as part of a hybrid approach during the transitional phase.

Post categorization, a migration roadmap is drafted, which includes the following phases:

1. **Phase 1: Pilot Migration**: This phase involves selecting a small, manageable high-priority service for migration. The selected service should serve as a pilot project to build confidence, refine the migration process, and prepare the team for larger-scale migrations. This phase includes:

   - Establishing the microservice design.
   - Implementing the CI/CD pipeline for automated deployment.
   - Introducing basic monitoring and logging capabilities.

2. **Phase 2: Core Services Migration**: Here, the major high-priority services are migrated. This phase is characterized by:

   - Scaling up the microservices infrastructure.
   - Expanding monitoring and advanced analytics.
   - Integrating services with new data management solutions.

3. **Phase 3: Dependency Decoupling**: In this phase, medium priority and some low-priority services that are tightly coupled with high-priority ones are migrated or rearchitected to become more independent. Key activities include:

   - Redesigning legacy integration patterns.
   - Removing redundant data storage.
   - Optimizing performance post-decoupling.

4. **Phase 4: Optimization and Fine-tuning**: The final phase involves the migration of remaining medium and low-priority services, along with ongoing optimization:

   - Tuning performance based on real-world usage data.

- Enhancing security and compliance measures as needed.
- Completing the documentation and final testing cycles.

Mapping these categories and phases clearly in the migration plan is critical to aligning migration activities with business priorities and technical capabilities. It ensures that resources are efficiently allocated throughout the migration process and helps set realistic expectations for all stakeholders involved in the transition.

Emphasizing iterative deployment allows for timely feedback on the system's performance and the flexibility to make adjustments prior to additional phases. This not only mitigates risks but also aligns the migration process with ongoing business requirements and potential market changes. Prioritizing components based on their business importance and readiness for migration maximizes the operational benefits and cost-savings potential of moving to a microservices and cloud-native architecture.

4.6 Selecting the Right Microservices and Cloud-Native Patterns

Selecting the appropriate microservices and cloud-native patterns is a critical step in the migration process as it sets the foundation for a scalable, maintainable, and efficient architecture. Given the complexity and the variety of patterns available, it is essential to understand the criteria impacting this decision and the implications of each pattern within the specific context of your project.

When selecting these patterns, the primary goal is to ensure that the architecture aligns with business requirements and leverages the advantages of a cloud-native environment. To start, let us delve into how different architectural styles can be matched with migration goals.

- **Decomposition by Business Capability:** For organizations prioritizing agility and scalability, decomposing the legacy application based on business capability yields manageable, loosely coupled, independently deployable microservices which align with specific business functions. This approach enhances business relevance and facilitates better team alignment.

- **Decomposition by Subdomain:** In scenarios where the application is complex, breaking it down into subdomains based on

99

Domain-Driven Design principles helps in managing complexity and interdependencies effectively.

- **Strangler Fig Pattern:** Recommended for highly sensitive production environments, this pattern involves gradually replacing specific pieces of functionality with new microservices. It serves as an incremental approach that minimizes risk by allowing the new and old systems to coexist during the transition period.

- **API Gateway Pattern:** Establishing an API gateway as a single entry point manages API versions and securitizes calls to internal services, which are dynamically routed to different backend services. This pattern is invaluable in managing microservices APIs for both internal and external clients.

- **Backend for Frontend (BFF) Pattern:** When different clients (e.g., mobile, web, desktop) require different views and interactions, this pattern advocates creating separate backend services tailored for each type of client to optimize communication and reduce front-end complexity.

Further, the selection process involves a detailed assessment of each potential pattern in light of the current legacy system's capabilities and projected needs. Here, several technical, operational, and business criteria are evaluated:

- **Performance:** Patterns need to be assessed for their potential to enhance system performance, including load balancing strategies, service discovery mechanisms, and dynamic scaling capabilities.

- **Fault Tolerance:** Assessing each pattern's capability to handle service failures without affecting user experience is crucial. Implementations like Circuit Breaker or Bulkhead can shield the system from cascading failures.

- **Security:** A key concern is ensuring that the patterns support robust security protocols for authentication, authorization, and data protection. The ability to integrate seamlessly with security tools and frameworks in the cloud-native ecosystem is also evaluated.

- **Technological Compatibility:** Compatibility with existing technology stacks and the potential need for additional tooling or technology changes need careful consideration.

100

The challenge lies not only in selecting the right patterns but also in adapting them to the specific nuances of the project and its operational context. As such, mapping technologies to business goals through a well-defined, iterative approach enhances the chances of successful migration. By iterating through this selection process, adjusting criteria, and validating against actual project outcomes, the architecture evolves to more effectively support strategic business objectives and operational requirements.

Throughout this selection phase, it is essential to ensure all system stakeholders are involved and informed about the rationale for the chosen patterns, anticipated changes, and expected benefits. This engagement fosters a collaborative environment and promotes an inclusive approach to tackling the complexities of migration.

By carefully selecting and adapting microservices and cloud-native patterns, the migrated system not only meets current technological standards but is also positioned well for future scalability and enhancements, reinforcing the organization's strategic objectives within its competitive landscape.

4.7 Risk Assessment and Mitigation Strategies

Effective risk management is paramount to ensure the success of migration projects from legacy systems to microservice architectures. This section details the systematic approach to identifying, analyzing, and mitigating potential risks associated with such transformative initiatives.

Identifying potential risks begins with a thorough analysis of the existing legacy system. Key factors such as system complexity, dependency on third-party services, and historical downtime records provide initial insights into potential vulnerabilities. Additionally, the experience and skill levels of the current IT staff in new technologies play a critical role in foreseeing challenges in both the migration and the maintenance phases post-migration.

The process of risk analysis involves categorizing identified risks based on their probability of occurrence and the potential impact on the migration process. This can be visually represented using a risk matrix. Common risks include technological mismatches, data migration failures, security breaches, and unexpected downtime.

- Technological risks arise from the incompatibility between legacy and new systems.

- Data-related risks concern the integrity and loss of data during its transfer from legacy structures to new storage formats.

- Security risks are heightened due to new interfaces and more complex connectivity options.

- Operational risks involve disruptions in business activities during the migration process.

After classifying and prioritizing risks, the next step is to develop a comprehensive mitigation strategy. This entails detailed plans to address each significant risk, leveraging best practices and lessons learned from similar previous projects. It also includes the setup of monitoring systems to track risk indicators during migration.

For increasing the robustness of data migration, techniques such as parallel runs and the use of data verification tools to confirm the integrity of the migrated data should be employed. Security risks can be mitigated by implementing up-to-date encryption methods and continuously testing the security of new services.

It is imperative to incorporate contingency planning. This includes predefined response strategies that address possible failures and allocate resources that can quickly remedy situations without jeopardizing the entire project timeline. For instance, in the case of critical system failures, having a rollback plan to restore systems back to their previous state can be crucial.

Ensuring continuous communication across all team members coupled with regular reviews of risk assessments are also vital. Changing conditions can alter risk dynamics considerably, thereby requiring the migration plan and strategies to be agile enough to adapt.

Regular training sessions for staff on the new system technologies and best practices will reduce operational risks by enhancing their understanding of the new system operations and maintenance. This proactive approach not only mitigates risk but also aids in the smooth transition to the new system.

By systematically identifying, analyzing, and mitigating risks, organizations can ensure fewer disruptions and maintain continuity of operations during the migration to microservices and cloud-native architectures. This disciplined approach towards risk management will contribute significantly to the success of the migration initiative, safeguarding both the technological investments and overall business interests.

4.8 Resource Allocation and Budget Planning

Effective resource allocation and budget planning are pivotal for the successful migration from legacy systems to microservices and cloud-native architectures. This section elucidates the methodology for estimating costs, allocating resources, and planning the budget throughout the migration process.

Allocating financial resources judiciously is the cornerstone of any migration project. It is imperative to categorize costs into different segments such as initial setup, training, implementation, and ongoing operational expenses. A robust estimation starts with a thorough analysis of the necessary resources for project execution which can be broadly classified into human resources, technology acquisitions, and operational overheads.

- Human resources involve costs related to staffing, which include hiring new talent or training existing employees. Consider the expertise required at various phases such as development, deployment, and maintenance.

- Technology acquisitions encompass the expenses on new software, updated hardware, or third-party services necessary for building a microservices architecture.

- Operational overheads include day-to-day running costs, unexpected expenses, and costs of transitioning from old systems to new ones.

Immediate cost calculations often follow the identification and categorization of these resources. Using historical data and predictive analytics can enhance the accuracy of these estimations. Tools like cost estimation software or services provided by cloud vendors (Amazon

Web Services, Microsoft Azure, etc.) offer detailed insights into the prospective expenditure patterns.

```
Example of a typical cost categorization:
- Initial Setup: 20% of total budget
- Training: 15% of total budget
- Implementation: 30% of total budget
- Operational Expenses: 35% of total budget
```

Transitioning to a more granular level, budget planning must align with the phased implementation approach defined earlier in the migration roadmap. Allocating a contingency budget for each phase can safeguard against possible financial overshoots due to unforeseen challenges.

Algorithm 3: Algorithm to estimate phase-specific migration budgets

---

Result: Develop an initial budget estimate for each phase of migration

1 initialization;
2 **for** *each phase in the migration plan* **do**
3 | estimate human resources costs;
4 | estimate technology acquisition costs;
5 | estimate operational overheads;
6 | adjust estimates based on historical data;
7 | add contingency allowance;
8 | summarize the phase budget;
9 **end**

Ensuring constant monitoring and revision of the budget as the project advances is crucial. This dynamic approach allows the migration team to stay agile and adapt to any changes effectively, reducing the risk of significant financial impacts.

Utilizing performance metrics such as cost variance (CV) and budget at completion (BAC) ensures that budget planning remains a continuous cycle rather than a one-time estimation. Performance indices are updated regularly to reflect the true financial state compared to the planned expenditures.

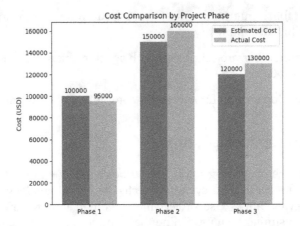

Regular reviews and adjustments in the resource allocation and budget planning processes ensure that each phase of the migration leverages the allocated resources efficiently and remains within financial bounds, contributing to the overall success and sustainability of the migration project.

4.9 Developing a Detailed Migration Roadmap

Developing a detailed migration roadmap is an essential component of transitioning from a legacy system to microservices and cloud-native architectures. This roadmap not only provides a structured timeline for project execution but also aligns the migration activities with business objectives and technical requirements.

Initial Steps in Roadmap Development

The first step in creating a migration roadmap is to consolidate the findings from the earlier phases of assessment and planning. This includes incorporating insights from the evaluation of the existing legacy system, the technical debt, and the specifically defined migration scope and phases. These inputs form the foundation for a coherent migration strategy.

- Establish migration milestones based on business priorities and technical complexity.

- Define clear project phases with specific objectives and expected outputs.

- Develop criteria for successful completion of each phase.

Timeline and Scheduling

The timeline of the migration should be carefully crafted, taking into consideration business cycles, expected technical challenges, and resource availability. Use project management tools to draw a Gantt chart or a similar visual timeline that outlines all major activities and their expected durations.

```
Example of a simplified Gantt chart entry:
- Phase 1: Data Assessment, Jan 2023 - Feb 2023
- Phase 2: Service Modelling, Mar 2023 - Apr 2023
```

Resource Assignment

Following timeline establishment, allocate resources effectively across planned tasks. This includes human resources, technologies (both existing and new), and financial resources. Assign project roles based on the skills and experience needed for each phase of the migration. Typical roles might include:

- Project Manager

- Systems Architect

- DevOps Engineer

- Legacy System Analyst

- Cloud Specialist

Integration and Testing Strategy

Integration and testing form crucial checkpoints in the roadmap. Develop a strategic approach to integrate new microservices with existing systems (where necessary) and plan comprehensive testing phases to ensure functional and performance standards are met. Include:

106

- Unit testing of new microservices

- Integration testing between the microservices and existing legacy components

- System-wide performance testing

Communication and Documentation

Effective communication mechanisms must be established to ensure all stakeholders are kept informed about the migration's progress and any issues that might arise. Create a communication plan detailing the methods and frequency of updates.

Documentation is equally important. Document each phase of the migration process, decisions made, and rationales behind them. This not only helps in maintaining clarity but also assists new team members to quickly come up to speed.

Contingency and Risk Management

Identify potential risks at each stage of the migration and develop contingency plans. Risks can range from data loss and security breaches to unexpected downtime and cost overruns.

- Data handling errors

- Security vulnerabilities

- Compliance issues

- Technological malfunctions or incompatibilities

Review and Adjustment Mechanism

Throughout the migration process, establish regular review points to assess the progress against the original objectives and KPIs. This allows for ongoing adjustments to the strategy in response to new challenges or opportunities.

Algorithm 4: Algorithm for Risk Assessment and Contingency Planning

---

Input: Identified risks
Output: Contingency strategies
1 **foreach** *risk* **do**
2   Assess the probability and impact of the risk
3   Develop mitigation strategies specific to the risk
4   Document the risk and corresponding response plan

Finalization of the Roadmap

Once all elements are defined, compile them into a comprehensive migration roadmap document. This document should clearly articulate the migration vision, broken down into structured and actionable phases. Ensure this final roadmap is approved by all key stakeholders to enable a unified approach to the migration initiative.

4.10 Stakeholder Engagement and Communication Planning

Effective stakeholder engagement and communication are paramount in the context of migrating legacy systems to microservices and cloud-native architectures. Involving stakeholders early and maintaining transparent communication throughout the project lifecycle helps in managing expectations, fostering collaboration, and ensuring alignment with the business goals of the migration.

Identifying Key Stakeholders: The first step involves identifying all potential stakeholders affected by the migration. These typically include business unit heads, IT staff, end-users, senior management, and external partners. It is crucial to understand their interests, influence, and level of impact on the project.

- Business unit heads are concerned with how the migration will affect the operations and performance metrics of their units.

- IT staff focuses on the technical details and the implications of the migration on existing processes.

108

- End-users are primarily concerned with how the migration might change their interaction with the system.

- Senior management will be interested in the strategic advantages of the migration and its alignment with broader business objectives.

- External partners might need to adapt their interfaces or operations to accommodate the new system architecture.

Developing a Communication Plan: Crafting a detailed and effective communication plan is essential. This plan should outline:

- The methods of communication to be used (meetings, email updates, workshops, etc.).

- The frequency of communication, which may vary between different stakeholder groups.

- Specific milestones at which communication is crucial (e.g., completion of phases, testing, deployment).

- Feedback mechanisms to gather inputs and concerns from stakeholders throughout the migration process.

In the communication plan, it is beneficial to include specific templates and tools for reporting so that information is presented consistently, making it easier for stakeholders to understand the progress and challenges of the migration.

Engagement Mechanisms: Engaging stakeholders is not solely about sending them updates but also involves actively soliciting their input and collaboration. Various mechanisms can be employed:

- Workshops and seminars to educate stakeholders about the benefits and challenges of migrating to microservices and cloud-native architectures.

- Regular steering committee meetings which include high-level stakeholders to discuss strategic issues and make crucial decisions.

- Surveys and feedback forms that enable stakeholders to express their concerns and suggestions regarding the migration process.

Monitoring and Adjusting the Communication Plan: The communication plan must be dynamic. It should be regularly reviewed and adjusted based on the following criteria:

- Stakeholder feedback — Are the stakeholders' needs being met? Are their concerns being addressed effectively?

- Migration progress — Does the communication plan need to be intensified or modified to address challenges or changes in scope?

Implementing an effective stakeholder engagement and communication plan facilitates a smoother transition by ensuring that all parties involved are informed and supportive of the migration objectives. Additionally, it plays a critical role in preempting resistance by addressing concerns proactively and realigning the project with the organization's strategic goals as necessary. Success in this regard contributes to a transparent, inclusive, and ultimately productive migration process.

4.11 Training and Skill Development for Teams

The transition from a traditional legacy system to modern, cloud-native microservices architectures demands a significant shift in the skillset and competencies of the involved IT teams. It is imperative that organizations equip their workforce with necessary technical skills and knowledge to support the new environment effectively. This section explores the imperative segments of training and skills development for these teams, covering core technologies, methodologies, and continuous learning frameworks.

Identifying Skill Gaps

Initial efforts in training must begin with an accurate assessment of existing skills against the skills needed for the new technology stack. This discrepancy forms the basis of the skill gap analysis.

- Analyze current team skills through surveys, interviews, and performance assessments.

- Compare existing skills with those required for technologies such as Docker, Kubernetes, CI/CD pipelines, and other cloud-native tools.

- Highlight gaps in advanced programming languages known to be essential in microservices environments, like Go and Scala.

Designing a Comprehensive Training Program

Following the identification of skill gaps, designing an appropriate training program tailors development needs to organizational goals. The training program should address both immediate skill shortages and long-term capability building.

- Incorporate modular training sessions segmented into foundational, intermediate, and advanced topics.

- Utilize a blend of learning approaches including classroom training, hands-on workshops, and e-learning modules.

- Focus training modules on both the theoretical aspects of microservices and cloud-native technologies, and practical, real-world application.

Implementation of Training Initiatives

Effective implementation of training programs is crucial for maximal benefit. It must be structured and timed to coincide with the various phases of the migration project.

- Schedule training sessions at optimal times during the migration process to ensure newly acquired skills are applied immediately.

- Provide access to cloud environments and microservices frameworks to allow real-time applications of skills learnt.

- Reinforce learning through regular refresher courses and updates on evolving technologies.

Monitoring and Evaluating Training Effectiveness

To ensure the training programs contribute positively towards the migration goals, continuous monitoring and evaluation are necessary.

- Establish benchmarks and performance metrics to assess the impact of training on team performance and migration success.

- Use regular feedback loops from employees to adjust and improve training methods and content.

- Integrate skills assessment at the end of each training module to measure knowledge acquisition and retention.

Promoting a Culture of Continuous Improvement

Migration to cloud-native architectures is not a one-time shift but a continuous evolution of technology and practices. Promoting an organizational culture that values ongoing learning and skill improvement is vital.

- Encourage teams to stay updated with the latest developments in technology by sponsoring participation in relevant conferences, webinars, and professional courses.

- Offer incentives for obtaining certifications in key technology areas such as cloud operations, data management, and security.

- Facilitate knowledge sharing among teams to foster a collaborative learning environment and accelerate collective problem-solving and innovation.

Effective training and skills development are critical enablers of a successful migration from legacy to cloud-native and microservice-based architectures. By strategically equipping teams with necessary skills, organizations not only enhance their technical capabilities but also empower their workforce to address the challenges of modern IT environments efficiently. This strategic alignment of skills with organizational migration goals is an essential underpinning of successful change management and the continuous evolution towards a more flexible and scalable technology infrastructure.

4.12 Setting up Key Performance Indicators (KPIs) for Migration Success

Key Performance Indicators (KPIs) provide measurable values that are crucial in observing the effectiveness and success of the migration process. They offer clear criteria for tracking progress, gauging performance, and identifying areas needing improvement during the migration from legacy systems to microservices and cloud-native architectures. This part discusses the setup and utility of KPIs critical in assuring that the migration achieves its intended goals.

Selection of KPIs: The selection of appropriate KPIs hinges on the specific objectives established earlier in the migration process. KPIs should be SMART: Specific, Measurable, Achievable, Relevant, and Time-bound. Furthermore, they need to align with both technical and business facets of the migration project to ensure balanced and comprehensive monitoring. Typical examples of KPIs for migration projects include system downtime during migration, response times before and after migration, user satisfaction ratings, and cost savings achieved through the migration process.

- `System Downtime`: Measures the total time the system is non-operational during the migration. A lower value indicates better performance in minimizing impact on business operations.

- `Response Time`: Compares the performance latency of the system before and after migration. A shorter response time after migration implies performance improvement.

- `User Satisfaction Rating`: Gauges the end-user satisfaction with the new system. This is typically assessed through surveys post-migration.

- `Cost Savings`: Examines the reduction in operational costs as a result of the migration, including long-term maintenance costs.

Implementation of KPI Monitoring: To monitor these indicators effectively, automated tools and dashboards are implemented. These tools provide real-time data analysis and visualization, which are essential for timely decision-making and adjustment strategies.

For example, consider a migration situation where response times are crucial. The following pseudocode outlines an approach for monitoring response times across both the legacy and migrated systems:

---

1 **if** *system* == *legacy* **then**
2   measure_response_time(legacy_system)
3 **else**
4   measure_response_time(migrated_system)

Regular Review and Adjustment of KPIs: KPIs are not static, and they should be reviewed periodically to reflect changes in migration strategies, unexpected challenges, and shifts in business objectives. This iterative review helps in keeping the migration aligned with business goals and the dynamic technological landscape.

For visual analysis and ongoing monitoring, creating charts that depict KPI trends over time can be beneficial. Below is an example using Python with libraries such as numpy, pandas, and matplotlib to plot response time data before and after migration.

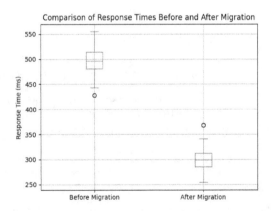

Ongoing Adjustment and Reassessment: As the migration progresses, it may be necessary to redefine KPIs or introduce new ones. This adaptability is crucial for keeping the migration efforts aligned with organizational targets and evolving industry standards.

Through the systematic setup, monitoring, and adjustment of KPIs, organizations can better manage the complex task of migrating to microservices and cloud-native architectures. The KPIs not only provide a quantifiable measure of success but also ensure that the migration process remains under continuous evaluation and improvement, thereby directly contributing to the achievement of desired strategic outcomes.

Chapter 5

Strategies for Decomposing a Monolithic System

Decomposing a monolithic system into microservices is a complex yet vital process for organizations seeking to increase their system's modularity and adaptability. This chapter explores various strategies and methodologies to effectively identify and separate functional components into independent services. The focus is on ensuring that each service can be developed, deployed, and scaled independently, which improves fault isolation and enhances the overall agility of the application development lifecycle.

5.1 Understanding Monolithic Systems and Their Challenges

A monolithic system is traditionally defined as a unified software entity in which components for input handling, processing, and output management are interwoven and interdependent. Such systems have typically been the foundation of many enterprise applications due to the straightforward development and deployment models they offer. However, they bring a set of inherent challenges which intensify as the scale and complexity of applications increase.

Scalability Challenges: Monolithic architectures often struggle with effective scalability. Scaling a monolithic application typically means operating multiple identical copies of the application behind a load balancer. This approach can lead to excessive resource consumption because each instance of the application handles the full set of functionalities, even if only a fraction of these functionalities is under high demand at any given time.

Difficulty in Implementing Changes: Any modification, no matter its size, requires redeploying the entire application. This tight coupling leads to high risk and complexity in introducing changes, as a single fault in any module could potentially compromise the entire system. The buildup of such interconnected code tends to evolve into what is often referred to as "spaghetti code," which is difficult to understand, modify, and maintain.

Technological Restraints: Monoliths often bind an organization to a specific technology stack. Over time, as these technologies become outdated, the entire application might need significant rewrites to accommodate new, more efficient technologies. This technology lock-in restricts an organization's agility and ability to adopt newer tools that enhance productivity and feature delivery.

Extended Downtime and Lower Availability: Due to the interconnected nature of monolithic applications, deploying updates or new features generally involves taking the system offline, leading to downtime. Recurring downtime for updates affects the availability and reliability of the system which, in turn, impacts customer satisfaction and trust.

Barrier to Continuous Integration/Continuous Deployment (CI/CD): Implementing Continuous Integration and Continuous Deployment is challenging in a monolithic setup due to the size and complexity of the application. The lengthy build and test cycles reduce development agility and delay the feedback loop essential for timely corrections and updates.

The convergence of these challenges necessitates exploring architectural paradigms that better align with the dynamic requirements of modern business operations. Microservices architectures present a viable alternative by promoting a decomposed approach towards application development, wherein each service is developed, deployed, and scaled independently. Moving forward, addressing these monolithic

challenges will set the stage for discussing and engaging with strategies that effectively decompose monolithic systems into microservices,
increasing system robustness, scalability, and developer productivity.

5.2 Identifying Components for Decomposition

Decomposing a monolithic system into microservices requires methodical identification of components that can function as independent
services. The process begins with a thorough analysis of the existing
monolithic architecture to understand the relationships and dependencies between various components. This analysis involves review-
ing the codebase, architecture documentation, and consultation with
stakeholders, including developers, system architects, and business
leaders, who understand the application's functioning and business
requirements.

Analysis of the Monolithic Architecture

To initiate, it is essential to map out a detailed architectural overview
of the existing system. This involves creating or revisiting architectural
diagrams that display the various components of the system and how
they interact. Through the use of Unified Modeling Language (UML)
diagrams, particularly class diagrams and sequence diagrams, one can
understand the flow of data and control across the system. Interaction
with system architects and senior developers helps in validating these
diagrams and understanding undocumented or obscure system behaviors.

Component Coupling and Cohesion

Key to identifying the components for decomposition is assessing the
degree of coupling and cohesion within the monolithic system. Components with high cohesion that perform a unique set of related functions
are ideal candidates to be evolved into microservices. Conversely,
components with high coupling need a detailed analysis as they may
be too dependent on other components, sharing data and behaviors.
Lowering the coupling before the actual decomposition can simplify
the process significantly.

```
1  // Example pseudo-code to assess component coupling
2  function assessCoupling(component):
3      connections = countExternalConnections(component)
4      if connections > threshold:
5          print("High coupling detected:", component)
```

```
High coupling detected: PaymentProcessing
```

For practical assessment, software tools like Structure101 and Lattix can be used to analyze and visualize the dependencies which aid in understanding component interactions more lucidly.

Business Domain Analysis

Alongside the technical aspect, the business domain analysis forms the crux of the initial phase of decomposition. This analysis focuses on business capabilities and how they are currently implemented in the system. It is crucial to identify domain boundaries as these will guide the formation of `Service Boundaries` in later stages. Techniques like Event Storming and domain story telling facilitate collaborative discovery and documentation of business processes and domain boundaries. These sessions should involve domain experts and product owners besides the technical team.

Utilization of Code Metrics

Quantitative analysis through code metrics also assists in identifying decomposition candidates. Metrics such as cyclomatic complexity, code churn, and coupling metrics are valuable. Tools like SonarQube or Code Climate provide insights into the health of various system components. Components with high complexity and frequent modifications are potential candidates indicating either problematic areas that need refactoring or areas subjected to frequent business rule changes, thus suitable for isolation as separate services.

- Cyclomatic complexity helps identify complex modules.

- Code churn indicates how often the component has changed.

- Coupling metrics highlight the interdependence between components.

Drawing on these analyses, one can start identifying and outlining the boundary of each potential component. This leads to an iterative process of refining these boundaries through further analysis and stakeholder feedback. The resulting components are evaluated against strategic business goals and IT capabilities to ensure alignment and the practical feasibility of maintenance post-decomposition.

Detailed documentation during this entire phase is paramount, as it serves as the foundational blueprint for the remaining decomposition process. Armed with this structured information and preliminary component boundaries, the project progresses into more advanced stages of decomposition where these components are gradually transformed into independent, deployable microservices.

5.3 Domain-Driven Design (DDD) Principles for Decomposition

Domain-Driven Design (DDD) is a conceptual approach primarily aimed at aligning complex software designs with an organization's business operations. Central to DDD is the development of an ubiquitous language that is shared between developers and domain experts, ensuring software precisely conforms to business needs. In the context of decomposing a monolithic system into microservices, DDD principles can provide systematic guidelines to identify natural boundaries within the system, allowing a clear pathway towards decoupling and enhanced modularity.

The primary principle of DDD in the realm of system decomposition is the concept of *Bounded Contexts*. A Bounded Context is a design pattern that defines clear boundaries encapsulating functionality and the data pertinent to a specific domain model. Each bounded context corresponds to a logical segment within the overall domain where a particular domain model applies. This segmentation is critical as it guides developers on how subsystems interact and integrate with one another, promoting a clear separation and preventing coupling within the system.

Implementing Bounded Contexts involves several key steps:

- Identifying the contexts: It requires a thorough analysis of the domain to outline distinct areas where different domain models

121

apply. These areas are guided by differences in terminology, processes, or data distinctiveness.

- Define the boundaries: Once identified, explicit boundaries separating each bounded context must be defined. These boundaries determine the scope of a microservice, ensuring that it only addresses concerns within its context and does not overstep into others.

- Context mapping: This involves outlining how different bounded contexts interact with one another. This mapping guides the communication and integration patterns between decomposed services, such ensuring the use of appropriately scoped interfaces and data transfer objects (DTOs).

Another crucial concept in DDD aiding in the decomposition process is the `Aggregate`. An aggregate is a cluster of domain objects that can be treated as a single unit for data changes. In defining aggregates, one designates one of the objects as an *Aggregate Root*, which is the only object within the aggregate that external objects are allowed to hold references to. This establishes clear ownership and boundaries for operations, which is particularly important when transferring monolithic components to microservices because it limits the scope of changes and the associated ripple effects across the system.

The process of identifying aggregates can be properly visualized through the following pseudocode, which considers domain entities and their relationships to determine roots:

Algorithm 5: Pseudo-algorithm for identifying aggregate roots within a bounded context

---

Data: Entity relationships within a bounded context
Result: Identify aggregate roots
1 **foreach** *entity in entities* **do**
2   **if** *entity has independent lifecycle and global identity* **then**
3 | Mark entity as potential aggregate root
4   **foreach** *related entity* **do**
5   **if** *dependency exists but does not necessitate direct modification* **then**
6 | Attach related entity under potential root

In summary, the application of Domain-Driven Design in system decomposition offers a structured approach to identifying service boundaries and ensuring each microservice encapsulates a distinct and coherent model of the domain. With clear delineation provided by bounded
contexts and a methodical aggregate design, systems can be effectively
decomposed into microservices that are autonomous, yet efficiently col-
laborate within the larger ecosystem. This however requires consistent
dialogue and collaboration between developers and domain experts
to align the software constructs with the actual business needs and
processes, encapsulating the essence of DDD.

5.4 Strangling the Monolith: Incremental De-composition

The strategy of "strangling" a monolith involves incrementally replacing specific parts of a monolithic application with microservices. This
approach is particularly effective in mitigating risk by allowing for
piecemeal improvements and validations without disrupting the entire
system. The process can be described in a series of detailed steps, each
focusing on isolating and transitioning particular functionalities from
the monolith to independently deployable services.

The initial step in this incremental decomposition approach is to create
a detailed map of the existing monolithic application. This involves
understanding the request flow, dependencies, and interactions within
the application. Typically, this is achieved by logging and monitoring
the system to capture current usage patterns and data flows.

```
Sample log output of request flow:
GET /product/details/1 -> Database query on Products table
POST /product/update -> Update operation on Products table
```

Following the mapping phase, the next step is to identify the seams
within the application. A seam is a place in the application where
software components interact in such a way that they can be sepa-
rated without extensive modification. Commonly, seams are identified
around business capabilities or functionalities that show a high degree
of cohesion but loose coupling with other parts of the system.

Once seams are identified, the next stage involves creating a proxy layer
that intercepts calls to these specific parts of the monolithic system.
This proxy serves as an intermediary, deciding whether to route a

request to the old monolith or to the new microservice based on certain rules or the maturity of the microservice.

```
1  from http.server import BaseHTTPRequestHandler, HTTPServer
2
3  class ProxyHandler(BaseHTTPRequestHandler):
4      def do_GET(self):
5          if self.path.startswith("/products"):
6              route_to_microservice(self.path)
7          else:
8              route_to_monolith(self.path)
9
10 def route_to_microservice(path):
11     # Code to redirect to microservice
12     pass
13
14 def route_to_monolith(path):
15     # Code to handle request via monolith
16     pass
```

The creation of microservices starts with building small, often singular function services that replicate the functionality found at the identified seams of the monolith. This is a crucial phase as it involves not only software development but also adapting data storage solutions to fit the needs of new, decoupled applications. Data that was once centrally stored must now be divided and managed across the newly created services. This step might involve data duplication initially, which can be addressed over time as the system evolves.

- Deploy the microservice in a controlled environment.

- Gradually shift traffic from the monolith to the microservice.

- Monitor the performance and functionality of the microservice closely.

- Scale up the microservice as confidence in its stability grows.

This stage is followed by a feedback loop consisting of monitoring, analyzing, and refining. The microservices are closely monitored for performance issues, bugs, and other problems. The insights gained from this monitoring are used to refine the microservice further and to decide on subsequent migrations.

The 'strangling' process is iteratively applied until the functionality provided by the monolith is fully replaced by microservices. At this point, the monolith can be decommissioned. The success of this methodology lies in its incremental nature, allowing problems to be localized and addressed promptly without cascading effects on critical

---

Data: Monitoring data from new microservice
Result: Improved version of microservice
1 initialization;
2 **while** *not converged* **do**
3   analyze the performance data;
4   **if** *anomaly detected* **then**
5   pinpoint the problem;
6   correct the issue;
7   redeploy;
8   **end**
9   collect new data;
10 **end**

---

system services. The transition is thus not only manageable but also conducive to continuous enhancement through feedback-oriented development practices.

5.5 Identifying and Extracting Microservices

Identifying and extracting microservices from a monolithic system is a pivotal task that influences the efficiency, reliability, and scalability of the resulting application architecture. This phase demands a meticulous examination of the monolith's business functionality and a systematic approach to service identification and isolation.

The first step in this process is the careful analysis of existing system functionalities and their interdependencies. This analysis can be facilitated by utilizing several techniques and tools designed for static and dynamic analysis of the source code. For example, static analysis tools like Structure101 and Lattix provide insights into the architectural dependencies and modules within the system. These tools generate diagrams and reports that help developers visualize the complexity and coupling between different parts of the application.

Dynamic analysis, on the other hand, involves techniques such as log analysis and monitoring runtime behaviors to understand how different parts of the system interact during execution. Tools like DynaTrace and NewRelic offer capabilities for tracing and profiling applications, which can be invaluable for recognizing runtime dependencies that are not evident in the codebase directly.

Once a comprehensive understanding of the system is achieved, the next step is to define the boundaries for potential microservices. This involves identifying logical groupings of functionalities that can operate as autonomously as possible. Applying Domain-Driven Design (DDD) principles, particularly the concept of 'Bounded Contexts', is crucial at this stage. Each bounded context represents a clear boundary, within which lies a distinct set of functionalities that can be developed, deployed, and scaled independently.

For instance, consider a typical e-commerce application. By analyzing the business domains, we can extract multiple microservices such as 'User Management', 'Product Management', 'Order Management', and 'Payment Processing'. Each of these services encompasses a discrete business capability and interacts with other services in a defined and controlled manner.

The process of physically separating these identified services from the monolith involves refactoring the existing codebase. The refactoring must ensure that each microservice only contains code and dependencies relevant to its functionality. Dependency management tools such as Gradle or Maven become instrumental here, as they aid in defining and managing service-specific libraries and frameworks without overlap.

Following the code separation, each microservice's endpoints need to be defined. These endpoints act as the communication interface with other services and should be designed to be as lightweight and non-restrictive as possible, often implemented using RESTful APIs or asynchronous messaging patterns like those provided by RabbitMQ or Kafka.

Now let us discuss an example to demonstrate this extraction process. Consider a part of a legacy monolithic application responsible for handling user authentication and profile management. The code snippet below illustrates a simplified method of extracting the 'User Management' microservice:

```
1  // Original Monolithic Code Base
2  public class UserService {
3      public User loginUser(String username, String password) {
4          // Authentication logic
5      }
6
7      public User updateUserProfile(int userId, User newDetails) {
8          // Update profile logic
```

```
 9       }
10    }
11
12    // Extracted Microservice for User Management
13    public class UserManagementService {
14        public User loginUser(String username, String password) {
15            // Authentication logic, potentially updated for microservice
16        }
17
18        public User updateUserProfile(int userId, User newDetails) {
19            // Update profile logic, refactored for microservice
20        }
21    }
```

After extracting the service, the communication between 'User Management' and other parts of the system would shift from direct method
calls to network-based API calls. This decoupling introduces need for
careful handling of data consistency and fault tolerance, techniques
such as Compensation Transactions or Eventual Consistency might be
employed.

The key to success in this phase is the rigorous testing of the newly
created services to ensure they perform as expected and adhere to the
defined contracts. This involves both unit testing individual components and integration testing the interactions using tools like JUnit for
Java applications.

Extracting microservices from a monolithic structure not only demands
technical expertise but also a deep understanding of the business domains. Through careful analysis, precise definition of service boundaries, and rigorous testing, one can ensure a smooth transition towards
a more resilient and scalable microservices architecture.

5.6   Service Boundaries and Bounded Contexts

Defining service boundaries is one of the most critical aspects of transitioning from a monolithic architecture to a microservices architecture. The concept of *bounded contexts*, as derived from Domain-Driven
Design (DDD), plays an essential role in this process. Essentially, a
bounded context defines the limitation of a specific domain model
within which a particular domain term or concept applies. Each
bounded context correlates to a microservice that encapsulates a specific functionality and its associated data model, thus ensuring a high
degree of modularity.

The first step in defining service boundaries is to conduct a thorough analysis of the existing domain. This involves identifying and categorizing domain entities and their relationships based on functionality and data coherence. Tools such as Entity-Relationship diagrams can be useful in visualizing these relationships. By studying these diagrams, one can pinpoint logical clusters of entities that interact frequently, which are candidates for forming individual microservices.

- Identifying logical clusters: This involves analyzing the functionalities that have high intra-cluster interaction and low inter-cluster communication.

- Defining APIs: Each bounded context should have a well-defined API, which acts as a contract for interaction with other microservices or external clients.

- Data ownership: Each bounded context owns its data schema and logic, making it the authority for that particular data set.

The implementation of these bounded contexts requires meticulous design to ensure consistency and integrity of the data exchanged across the microservices. For instance, when a business operation spans multiple bounded contexts, a transaction management strategy should be employed.

To illustrate, consider an e-commerce application that includes product management, order processing, and customer management. These functionalities can be represented as separate bounded contexts:

Product Manage- $\xrightarrow{\text{Uses}}$ Order Processing $\xleftarrow{\text{Uses}}$ Customer Management
ment   ment

In this scenario, the Service for Product Management might only need minimal details from the Customer Management service, like customer IDs or status flags, reducing the coupling between these services.

Another critical element in defining boundaries is understanding the commonality and variability of the domain model. It is crucial to distinguish features that are stable across the domain from those that are prone to frequent changes. This distinction helps in designing services that are robust and require less frequent modifications.

The deployment of bounded contexts enhances the scalability and resilience of the system. It enables individual services to be scaled based on their specific load and performance requirements without affecting

---

Algorithm 6: Algorithm to define service boundaries in a monolith decomposing process

---

Result: Define Service Boundaries
1 initialization;
2 **while** *Not at end of entity list* **do**
3   identify potential entity cluster;
4   **if** *high intra-cluster cohesion* **then**
5   mark as potential bounded context;
6   define provisional API;
7   specify data ownership rules;
8   **else**
9   examine inter-cluster interactions;
10   adjust cluster boundaries;
11   **end**
12 **end**

---

other services. Additionally, failure in one bounded context does not necessarily compromise the entire system, achieving fault isolation.

This approach has implications for the deployment lifecycle as well. Each microservice can be developed, deployed, and maintained independently, which significantly shortens the development cycle and facilitates continuous deployment and integration practices.

The strategic separation into bounded contexts helps elucidate the importance of context and interaction within the domain, thereby not only streamlining the development process but also enhancing the service's adaptability and performance.

5.7 Data Decomposition Strategies

Decomposing the data layer in a monolithic system to fit a microservices architecture is a critical process that requires meticulous planning and execution. The primary goal of data decomposition is to ensure that each microservice is autonomous and owns its domain data, thereby eliminating any dependencies that could hinder the individual scalability and resilience of each service.

Identifying Data Ownership

The first step in data decomposition is to clearly define the ownership of data entities according to the domain boundaries established during the application's domain analysis. This involves mapping data entities to corresponding microservices, ensuring that each microservice interacts primarily with its own database schema.

- Determine which microservice has the authority to perform Create, Read, Update, and Delete (CRUD) operations on each data entity.

- Analyze transaction boundaries to make sure that data consistency is maintained even when operations span multiple microservices.

- Consider using domain events to manage data coherence across bounded contexts in cases where outright ownership is ambiguous.

Database Per Service

Implementing a database-per-service model is a widely accepted strategy that supports the encapsulation of each microservice. This model prevents different services from accessing the same database, thus enforcing independence in terms of data management and evolution.

- For each microservice, set up an independent database instance where possible.

- Use polyglot persistence if necessary, where different database technologies are utilized depending on the service-specific needs.

- Ensure transactional integrity and latency management through patterns like SAGA or two-phase commit where strictly necessary.

Data Migration Tactics

Data migration involves moving subsets of data from the monolithic system's centralized database to the microservices' databases. Here, special care must be taken to handle migrations incrementally while maintaining system availability and data integrity.

```
1  /* Example of a simple data migration script */
2  SELECT * INTO TempOrders FROM Orders WHERE order_date >= '2023-01-01'
3  UPDATE Orders SET migrated = 1 WHERE order_date >= '2023-01-01'
```

```
Output of SELECT COUNT(*) FROM TempOrders:
1000 records
```

Handling Shared Data

Deciding how to handle shared data among microservices is crucial for preventing data duplication and ensuring consistency.

- Use a shared data model only if absolutely required. Prefer replicating data locally and rely on eventual consistency.

- Establish mechanisms for inter-service communication such as RESTful APIs or asynchronous messaging for accessing shared or common data.

Dealing with Foreign Key Relationships

In a distributed architecture, foreign key relationships that enforce data integrity in traditional relational database systems are challenging to maintain.

```
1  /* Handling foreign key relationships in services */
2  ALTER TABLE Orders DROP CONSTRAINT FK_CustomerID
```

```
Output of SQL operation:
Constraint 'FK_CustomerID' is dropped successfully.
```

Data Consistency and Integrity Strategies

Ensuring data consistency in a microservices environment, where each service may handle its data independently, is essential. Employ compensating transactions, domain event patterns, and eventual consistency where appropriate.

131

Algorithm 7: Pseudocode for a compensating transaction

Result: Ensure data consistency using compensating
transactions

1 operation result ← PerformCriticalUpdateOperation()
2 **if** *operation result is successful* **then**
3 | CommitTransaction()
4 **else**
    | /* Operation failed, start compensating
    | transaction   */
5 | RollbackOperation()
6 **end**

Implementation Considerations

Implementing data decomposition strategies should be guided by comprehensive logging and monitoring to track the flow of data and understand the impact of the changes. This aids in detecting anomalies early and adjusting strategies accordingly.

- Rigorous documentation of all changes to the data schema and interfaces should be maintained.

- Changes to the database schema should be applied incrementally using version-controlled migration scripts.

Through careful consideration and meticulous implementation of these strategies, organizations can ensure that their transition to a microservices architecture is successful in terms of data management. This approach not only helps in maintaining data integrity and consistency but also supports the overall scalability and resilience of the system.

5.8 Refactoring the Database for Decoupled Services

When decomposing a monolithic application into microservices, one of the most challenging aspects is to refactor the database to support the newly created services adequately. Each service should own its database schema and data to ensure loose coupling and independent scalability. This section discusses strategies for refactoring a monolithic database into multiple databases corresponding to their respective services.

Step 1: Identifying Service-Specific Schemas The initial step in database refactoring involves identifying the data requirements for each microservice. This step typically stems from the domain models defined using Domain-Driven Design (DDD) principles.

- Analyze the existing database schemas to understand data usage patterns.

- Map entities and relationships to corresponding services identified during the decomposition phase.

- Define schemas for each service, ensuring they include only the data that service is responsible for.

Step 2: Creating Isolation at the Data Layer After mapping entities to services, create isolation at the data layer to support the independence of each microservice.

- Implement separate database instances for each microservice wherever feasible. This approach maximizes data isolation and reduces the impact of service-specific schemas on other services.

- Use schema prefixes if separate databases are not viable due to operational constraints or costs.

Step 3: Data Migration Strategy Data migration is critical and needs a careful and planned approach.

- Develop scripts to migrate data from the monolithic schema to the new service-specific schemas.

- Ensure data integrity and consistency during the migration phase.

- Sequence the migration to minimize downtime. Incremental migration strategies, like the Expand and Contract pattern, are recommended.

Step 4: Modifying Application Code Application code must be modified to adapt to the new database architecture. This involves updating data access layers within each microservice.

```
1  // Example code for updating data access layer to new schema
2  public class ProductService {
3     public void updateProduct(Product product) {
4        // Adjusted to new schema
5        String query = "UPDATE product_service.products SET name=?, price=? WHERE id
          =?";
6        // Execute query
7     }
8  }
```

Step 5: Implementing New Data Management Policies New data management policies should be implemented to govern data operations within a distributed system context.

- Define data governance rules for each service, including data ownership, data retention, and legal compliance.

- Set up data validation and error handling mechanisms specific to each microservice's needs.

Challenges and Considerations Several challenges can arise during the database refactoring process:

- Ensuring transaction consistency across services can be complex in a distributed environment.

- Handling distributed data queries that span multiple microservice databases requires implementing either a federated database layer or specific aggregation services.

- Monitoring and managing performance overhead due to increased communication between services.

As the database is progressively decoupled, ongoing monitoring and iterative review of the implemented strategies are essential to ensuring that the system adapts well to changes and continues to meet business requirements efficiently. This thorough approach enables organizations to achieve a level of agility and reliability that keeps pace with modern software development needs.

5.9 Managing Dependencies in a Gradually Decoupled System

As the decomposition of a monolithic system progresses, one of the critical areas that require meticulous attention is the management of dependencies among the emerging microservices. To ensure a smooth transition and effective operation of both the existing monolithic system and the new microservices, it is imperative to adopt a strategic approach to dependency management. This involves identifying, analyzing, and restructuring dependencies so that each service can operate as independently as possible, thus minimizing the impact on other services within the ecosystem.

Identifying Dependencies

The first step in managing dependencies is to identify and categorize them. Dependencies in a monolithic system can be broadly classified into several types:

- **Code Dependencies**: These occur when classes or functions are directly invoked by other parts of the system.

- **Data Dependencies**: These arise when different parts of the system share the same data model or database.

- **Resource Dependencies**: These include shared external libraries or frameworks needed by multiple parts of the system.

Identifying these dependencies requires thorough analysis and often involves tools that can perform static code analysis or dynamic monitoring to track interactions between different parts of the system.

Analyzing and Prioritizing Dependencies

Once dependencies have been identified, the next step is to analyze their impact and decide which are critical and need to be addressed immediately. This analysis should consider factors such as:

- **Frequency of Interaction**: Dependencies that are used frequently are likely to pose higher risks and complexities during decomposition.

135

- **Criticality**: The importance of the dependent operation to the system's overall functionality.

- **Tightness/Coupling**: The degree to which components are dependent on each other. Loosely coupled dependencies are easier to manage and modify.

Prioritizing dependencies based on these factors helps in planning the sequence of microservices extraction, ensuring that changes cause minimal disruptions to system operations.

Strategies for Dependency Isolation

To manage dependencies effectively, isolation strategies must be employed. This can be done through several approaches:

- **Interface Segregation**: Implement interfaces that allow microservices to communicate without needing direct knowledge of each other's implementations.

- **Service Facades**: Use facades to provide a simplified interface to complex subsystems, thereby reducing direct dependencies.

- **Event-Driven Architecture**: Replace direct inter-service function calls with asynchronous message-passing mechanisms that allow services to react to events rather than directly invoke other services.

Implementing these strategies often involves refactoring the existing monolith's codebase to introduce abstractions that make the dependencies manageable and isolate them effectively.

Refactoring to Reduce Dependencies

Refactoring is a critical activity in managing dependencies by altering the existing code without changing its external behavior to reduce tight coupling. Typical refactoring techniques include:

- **Extracting Interfaces**: Creating interfaces for services that abstract the underlying implementations.

136

- **Decomposing Database Schemas**: Reducing database coupling by segmenting the monolith's database schema into schemas particularly managed by the respective microservices.

- **Adapting Module Pathways**: Changing how modules interact to change their relationship from a direct invocation to a mediated communication through APIs or events.

Each of these techniques requires careful planning and execution to ensure that they do not introduce new issues or significantly disrupt the existing system's operations.

Testing and Validation

After refactoring and applying isolation strategies, thorough testing and validation are essential to ensure that the system remains stable and functional. This should include:

- **Unit Testing**: Testing individual microservices in isolation to ensure that they function correctly independently.

- **Integration Testing**: Testing the interactions between microservices to ensure that they communicate and function together as expected.

- **System Testing**: Conducting tests on the entire system to ensure that it meets the requirements and behaves as intended.

The testing phase should employ automated testing frameworks to manage the increased complexity and ensure consistency across different testing cycles.

Through diligent monitoring and iterative refinement, dependency management can transition a monolithic architecture into a robust, independently scalable microservices architecture, thus ensuring future adaptability and resilience.

5.10 Testing Strategies for Transition Phases

Testing strategies during the transition phases of decomposing a monolithic system into microservices are critical to ensure the reliability, functionality, and performance of both the legacy system and the new microservices architecture. As changes are incrementally made, a meticulous testing approach helps in minimizing disruptions to the existing system, while accurately validating the functionalities of newly created services.

Integration Testing

Integration testing is pivotal in verifying the interactions between the old monolithic components and the new microservices. It ensures that newly developed services integrate correctly with the unmodified parts of the monolith and with each other. This involves testing APIs, data flows, and service dependencies.

A robust approach is to employ Contract Testing. Contract tests assert the communication contract between two services, such as a response to a given request. Here is an example of a contract test setup in Python using the pact framework:

```
from pact import Consumer, Provider
pact = Consumer('ConsumerService').has_pact_with(Provider('ProviderService'))
(pact.given('Valid request data for service')
    .upon_receiving('a request for data from ProviderService')
    .with_request(method='GET', path='/data')
    .will_respond_with(200, body={'data': 'valid data'}))

def test_provider_service():
    with pact:
        response = requests.get('http://ProviderService/data')
        assert response.json() == {'data': 'valid data'}
```

Service Virtualization

Service virtualization becomes significant when implementing new microservices that interact with unstable or incomplete services. It simulates the behavior of these services by creating realistic test environments where not all services are present or finalized. This method supports continuous testing even when components of the system are in development.

End-to-End Testing

End-to-end testing confirms that the entire integrated system performs as expected after introducing new services or after making changes to the existing monolith. Automating these tests can significantly reduce the testing time and effort. Selenium or Cypress are popular tools that can be used for this purpose:

```
1  from selenium import webdriver
2  driver = webdriver.Chrome()
3  driver.get("http://localhost:3000")
4  assert "Your Application Title" in driver.title
5  driver.quit()
```

Testing Data Integrity

Testing for data integrity is essential when migrating or duplicating functionalities that handle data across the monolithic and the microservices boundaries. This involves verifying that data is consistently and accurately processed, stored, and retrieved across multiple components of the system. Techniques like checksum verification, comparison tests, and employing temporary data duplication validation rules are commonly used.

Shadow Testing

Shadow testing involves routing real-time data to both the old and new systems simultaneously and comparing the responses from both systems. This method can detect discrepancies and performance issues without affecting production traffic. It ensures that the new service can handle actual workload scenarios before it fully replaces functionalities in the legacy system.

Canary Releases

Canary releasing is a technique used to roll out the new microservice to a small subset of users prior to a full release. It tests the stability and performance of the service under real-world operating conditions. This incremental approach to release allows detection and mitigation of issues without impacting the entire user base:

```
Initial release to 5% of the user base.
Monitor performance metrics and user feedback.
Expand to 20% of the user base.
Full rollout after ensuring no critical issues are reported.
```

The effectiveness of testing during the transition to microservices is enhanced by focusing on these strategic approaches. Together with

139

automated deployments and continuous integration, these testing techniques aid in maintaining system reliability and user trust during the critical phases of system decomposition.

5.11 Monitoring and Feedback Mechanisms During Decomposition

The deployment of monitoring and feedback mechanisms plays a critical role in the successful decomposition of a monolithic system into microservices. As the migration progresses, these mechanisms provide crucial insights into the system's operational behavior, identify performance bottlenecks, and aid in verifying the functional correctness of newly introduced microservices.

Establishing Baseline Metrics:

Prior to beginning the decomposition process, it is essential to establish baseline metrics for the current monolithic system. These metrics will serve as a reference point to assess the impact of changes made during the decomposition. Key performance indicators (KPIs) to monitor include:

- Response time

- Throughput

- Error rates

- Resource utilization (CPU, memory, and disk I/O)

Gathering these metrics requires the integration of system monitoring tools. Popular choices include Prometheus, which can capture time-series data about system operations, and Grafana for visualizing the metrics.

Logging Strategy:

Implementing a comprehensive logging strategy is imperative. Logs from the monolithic system and from each of the microservices should be centralized to allow for correlated analysis. This is instrumental in diagnosing issues that may span multiple services. Structured logging should be employed, wherein logs are generated in a uniform format (such as JSON), making them easier to analyze programmatically. Tools like ELK Stack (Elasticsearch, Logstash, and Kibana) or Splunk can be used to manage log data.

```
1   // Example of structured logging in JSON format
2   logger.info({
3       "event": "response_sent",
4       "status_code": 200,
5       "transaction_id": "abc123"
6   });
```

Tracing Transaction Paths:

As interactions within a monolithic system can be complex and obscured, it is important to implement distributed tracing. This technique traces the path that a transaction or a request takes through the different components of the system. Each transaction is tagged with a unique identifier, and tracing data is collected. This practice not only helps in understanding dependencies but also in spotting performance bottlenecks.

Tools like Jaeger or Zipkin can be implemented for distributed tracing. These tools provide a visual representation of the transaction paths and timings involved in each service call.

```
1   // Example of initiating a trace with a unique transaction ID
2   tracer.startSpan("transaction_id", {
3       "transaction_id": "xyz789",
4       "service_name": "user_service"
5   });
```

Real-Time Performance Monitoring:

During and after the decomposition, real-time performance monitoring of each microservice is critical. Each service should be independently monitored to detect any deviations from expected behavior. Metrics to be collected include:

- Latency per service endpoint
- Service error rates
- Service throughput

Setting up alerts based on these metrics will help in quickly identifying and rectifying issues in a specific service without impacting the entire system's functionality.

Feedback Mechanisms:

Regular feedback mechanisms should be instituted. This includes automated alerts, dashboards, and regular reports to stakeholders about the migration's progress. Feedback from real users is also invaluable. Mechanisms such as feature flags can be used to gradually expose new microservices to users in a controlled manner, gathering user feedback to guide further development and refinement.

```
Alert: Service 'payment_processor' exceeding error threshold.
Error rate: 5.2%
Timestamp: 2023-09-15 14:22:03
```

Maintaining a dynamic monitoring and feedback environment fosters a robust decomposition process by facilitating prompt detection of issues and adjustments. This proactive approach minimizes disruptions and ensures continual system improvement as it evolves from a monolithic architecture into a distributed suite of microservices.

5.12 Best Practices and Pitfalls in Monolith Decomposition

Decomposing a monolithic application into microservices is a critical step in improving an application's scalability, maintainability, and deployment flexibility. This section delves into essential best practices and highlights common pitfalls that teams might encounter during the decomposition process.

Best Practices

Decomposing a monolithic system effectively requires adherence to several best practices, which ensure that the process minimizes disruptions and maximizes the system's overall effectiveness.

- **Incremental Decomposition:** Rather than attempting a full decomposition all at once, it is advisable to break down the monolith incrementally. This approach helps in minimizing risk by allowing partial validations and adjustments based on feedback from each phase.

- **Define Clear Interfaces:** Each service should have a clearly defined API that encapsulates its functionality, thereby reducing dependencies on internal implementation details of other services. This practice facilitates easier modification and scaling of individual services.

- **Automate the Deployment Process:** Implementing continuous integration and continuous deployment (CI/CD) practices is crucial. Automation of the build, test, and deploy processes ensures that changes can be delivered quickly and reliably.

- **Focus on Independent Scalability:** Design services such that they can be scaled independently based on their specific load and performance requirements. This involves careful consideration of resource management and load balancing strategies.

- **Implement Service Monitoring:** Deploying monitoring and logging mechanisms across all services allows for proactive management of the system. Effective monitoring helps in identifying performance bottlenecks and potential points of failure early in the transition process.

Pitfalls to Avoid

Awareness of common pitfalls in the decomposition process is equally critical as following best practices. Noting these pitfalls can serve as precautionary measures for planning and executing the transition.

- **Inadequate Planning:** Insufficient understanding of the domains involved may lead to inappropriate service boundaries. This can result in services that are either too large and encompassing or too fine-grained, leading to chatty microservices.

- **Overlooking Data Consistency:** Decoupling services without a strategy for data consistency can introduce data synchronization challenges across services. It is important to employ comprehensive strategies, such as eventual consistency or distributed transactions where necessary.

- **Ignoring Fault Tolerance:** Services should be designed to be resilient; ignoring fault tolerance can lead to cascading failures in a microservices architecture. Implementing patterns such as Circuit Breaker or Bulkhead can mitigate these risks.

- **Neglecting Performance Testing:** It is vital to simulate real-world loads and conduct thorough performance testing during and after the decomposition. Performance bottlenecks might not become apparent until the system is operating under stress.

143

- **Cultural Resistance:** Organizational culture plays a significant role in the success of any major transformation. Resistance from development teams accustomed to the monolithic paradigm can derail progress. Effective communication and involving all stakeholders in the transition process are crucial in managing this change.

To navigate around these pitfalls, continuous adjustment and adherence to the laid-out best practices are indispensable. Adopting a methodical approach, fostering collaboration across teams, and maintaining a clear focus on the end goals of scalability, reliability, and performance will empower organizations to tackle the complexities of monolith decomposition effectively.

Chapter 6

Data Management in Microservices

Effective data management is a cornerstone of successful microservices architectures, where each service manages its own data autonomously. This chapter addresses the challenges and strategies associated with data persistency, consistency, and synchronization across distributed services. It emphasizes the importance of implementing resilient, loosely coupled data models that facilitate service scalability and maintain system integrity in a microservices environment.

6.1 Introduction to Data Challenges in Microservices

Microservices architecture introduces a paradigm where applications are structured as collections of loosely coupled services, each encapsulating a specific business capability. This architectural style inherently complicates data management due to its distributed nature, necessitating deliberate strategies to handle data consistently and efficiently across services. This section delves into the primary data challenges encountered in microservices environments, including data persistence, maintaining consistency, and fulfilling transactional requirements.

145

Data persistence in a microservices architecture requires each service to be responsible for its own database, which prevents data entanglements and conflicts that typically occur in monolithic applications where multiple modules interact with the same database. An exemplary implementation in a product inventory system could involve separate services for user handling, product management, and order processing, each with its own unique database schema.

```
1   CREATE TABLE products (
2       id INT AUTO_INCREMENT PRIMARY KEY,
3       name VARCHAR(255) NOT NULL,
4       price DECIMAL(10, 2) NOT NULL
5   );
6
7   CREATE TABLE orders (
8       id INT AUTO_INCREMENT PRIMARY KEY,
9       product_id INT NOT NULL,
10      quantity INT NOT NULL,
11      status ENUM('pending', 'completed') NOT NULL,
12      FOREIGN KEY (product_id) REFERENCES products(id)
13  );
```

Consistency across distributed systems is pivotal, especially in scenarios where business processes span multiple services. Achieving strong consistency, however, can severely impact system performance and availability, leading to a preference for eventual consistency in many microservices architectures. Eventual consistency allows for temporary discrepancies in data across services, which can be resolved using asynchronous processes.

For instance, when a product's price is updated, the product service publishes an event to a message bus, which is then consumed by the order service to update any pending orders with the new price:

```
1   UPDATE orders SET price = new_price WHERE product_id = updated_product_id;
```

Output:
35 rows updated.

Transactional management in microservices often adheres to the BASE (Basically Available, Soft state, Eventual consistency) model instead of the traditional ACID (Atomicity, Consistency, Isolation, Durability) properties found in monolithic systems. This shift necessitates implementing strategies such as the Saga pattern, where a series of local transactions are linked through a sequence of events, or compensation transactions, which help in reverting operations in case of a failure in a subsequent step.

When a new order is placed, a saga could begin by reserving a product, then attempting a payment process, and finally, confirming the order.

146

If the payment fails, a compensatory transaction is initiated to release the product reservation.

Algorithm 8: Example of a Saga implementation for handling orders

---

    Data: Order details
    Result: Handle Order
1 initialize transaction
2 **if** *reserveProduct() and processPayment()* **then**
3 | confirmOrder(); emitEvent('OrderConfirmed');
4 **else**
5 | compensateReserve(); emitEvent('OrderFailed');
6 **end**

Each of these strategies emphasizes the need for thoughtful design and robust mechanisms to handle data efficiently in a distributed system, aligning with microservices principles while ensuring data integrity and a responsive user experience. These issues are foundational, setting the context for deeper exploration of specific solutions in subsequent sections focused on data persistency, consistency techniques, and other advanced data integration patterns.

6.2 Database Per Service: Implementation and Benefits

The implementation of a database-per-service model typifies a foundational strategy in the realm of microservices. At its core, this approach entails provisioning a separate database for each microservice. This ensures that the service is the sole entity managing and accessing its respective data. This section delineates the protocols for implementing this architecture and reviews its consequent benefits.

Architectural Setup

Ensuring a robust division of database resources among services requires a well-structured architectural setup. The following steps outline the typical procedural sequence:

- **Service Definition:** Each microservice should be defined around a business capability, focusing on a singular aspect of the application's functionality. This includes outlining the data needs intrinsic to the service.

- **Database Selection:** For each microservice, choose a database that serves its specific needs. For instance, a service handling complex transactions might utilize a relational database, whereas a service requiring rapid, non-relational lookups might be better served by a NoSQL database.

- **Isolate Database Schemas:** Each service's database schema should be private and inaccessible to other services. This isolation enhances security and prevents any undesirable inter-service interference.

- **API Layer Integration:** Microservices communicate using well-defined APIs instead of direct database calls to other services. This shields the services from changes in database implementation and ensures a loose coupling among them.

Code needed for initializing separate databases for each microservice can be represented as follows:

```
# Python pseudocode for initializing databases using SQLAlchemy
from sqlalchemy import create_engine

def init_db(service_name, db_type, connection_string):
    engine = create_engine(connection_string)
    if db_type == 'SQL':
        # Perform SQL-specific initialization
    elif db_type == 'NoSQL':
        # Perform NoSQL-specific initialization
    return engine

service_dbs = {
    'order_service': init_db('order_service', 'SQL', 'postgresql://...'),
    'inventory_service': init_db('inventory_service', 'NoSQL', 'mongodb://...')
}
```

Benefits

Implementing a database-per-service model yields several significant benefits which contribute to the efficiency and effectiveness of using microservices:

148

- **Decoupling:** By segregating databases based on service, systems avoid tight coupling, leading to easier scaling, fault isolation, and better fault tolerance.

- **Optimized Performance:** Data management that is closely tailored to the needs of each specific service often yields improved performance. Services can interact with their databases using techniques that are best suited to their unique data access patterns.

- **Independence in Scaling:** Services can scale independently, as they are not bound by centralized data throughput constraints. This facilitates a more efficient use of resources and a more responsive scaling process.

- **Flexibility in Technology Choices:** Teams can select different database systems that are optimal for the specific requirements of each service (e.g., SQL vs. NoSQL), leading to performance optimizations and the easy inclusion of new technologies.

Design Considerations

However, this architecture is not without its challenges and requires careful consideration of transaction management across services, data duplication issues, and the complexity introduced by maintaining multiple databases. Strategies like Event-driven architecture and tools such as API gateways can mitigate these drawbacks and are discussed in later sections.

The implementation of a database dedicated to each microservice is conducive to a robust, scalable, and efficient system. It promotes resilience and facilitates the microservices architecture's fundamental goal: building a system with independently deployable, modular components that align closely with organizational goals.

6.3 Data Consistency in Distributed Systems

In distributed systems, particularly within microservices architectures, ensuring data consistency represents a significant challenge due to the decentralized nature of data management. Each service in a microservices environment typically manages its own database, potentially leading to scenarios where data consistency across different services can become compromised without proper handling.

Understanding Data Consistency Models: Data consistency can be understood through several models, each providing a different level of guarantee regarding how data is synchronized across different nodes in a system.

- **Strong Consistency:** Every read receives the most recent write or an error.

- **Eventual Consistency:** Updates will propagate to all nodes eventually, and if no new updates are made to a particular data item, eventually all accesses will return the last updated value.

- **Causal Consistency:** If process A communicates an update to process B, a subsequent read from process B will reflect that update, and any further updates that causally follow from it.

Achieving Strong Consistency: Implementing strong consistency requires a method to ensure that all copies of a distributed data item agree on a single, consistent value. This often entails using synchronization mechanisms that delay operations to achieve uniformity, potentially impacting system performance. One common approach is the use of distributed transactions with two-phase commit (2PC) protocols.

```
1  // Example of a simple two-phase commit protocol
2  BEGIN TRANSACTION
3  // Phase 1: Voting
4  Prepare all nodes to commit the transaction;
5  If all nodes vote 'yes', proceed; else rollback;
6  // Phase 2: Commit/Rollback
7  Commit transaction on all nodes;
8  END TRANSACTION
```

However, the two-phase commit protocol doesn't scale well due to its blocking nature and its susceptibility to failures; if any node fails during the transaction, recovery can be complex and time-consuming.

Eventual Consistency Strategies: An alternative to strong consistency is eventual consistency, which allows for greater performance and availability but at the cost of having temporary inconsistencies. This model is particularly effective in environments where operational conditions can tolerate some inconsistencies for the benefit of achieving higher throughput and availability.

To implement eventual consistency, techniques such as Conflict-free Replicated Data Types (CRDTs) and version vectors are employed.

150

These methods allow concurrent updates that are mathematically guaranteed to converge to a consistent state without requiring immediate synchronization.

```
1  // CRDTs Counter Example
2  incrementCounter(nodeId) {
3      counters[nodeId] += 1; // Increment the counter for the current node
4  }
5
6  getTotal() {
7      return sum(counters.values()); // Sum the counters from all nodes
8  }
```

Hybrid Approaches: In practical scenarios, a hybrid approach often offers a balance between strong and eventual consistency, adapting based on specific domain needs or transactional requirements. Techniques such as the Saga pattern allow for implementing business transactions that span multiple services without needing distributed transactions. Instead of relying on lock-based mechanisms, Sagas orchestrate transaction sequences, where each service executes its transaction and publishes events that trigger the next step in the saga.

Algorithm 9: Pseudocode for a basic Saga Execution Procedure

   Input: TransactionSteps
   Output: SagaExecutionResult
1 **begin**
2   foreach (Step in TransactionSteps) ExecuteStep(Step)
3   **if** *StepExecutionFails* **then**
4   ExecuteCompensatingTransactions()
5   break
6   PublishSuccessEvent()

The choice of consistency model and method should be dictated by the service's business requirements and the acceptable trade-offs between consistency, availability, and partition tolerance, famously known as the CAP theorem.

By thoughtfully applying these strategies, systems can maintain high levels of data integrity and consistency even in a distributed, microservices architecture, allowing businesses to leverage the scalability and flexibility that microservices provide while minimizing the risk of data anomalies. This approach also facilitates the resilience of the system, helping to ensure that service disruptions are gracefully handled with minimal impact on the user or consuming services.

6.4 Data Integration Patterns in Microservices

In microservices architectures, each service is expected to operate as an independent entity, handling its own data management and business logic, which introduces challenges in maintaining data consistency and integrity across the system. To address these challenges, several data integration patterns have been developed. These patterns facilitate efficient data exchange and synchronization between different microservices, thereby enhancing the system's overall functionality and user experience.

API Composition

The API Composition pattern consists of building a composite API that gathers data from the individual microservices. This pattern dictates that when a client makes a call to obtain aggregated data, the application will perform separate calls to the involved services and then synthesize the results. This approach is synchronous and usually implemented through simple REST or GraphQL APIs.

The code snippet below demonstrates a simple implementation of an API gateway that employs the API composition pattern:

```
1  import requests
2
3  def get_user_details(user_id):
4      user_data = requests.get(f"https://user-service/{user_id}").json()
5      user_orders = requests.get(f"https://order-service/users/{user_id}/orders").
           json()
6      return { "user": user_data, "orders": user_orders }
```

This method, while directly reliant on the responsiveness of the called services, allows for real-time data integration but introduces a point of failure in the form of network dependence.

Database Sharing

Another approach is Database Sharing, where multiple services are allowed to access the same database schema. This can simplify data access and improve performance but goes against the principle of microservices managing their own database, potentially leading to high coupling and thus reducing the microservices' independence and resilience.

Consider the following risks associated with the database sharing pattern:

- High coupling between services sharing the database schema.
- Increased risk of transaction conflicts due to concurrent access.
- Difficulty in scaling due to shared database resources.

SAGA Pattern

The SAGA Pattern is an effective solution for managing distributed data consistency without enforcing distributed transactions. A SAGA is a sequence of local transactions where each transaction updates data within a single service. On transaction failure, compensating transactions (or SAGA steps) are triggered to ensure data consistency.

Example of a SAGA implemented through an event-driven approach:

```
1   def process_order(order_id):
2       # Service A creates an order
3       create_order(order_id)
4       emit("order_created", order_id)
5
6   def handle_order_created(order_id):
7       # Service B performs payment transaction
8       if perform_payment(order_id):
9           emit("payment_successful", order_id)
10      else:
11          emit("payment_failed", order_id)
12          # Compensating transaction could be invoked here
13
14  def handle_payment_failure(order_id):
15      # Compensate by cancelling the order
16      cancel_order(order_id)
```

Each step within the SAGA emits an event, which is then handled by other services or by itself to proceed to the next step or to roll back the process through compensating actions.

Change Data Capture

Change Data Capture (CDC) involves monitoring and capturing changes in a service's database and then forwarding these changes to

153

other interested services or data stores. This approach allows services to react to data changes asynchronously, reducing the immediate load on the system and providing a robust mechanism for keeping disparate service data in sync without direct coupling.

To implement CDC, tools like Debezium or Apache Kafka can be utilized:

```
1   # Example configuration snippet for setting up Debezium with Kafka
2   # This is typically done through configuration files rather than code.
3   debezium.source.connector.class=io.debezium.connector.postgresql.PostgresConnector
4   debezium.source.offset.storage=org.apache.kafka.connect.storage.
        KafkaOffsetBackingStore
5   debezium.source.database.hostname=postgres.example.com
6   debezium.source.database.user=dbuser
7   debezium.source.database.password=dbpassword
```

The effective use of these data integration patterns will depend on specific use cases and requirements of the microservices architecture. Choices among these patterns should consider factors such as data consistency needs, performance requirements, and the overall design philosophy of the system. Each pattern offers unique advantages and comes with its own set of trade-offs. A profound understanding of these patterns and their implications is crucial for designing robust microservices architectures that handle data efficiently and reliably.

6.5 Eventual Consistency and Compensation Transactions

Eventual consistency is a consistency model employed in distributed systems, such as those based on microservices, where it is understood that all changes to a piece of data will eventually propagate through the system and become consistent. Unlike strong consistency models where data is immediately consistent across all nodes, eventual consistency allows for temporary discrepancies in exchange for increased system availability and resilience.

Definition and Relevance in Microservices: Microservices architectures often involve multiple instances of data storage, and coordinating them in real-time can be impractically expensive or even impossible in terms of processing resources and network latency. Hence, eventual consistency is a pragmatic solution for data management across the multiple, independently operated services that characterize microservices environments.

154

Impact on System Design: Adopting eventual consistency necessitates careful design consideration. Systems must be tolerant of data appearing slightly out of sync temporarily. Developers need to design application workflows that can handle this inconsistency, including user interfaces that may need to manage user expectations about the freshness of the data displayed.

Compensation Transactions In systems with eventual consistency, operations that span multiple services cannot rely on traditional atomic transactions. Instead, they often implement a strategy based on compensation transactions. Here, each step of an operation stores enough information so that any action can be reversed or adjusted if the overall process fails at a subsequent step.

Implementing Compensation Transactions: Let's explore how compensation transactions can be implemented to handle failures in a distributed, eventually consistent system.

Algorithm 10: Compensation Transaction Workflow

Data: Operations that span multiple services
Result: State consistency across services in the case of failure
1 1. Initiate operation
2 2. Execute local transaction
3 3. Record state changes and necessary compensatory actions in a log
4 4. Attempt to commit changes
5 5. **if** *commit fails* **then**
6 | Execute compensatory actions recorded in step 3 to revert or correct state
7 | Log compensatory action results
8 **end**
9 **return** final state

Examples of Compensation Transactions in Practice Consider an online shopping system implemented with microservices where a user places an order (service A) which then checks inventory (service B) and schedules delivery (service C). If scheduling the delivery fails, a compensation transaction must cancel the order and update inventory, reversing the earlier steps.

A practical application may look like the following:

```
1  def place_order(order_id, product_id, quantity):
2      inventory_service.reduce_inventory(product_id, quantity)
3      try:
4          delivery_service.schedule_delivery(order_id, product_id)
5      except DeliveryException:
6          inventory_service.increment_inventory(product_id, quantity)
7          order_service.cancel_order(order_id)
```

Compensation transactions ensure that the system can maintain data integrity without requiring immediate consistency, thus respecting the distributed nature of microservices.

Moreover, the eventual consistency approach provides a flexible and scalable method to build large-scale distributed systems, although it adds complexity in terms of system design and error handling. Designing for eventual consistency typically involves implementing robust logging and monitoring to detect and rectify discrepancies in the data state actively.

This approach requires a shift in understanding traditional database transactions, urging developers and system architects to think deeply about data flows, dependencies, and the user experience in cases of inconsistency. The focus moves from preventing inconsistencies to managing them effectively when they occur, which is a foundational shift in building resilient, distributed systems. The utilization of logging, monitoring, and comprehensive compensatory measures forms the bedrock for successful implementation in a microservices architecture.

6.6   Using Event Sourcing in Microservices

Event Sourcing represents a foundational concept in the structuring of data storage and management within the context of microservices architectures. In essence, Event Sourcing involves storing the changes to the system's state as a sequence of events. Instead of recording just the current state of data in a domain entity, each state-changing operation is captured as a unique event that includes full contextual details. This allows the system to reconstruct past states and provides extensive audit and historical data-analysis capabilities.

Fundamentals of Event Sourcing

Event Sourcing fundamentally shifts how data is stored and managed. Traditionally, an application might store the current state of an entity, such as a user profile or a bank account balance, directly in a database table. When changes occur, the table is updated to reflect the new state. Under Event Sourcing, these modifications are not directly applied to the state but are described as an ongoing list of event records:

Listing 6.1: Traditional vs Event Sourced Data Modification Example

```
1   -- Traditional Update
2   UPDATE account SET balance = balance + 100 WHERE account_id = 123;
3
4   -- Event Sourcing Insertion
5   INSERT INTO event_store (event_type, account_id, amount) VALUES ('credit', 123,
        100);
```

Each event (e.g., 'credit' or 'debit') describes an action that affects the entity, annotated with sufficient data (e.g., amount, affected account) to reflect the impact independently of other events.

Benefits of Using Event Sourcing

The adoption of Event Sourcing in microservices architectures yields several critical benefits:

- **Auditability:** Each event represents an exact, immutable log of actions made to the data. This traceability is invaluable for audits and compliance, as well as for debugging and understanding the history of data changes.

- **Replayability:** Systems can reconstruct past states by replaying the events up to any point in time. This ability makes features like historical analysis, undo functionality, and predictive modeling feasible.

- **Resilience:** By decoupling data operations into discrete events, systems can handle partial failures more gracefully. For example, if the application fails while processing an event, the event can be retried without risking the corruption of the entity's current state.

- **Scalability:** Event-driven architectures inherently support distributed processes. This capability aligns well with microservices

157

principles, allowing different parts of an application to scale independently based on distinct workloads.

Challenges with Event Sourcing

While Event Sourcing offers substantial benefits, it introduces complexities that need to be managed:

- **Event schema changes:** As the system evolves, so too will the events. Managing changes to event structure—such as adding new fields or changing event semantics—requires careful handling to prevent issues with historical event replay.

- **Data volume:** Since events are stored perpetually, the volume of data in the system can grow significantly. Effective strategies for event data storage, querying, and archival become crucial.

- **Learning curve:** Teams may find the event-centric paradigm shift challenging initially, as it requires different thinking about data consistency, transactions, and error handling.

To cater to the operational needs and overcome challenges associated with Event Sourcing, services often employ related patterns such as Command Query Responsibility Segregation (CQRS). CQRS separates the read (query) aspect of a system from the write (command) aspect, using views or projections of the event store for queries, and processing commands by appending new events.

Such division is illustrated with the following conceptual diagram:

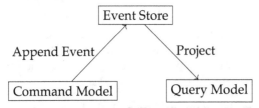

This abstraction allows different microservices or components within a service to individually scale and evolve as necessary, embracing the decentralized nature of microservices while adhering to the principles laid out by Event Sourcing. Implementing efficient and scalable Event Sourcing mechanisms will therefore not only strengthen the data management practices but also reinforce the overall architectural resilience of the system.

6.7 Implementing Command Query Responsibility Segregation (CQRS)

Command Query Responsibility Segregation (CQRS) is an architectural pattern that separates read operations from write operations into different models, allowing each to be optimized independently. This section dives into the practical details of implementing CQRS in a microservices architecture, addressing design, deployment, and potential challenges.

CQRS fundamentally divides the application into two layers: Command Model for handling updates to data, and Query Model for handling data retrieval. This separation enhances performance, scalability, and security by allowing these models to evolve according to their specific operational demands without affecting each other.

Designing the Command and Query Models

In CQRS, the Command Model encapsulates the business logic and rules required to alter data states. This involves creating commands, which are operations that cause state changes. Each command should be validated and translated into events that represent actual changes to the data. The following is an example of a simple command model pseudocode:

Algorithm 11: CreateUserCommand Model

   Data: Username, Password
   Result: Boolean indicating success or failure of operation
  1 validation = ValidateData(Username, Password);
  2 **if** *validation is successful* **then**
  3 | RaiseEvent('UserCreated');
  4 | **return** *True*;
  5 **else**
  6 | **return** *False*;
  7 **end**

The Query Model, on the other hand, deals with data presentation and retrieval requirements. It feeds from the same data sources but is structured and optimized for fast read-access patterns. The structure of the Query Model might denormalize data and create materialized views that are kept up-to-date with the underlying data stores through event listeners or similar synchronization techniques.

159

Implementation Strategies

Implementing CQRS in a microservices environment involves several key considerations:

- **Event Sourcing:** Often used in conjunction with CQRS, event sourcing ensures that all changes to application state as a result of command execution are stored as a sequence of events. These events then provide the means to reconstruct the past states of an entity.

- **Service Boundaries:** Properly defining the boundaries of services is crucial. Commands and queries should be scoped within clearly defined service contexts, aligning service boundaries with business capabilities.

- **Data Storage:** Deciding on the type of storage for commands and queries can vary based on specific requirements such as latency, throughput, and consistency needs. While commands may use transactional databases to enforce consistency, queries might rely on fast-read optimized data stores.

- **Data Synchronization:** Maintaining consistency between command and query databases is essential. This can be achieved using asynchronous mechanisms to update query databases after commands have modified the command-side data.

Example: Synchronizing Command and Query Models

Let's illustrate the synchronization between Command and Query models using a simple scenario in a banking application where a new account is created and then queried.

```
1   // Command Side
2   public void Handle(CreateAccountCommand command) {
3       if (ValidateCommand(command)) {
4           Account account = new Account(command.AccountId, command.Owner);
5           accountRepository.save(account);
6           eventBus.raise(new AccountCreatedEvent(account));
7       }
8   }
9
10  // Query Side (Event Handler)
11  public void On(AccountCreatedEvent event) {
12      viewModelStore.save(new AccountViewModel {
13          AccountId = event.AccountId,
14          Owner = event.Owner,
15          Balance = 0 // default balance
16      });
17  }
```

In this example, the command model handles the creation of a new account which, upon successful validation and creation, raises an event that the query model listens to. The query model consumes this event to create and store a view model for queries, effectively keeping the query data store synchronized with the command side.

Potential Challenges

Implementing CQRS can introduce complexity to the system architecture:

- **Complexity in Handling Data Consistency:** Eventual consistency is a common approach in CQRS which can lead to complex handling of data states across components.

- **Increased Effort for Implementation:** Separating command and query functionalities might require more initial setup and ongoing management than a traditional CRUD model.

- **Tooling and Expertise:** Effective use of CQRS often requires sophisticated tooling and developer expertise in designing and maintaining the separate models and their interactions.

In environments where distinct scalability and performance characteristics for read and write operations are vital, the benefits of CQRS can significantly outweigh these challenges. Proper implementation fosters enhanced maintainability, scalability, and responsiveness, contributing to a robust and flexible application ecosystem in microservices architectures.

6.8 Data Replication and Synchronization Techniques

To ensure high availability, fault tolerance, and low-latency data access across geographical locations, data replication and synchronization are critical in a microservices architecture. This section explores techniques designed to effectively manage the replication and synchronization of data in distributed environments inherent to microservices architectures.

Master-Slave Replication: One common approach is master-slave replication, where one data store (master) handles write operations, and multiple copies of that data store (slaves) handle read operations. The key advantage of this pattern is the enhancement of read scalability since read requests can be distributed across several slave nodes. The primary challenge, however, is ensuring that the data within the slaves is synchronized promptly with the master without significant latency. Failed synchronization can lead to stale data being served from the slaves.

```
1   # Python pseudocode to demonstrate master-slave synchronization
2   def replicate_data(master_data):
3       for slave in slaves:
4           try:
5               # Update slave's dataset with data from master
6               slave.update(master_data)
7           except Exception as e:
8               # Handle any exceptions during update, possibly logging or retrying
9               handle_exception(e)
```

Multi-Master Replication: Unlike master-slave, multi-master replication allows multiple nodes to handle write operations. Conflict resolution becomes significant here since multiple nodes might attempt to update the same piece of data concurrently. Recorded conflicts require automated resolution strategies, which could be complex based on the criteria defined by the consistency requirements of the application.

```
1   # Python pseudocode for conflict resolution in multi-master replication
2   def resolve_conflict(data_instances):
3       # Define rules or algorithms for determining which data remains valid
4       return max(data_instances, key=lambda instance: instance.timestamp)
```

Database Synchronization: This involves establishing a coherent set of protocols that ensure data updates in one database are reflected across other databases involved in the distributed system. Techniques such as version vectors and transaction logs are used to keep track of changes and sequence data updates accurately and reliably.

Change Data Capture (CDC) and Event Triggering: CDC tools track changes in the database and create corresponding event messages which are published to subscribers or middleware systems designed for event processing. These messages aid in triggering specific actions or synchronizations across the microservices. Tools such as Apache Kafka can be utilized for real-time data streaming and synchronization.

```
1   # Python pseudocode for generating events on data change using CDC
2   def capture_data_changes(db_state_previous, db_state_current):
3       changes = diff(db_state_previous, db_state_current)
4       events = generate_events(changes)
5       publish_events(events)
```

- **Reduce Latency:** Effective methods like locate data centers closer to user bases and optimizing database and query design can significantly reduce latency issues.

- **Data Consistency:** Employ consistency mechanisms such as synchronous writes or consensus algorithms to maintain a consistent state across all copies.

- **System Reliability:** Ensure the system's robustness can handle node or network failures gracefully without data loss.

Synchronizing databases in microservices involves various challenges and complexities often necessitated by the architectural distinctions. The techniques highlighted above are not exhaustive but represent a fundamental approach to achieving robust data replication and synchronization in a microservices ecosystem. Choosing the right strategy depends heavily on the specific requirements and constraints of the system under development. Each technique comes with its trade-offs regarding consistency, availability, latency, and complexity. Hence, careful consideration must be taken to align the replication and synchronization strategies with the overall system's resilience and performance objectives.

6.9 Handling Shared Data in Microservices Architecture

Handling shared data in a microservices architecture requires careful consideration to ensure that data consistency is maintained without compromising the principles of loose coupling and service autonomy. This section explores the challenges and techniques for managing shared data across microservices effectively.

Shared data poses significant challenges in microservices environments due to the distributed nature of the system. Services often need access to the same data to perform their functions, which can lead to problems such as data duplication, inconsistencies, and higher complexity in data management.

To address these challenges, several techniques can be employed:

- Database-per-service model

- API composition

- Command Query Responsibility Segregation (CQRS)

- SAGA patterns

Database-per-service model is a strategy where each microservice owns and manages its own database schema. This model avoids data inconsistency and promotes service autonomy by ensuring that services do not directly access the databases of other services. For shared data requirements, services can employ APIs to expose necessary information.

```
Example: A Customer Service and an Order Service each use their own databases
but must share customer data. The Customer Service exposes an API that the
Order Service can use to retrieve customer details safely.
```

API composition is another technique used to handle shared data. In this approach, a separate service acts as a composite layer that aggregates data from multiple underlying services. This service can cache the data for performance improvements but must have mechanisms to ensure cache consistency.

```
1  GET /composite/customer-details/{customerId} {
2      // Retrieve customer from Customer Service
3      // Retrieve customer's orders from Order Service
4      // Aggregate data
5      return aggregatedCustomerDetails;
6  }
```

Command Query Responsibility Segregation (CQRS) offers a refined model to deal with read and write operations separately. By using different models for updating information (Command model) and for reading information (Query model), it can efficiently handle shared data by synchronizing the read model asynchronously with the write operations.

---

1 **begin**
2   // Command Model Processing extract data from Command Model;
3   apply business rules;
4   update the write database;
5   // Asynchronously update Read Model on Event (DataChanged) { update read database from write database;
6   }

164

The SAGA pattern helps in maintaining data consistency across different services by managing each business transaction as a sequence of
local transactions. Each local transaction updates data within a single
service and publishes an event; subsequent local transactions can then
be triggered by these events in other services.

```
1    // Example of a SAGA orchestrating customer onboarding
2    begin transaction
3        // First microservice transaction
4        create customer record
5
6        // On success, publish customer created event
7        publish event(customerCreated)
8
9        // Second microservice responds to event
10       create billing account
11       if (failure) {
12           compensate previous transactions
13       }
14   end transaction
```

Effective handling of shared data in microservices involves selecting
appropriate strategies based on specific system requirements and characteristics. This ensures maintained data integrity and consistency
while promoting the isolation and autonomy of individual services.

6.10   Securing Data in a Microservices Environ-
ment

Data security in a microservices architecture presents unique challenges due to the distributed nature of services, the multiple interaction
points between services, and the various data storage systems used
by each service. Addressing these challenges requires a structured approach that encompasses data encryption, secure data access policies,
and regular audits.

- **Encryption of Data at Rest and in Transit**: Ensuring that data
  is encrypted both when it is stored (at rest) and as it moves
  between services (in transit) is fundamental. For data at rest,
  widely adopted algorithms such as AES (Advanced Encryption
  Standard) should be used. This approach prevents unauthorized
  access even if physical security measures fail or storage units are
  compromised.

- **Secure Data Access Controls**: Implementation of comprehensive
  access control mechanisms is critical. This includes the use of

role-based access controls (RBAC) to ensure that only authorized entities can access or manipulate the data. Each microservice should enforce authentication and authorization protocols such as OAuth2.0 and JWT (JSON Web Tokens) to manage access rights.

- **Audit Trails**: Maintaining detailed and comprehensive logs of data operations by services allows monitoring of who accessed what data and when. This is essential not only for security audits but also for fulfilling regulatory requirements for data tracing.

Data across multiple microservices must be protected under consistent security protocols. The following strategies are crucial for safeguarding data within a microservices ecosystem:

- Uniform security standards implementation across services.
- Regular security audits and penetration tests.
- Continuous monitoring of network traffic and irregular access patterns.

The specific implementation of security measures often includes setting up secure communication channels. Utilizing protocols such as TLS (Transport Layer Security) ensures that data transmitted over networks remains secure from eavesdropping and man-in-the-middle attacks. Here is an example of configuring a microservice to use HTTPS, a protocol built upon TLS, for secure communication:

```
1   from flask import Flask
2   import ssl
3
4   app = Flask(__name__)
5
6   context = ssl.SSLContext(ssl.PROTOCOL_TLS_SERVER)
7   context.load_cert_chain('yourserver.crt', 'yourserver.key')
8
9   if __name__ == '__main__':
10      app.run(ssl_context=context)
```

This script sets up a basic server using the Flask framework in Python and configures it with TLS encryption using a server certificate and a private key. The microservice initiated via this script will then only accept secure connections, thereby safeguarding data in transit.

For regularly auditing and updating security configurations, automation tools can play a significant role. They can help implement consistent security policies and react quickly to any potential breach by analyzing logs and detecting abnormal patterns. Here is an example of how anomaly detection can be scripted:

```
1   # Import necessary libraries
2   from sklearn.ensemble import IsolationForest
```

```
3   import pandas as pd
4
5   # Sample dataset for analysis
6   # Assuming continuation of data entries with ellipsis, which should be replaced with
        actual data.
7   data = pd.DataFrame({
8       'time_stamp': ["2021-07-01 12:00:00", "2021-07-01 12:00:10", "2021-07-01
            12:00:20", "2021-07-01 12:00:30"],
9       'service_name': ["Payment", "Authentication", "Payment", "Authentication"],
10      'data_accessed': ["Sensitive", "Non-sensitive", "Sensitive", "Non-sensitive"],
11      'user_id': [101, 102, 101, 103]
12  })
13
14  # Training the model on the historical data
15  # Ensure that the feature used for training the model is numeric and makes sense for
        anomaly detection.
16  model = IsolationForest(n_estimators=100, max_samples='auto', contamination=float
        (0.02), max_features=1.0)
17  model.fit(data[['user_id']]) # Training only on 'user_id' may not be very
        meaningful for real scenarios.
18
19  # Predicting anomalies
20  data['scores'] = model.decision_function(data[['user_id']])
21  data['anomaly'] = model.predict(data[['user_id']])
22  print(data)
```

This Python script leverages the Isolation Forest algorithm to detect anomalies in access patterns, which can indicate potential security breaches. The model is trained on historical data and can then be used to classify new data entries as normal or atypical.

Securing data in a microservices environment, thus, involves orchestrating multiple strategies from encrypting data to implementing stringent access controls and routinely conducting security audits. By adopting these measures, organizations can safeguard their data across microservices and mitigate risks posed by the distributed nature of a microservices architecture. This, in turn, not only protects the data but also reinforces the trust that stakeholders place in the digital infrastructure.

6.11   Data Monitoring and Health Checks

Effective data monitoring and regular health checks are essential in ensuring the robustness and reliability of microservices architectures. Unlike monolithic systems where centralized monitoring might suffice, microservices require a more distributed approach to monitoring due to their distributed nature.

Defining Key Performance Indicators

The first step in establishing an effective monitoring system is to define key performance indicators (KPIs) for each microservice. These KPIs should be directly linked to the service's functionality and the overall system's health. Common KPIs include:

- Response time

- Error rates

- Throughput

- Resource utilization (CPU, memory, disk IO, etc.)

Log Aggregation and Analysis

Given the distributed nature of microservices, log aggregation becomes a foundational step for effective monitoring. Each microservice should be configured to send logs to a centralized logging system where they can be correlated and analyzed. Tools such as ELK Stack (Elasticsearch, Logstash, and Kibana) or Splunk are commonly utilized for log aggregation purposes.

```
1  # Configuring a microservice to send logs to a centralized system
2  logger.addHandler(logging.StreamHandler(sys.stdout))
3  logger.addHandler(logging.handlers.HTTPHandler(
4      'http://logserver.example.com:9200',
5      '/log',
6      method='POST',
7  ))
```

Implementing Health Check APIs

It is important to implement health check APIs for each microservice. These APIs return the status of the microservice and are critical for orchestrators like Kubernetes or Docker Swarm to ensure service availability and reliability.

```
1  from flask import Flask, jsonify
2
3  app = Flask(__name__)
4
5  @app.route('/health', methods=['GET'])
6  def health_check():
7      # Implement checks here
8      return jsonify({'status': 'UP'}), 200
```

Using this code, the health status of the microservices can be continuously monitored by orchestration tools which can take automated actions such as restarting unhealthy service instances.

Metrics Collection

Metrics collection is another pillar of effective microservices monitoring. Tools such as Prometheus or Graphite can be used to collect various metrics from microservices. These metrics are invaluable for proactive monitoring and can trigger alarms when anomalies are detected.

```
1  # Java example to expose service metrics
2  registry = new CollectorRegistry();
3  Gauge duration = Gauge.build()
4      .name("requests_duration_seconds")
5      .help("Request duration in seconds.")
6      .register(registry);
```

Distributed Tracing

Distributed tracing is essential for debugging and monitoring complex interactions between microservices. OpenTracing, an API standard for distributed tracing, provides tooling for capturing the flow of transaction requests through microservices architectures.

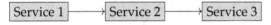

Alerting and Notification

Alerting mechanisms need to be set up to notify the development and operational teams if something goes wrong. Alerts can be based on thresholds set on KPIs or the output of log analysis.

```
ALERT HighErrorRate
  IF rate(errors_total[5m]) > 0.05
  FOR 10m
  LABELS { severity = "critical" }
  ANNOTATIONS {
    summary = "High error rate detected",
    description = "More than 5% errors observed in the last 10 minutes."
  }
```

The appropriate handling and response to these alerts ensure that issues can be addressed before they affect the system's stability or the user's experience.

This structured approach to data monitoring and regular health checks is vital to ensuring that microservices operate efficiently and effectively under the dynamics of scaling and distributed processing. Adaptation of these monitoring practices to specific service and architecture needs will aid in maintaining operational excellence and achieving high system reliability.

6.12 Strategies for Data Migration in Microservices

Data migration in microservices architectures involves moving data from a monolithic system or from older microservices to newer ones while ensuring that the data remains consistent, complete, and accessible. It is generally fraught with challenges owing to the distributed nature of microservices, which often implies multiple databases and differing data management strategies.

Decomposing the Monolithic Database: The initial step in data migration is the decomposition of the existing monolithic database into a set of databases that align with targeted microservices. This decomposition should be fine-grained enough to allow each microservice autonomy over its data, yet it must ensure that interdependencies are managed robustly.

```
1  // Example of a basic database decomposition strategy in pseudo-code
2  For each microservice {
3      Identify data ownership and boundaries;
4      Create individual schema based on service needs;
5      Migrate relevant data from monolith to the new schema;
6  }
```

Incremental Migration Strategies: Incremental migration is crucial in maintaining service availability and minimizing risk during the transition. The Strangler Fig Pattern, often employed here, involves gradually replacing specific pieces of functionality within the old system with new applications and microservices. This can often mean running old and new systems in parallel, necessitating a robust data synchronization mechanism.

```
Output after applying Strangler Fig Pattern:
- Step 1: Legacy and microservice databases operate concurrently.
- Step 2: Data flows bidirectionally but is prioritized towards the new service.
- Final Step: Legacy system is fully decommissioned, and microservice becomes the sole data owner.
```

Data Synchronization and Consistency: Ensuring data remains consistent across distributed systems is paramount. Techniques such as Change Data Capture (CDC) can be utilized to synchronize data between microservices. CDC tracks changes in a database and propogates them to other systems as events.

- Use transaction logs to capture changes in the source database.

- Publish changes to a message queue which acts as an event source for other services.

- Subscriber microservices process these messages to maintain data consistency.

Data Transformation: Data transformation is often required during migration, as different microservices might need data in different formats. This demands careful design to avoid complex transformations that can impact performance. Use lightweight transformation logic that can be encapsulated within the microservices themselves if possible.

```
1  // Example of a simple data transformation in Java
2  public class DataTransformer {
3      public NewDataFormat transform(OldDataFormat oldData) {
4          NewDataFormat newData = new NewDataFormat();
5          newData.setRelevantField(oldData.getCorrespondingField());
6          return newData;
7      }
8  }
```

Legacy Data Archiving: Once data migration is complete, legacy data, unless absolutely necessary, should be archived. Archiving older data is crucial to maintain system performance and reduce operational costs. Ensure compliance with legal and business retention policies while designing the archiving strategy.

```
Data archiving status:
- Legacy data stored securely in read-only format.
- Access restricted to administrative use only.
- Archived from active databases to improve performance.
```

The above strategies provide a broad framework to plan data migration in a microservices context. Each organization must adapt these strategies based on its specific business conditions, existing systems architecture, and future scalability expectations. By emphasizing a methodical, iterative approach to both migration and post-migration operations, enterprises can transition smoothly without jeopardizing data integrity or disrupting ongoing business processes.

Chapter 7

Migration to Cloud Platforms

Migrating to cloud platforms involves shifting applications, data, and other business elements from on-premise servers to cloud environments, which offer more robust scalability, flexibility, and cost-efficiency. This chapter discusses the various cloud service models, such as IaaS, PaaS, and SaaS, and provides a step-by-step approach to planning, executing, and optimizing the migration process. The emphasis is on minimizing downtime and ensuring data integrity while leveraging the full potential of cloud capabilities.

7.1 Overview of Cloud Platforms and Their Offerings

Cloud platforms provide a suite of infrastructural, platform, and software services that radically transform traditional IT capabilities. These platforms are built on virtualized hardware and managed via a network, typically the internet, offering substantial advantages in terms of scalability, cost, and efficiency over on-premise solutions.

In the context of cloud computing, there are three primary models of cloud services: Infrastructure-as-a-Service (IaaS), Platform-as-a-Service (PaaS), and Software-as-a-Service (SaaS). Each model offers different levels of control, flexibility, and management, which can influence the decision-making process for organizations aiming to migrate their operations to the cloud.

Infrastructure-as-a-Service (IaaS) provides virtualized physical computing resources over the Internet. IaaS includes offerings such as virtual server space, network connections, and bandwidth. The provider manages the infrastructure, while the user manages the operating systems, storage, and deployed applications.

Platform-as-a-Service (PaaS) offers a development and deployment environment in the cloud, including tools to develop, test, and host applications. PaaS is designed to simplify the process of coding new applications with pre-built backend infrastructure and middleware. It abstracts much of the system management hassle, which allows developers to focus on application logic and functionality.

Software-as-a-Service (SaaS) delivers software applications over the internet, on a subscription basis. SaaS providers manage the infrastructure, middleware, app software, and app data. This model is ideal for those who want an out-of-the-box solution that is ready to use with minimal configuration and offers compatibility with all users' platforms.

Each model is designed to address different needs and offers varying degrees of cost savings, operational efficiency, and speed to market. For instance, IaaS is highly flexible and cost-effective for large-scale computing tasks that do not demand large capital investments in hardware. On the other hand, SaaS could be more suitable for applications that require broad distribution or quick, low-cost deployment. PaaS sits in between these two, providing a balanced environment that reduces the need for extensive coding and system management while offering some flexibility in hosting customized applications.

In addition to these categories, cloud platforms may come in various deployment models:

- **Public Cloud**: Services are delivered over the public internet and shared across organizations. This model offers vast economies of scale and agility but may be less suited for applications requiring complex security and data residency compliance.

- **Private Cloud**: Infrastructure and services are maintained on a private network. These are often used by organizations with strict data control, security, and compliance needs.

174

- **Hybrid Cloud**: Combines public and private clouds, allowing data and applications to be shared between them. This model provides the versatility of the public cloud while retaining the control of critical operations in a private environment.

- **Community Cloud**: Infrastructure is shared among organizations with common concerns and considerations, possibly related to security, compliance, or jurisdiction.

Popular cloud platform providers include Amazon Web Services (AWS), Microsoft Azure, and Google Cloud Platform (GCP), each with their own unique services, pricing structures, and specific advantages. AWS, for instance, is widely recognized for its reliability, scalability, and vast array of services. Azure integrates deeply with Microsoft's software ecosystem, making it ideal for organizations that rely heavily on Microsoft tools and services. Google Cloud, on the other hand, offers cutting-edge AI, machine learning, and data analytics capabilities.

The selection of cloud services and the appropriate model of deployment very much depend on a strategic fit for the organization's specific requirements, budget, and long-term IT goals. Thus, an understanding of these foundations is crucial to effectively leveraging the power of cloud technologies.

7.2 Choosing the Right Cloud Platform for Your Needs

Selecting an appropriate cloud platform is critical for the success of your migration project. This decision should be based on various criteria including the specific needs of the business, the technical requirements of the applications, and the budget constraints. The process of identifying the right cloud platform involves a comprehensive evaluation of the features, services, cost structures, and support systems of different cloud providers.

To navigate this decision, businesses typically start by examining the types of cloud services required—Infrastructure as a Service (IaaS), Platform as a Service (PaaS), or Software as a Service (SaaS). Each of these service models offers distinct advantages and is suitable for different types of applications and business needs.

- IaaS provides virtualized computing resources over the internet. IaaS is highly flexible and offers complete control of the computing infrastructure. It is ideal for businesses with unique or highly specialized configuration needs.

- PaaS provides a platform allowing customers to develop, run, and manage applications without the complexity of building and maintaining the infrastructure typically associated with developing and launching an app. PaaS can dramatically increase developer productivity and time-to-market.

- SaaS delivers software applications over the Internet, on a subscription basis. It eliminates the need to install and run applications on individual computers or in data centers, reducing the effort of maintenance and support.

Once the service model is chosen, several other factors should be considered to choose the right provider. These include:

- **Scalability**: The platform should be able to scale resources up or down as needed without requiring a significant lead time or excessive costs.

- **Security**: Security features and compliance with relevant standards (such as GDPR, HIPAA) are crucial. The platform should provide robust security measures including data encryption, firewall configurations, and intrusion detection systems.

- **Reliability**: Look for platforms with high availability and strong disaster recovery capabilities.

- **Cost Efficiency**: Analyze the cost structure of each platform, including hidden costs like data transfer fees. The goal is to avoid unexpected expenses that could impact the financial aspect of running applications in the cloud.

- **Support and Services**: Consider the support services provided by the vendor. Efficient customer support and professional services can be valuable to solve potential issues during and after migration.

- **Geographical Location**: The region in which the data centers are located can affect latency and also compliance with data sovereignty laws.

- **Technology Ecosystem**: Ensure that the cloud platform is compatible with the existing technology stack used by your business. This includes compatibility with current development tools, databases, and applications.

Furthermore, it is advisable to conduct a pilot project before fully committing to a cloud platform. This involves deploying a portion of your applications to evaluate the platform's performance in a controlled setting. The insights garnered from the pilot test can help finalize the decision and establish trust in the platform's capabilities.

To illustrate how a cloud platform's performance can be evaluated, consider an analysis using the following Python code snippet within a pilot project, which uses APIs provided by the cloud service to measure response times and resource usage:

```
1   import time
2   import requests
3
4   # Measure the response time for a cloud service API
5   endpoint = "https://api.yourcloudplatform.com/data"
6   start_time = time.time()
7   response = requests.get(endpoint)
8   end_time = time.time()
9
10  # Print response time in milliseconds
11  print(f"API Response Time: {(end_time - start_time) * 1000} ms")
```

Lastly, adhering carefully to the selection criteria discussed ensures that the chosen cloud platform supports achieving the strategic business goals and aligns with the overall IT infrastructure, thereby facilitating a successful migration to the cloud platform.

7.3 Cloud Migration Models: IaaS, PaaS, SaaS

Cloud migration models are fundamental to understanding how businesses can leverage various service offerings to enhance their operational efficiency and scalability. Three primary models dominate the landscape: Infrastructure as a Service (IaaS), Platform as a Service (PaaS), and Software as a Service (SaaS). Each model offers distinct features and benefits suited for different migration needs and organizational strategies.

Infrastructure as a Service (IaaS) serves as the baseline layer in cloud computing models, providing virtualized computing resources over the Internet. IaaS allows businesses to rent infrastructure like servers, storage, and networking hardware, alongside the flexible scaling options depending on their immediate needs. Being the most flexible of all cloud services, IaaS offers significant control over hardware infrastructures but requires more management and maintenance from the user's side.

A profound advantage of IaaS is its flexibility to facilitate experimental, temporary, or fluctuating projects. As a result, it is particularly beneficial for small to medium-sized enterprises (SMEs) that do not seek to invest heavily in physical hardware or firms that experience highly variable workloads.

Example usage of IaaS in a typical migration could be demonstrated with the migration of a company's storage and backup systems. The migration process can be illustrated through the following pseudo-algorithm implemented by DevOps:

Algorithm 12: Data Migration to IaaS cloud storage

   Data: Enterprise on-premise data
   Result: Data migrated to cloud-based storage
1 initialization;
2 **while** *Data exists* **do**
3   read data from on-premise system;
4   transfer data to IaaS-based storage solution;
5   verify integrity of the transferred data;
6   log transfer details;
7   remove data from local source if verified;

Platform as a Service (PaaS) builds upon the infrastructure services provided by IaaS, offering additional layers such as operating systems and middleware, while also handling much of the management of underlying infrastructure. This enables developers to focus more on the deployment and management of their applications. PaaS is ideally suited for developers seeking to build applications without the hassle of managing the underlying hardware and software layers.

The key benefit of PaaS is its ability to simplify complexities in software development by providing pre-configured features and a development framework, which can significantly reduce the development time and costs. Commonly utilized by development teams to streamline workflows in cloud-native application development, PaaS ensures that teams can concentrate on creating high-quality applications without worrying about underlying system maintenance.

178

Software as a Service (SaaS) offers completely managed software applications to users over the internet. Users do not need to handle installation, maintenance, or updates of the software, as these responsibilities are handled by the service provider. The accessibility and minimal input required from the user make SaaS an attractive option for businesses of all sizes, facilitating solutions from email systems to complex enterprise applications like Customer Relationship Management (CRM) and Enterprise Resource Planning (ERP).

An example of using SaaS in the business context could include a company transitioning its email systems to a SaaS provider, thus eliminating the need for internal server maintenance and updates as shown below:

```
Migration Process: Email system -> SaaS provider
Result: Reduced IT overhead, enhanced scalability, and better resource allocation
```

Overall, the selection between IaaS, PaaS, and SaaS should be dictated by the specific business needs, operational priorities, and the intended level of control over IT infrastructures. By appropriating the correct model, businesses can not only ensure a smooth transition to the cloud but also harness the full potential of their cloud environment to align with their long-term strategic goals.

7.4 Pre-migration Preparation and Checklist

Migrating to a cloud environment necessitates comprehensive planning and preparation to ensure a successful transition. This section delineates critical steps and considerations for organizations to prepare for cloud migration.

Inventory Assessment of IT Assets

The initial step in preparing for migration involves performing a thorough assessment of the current IT assets. This includes cataloging all hardware, software, network configurations, and data. Solutions to automate the discovery of these assets can facilitate this process, providing detailed insights into system dependencies and resource utilization.

```
1  # Example Python code to list all servers in an IT environment using a hypothetical
     library
2  import asset_discovery_library
3
```

179

```
4    # Initialize the discovery system
5    discovery_system = asset_discovery_library.initialize()
6
7    # Perform discovery
8    servers = discovery_system.discover_servers()
9
10   # Output the list of servers
11   print("Discovered servers:")
12   for server in servers:
13       print(server)
```

The output from such an operation might typically look like this:

```
Discovered servers:
Server1
Server2
Server3
...
```

Defining Migration Goals and Objectives

It is crucial to clearly define the goals and objectives of migration. These can vary from enhancing performance, increasing business agility, cost reduction, to improving disaster recovery strategies. Goals should be Specific, Measurable, Achievable, Relevant, and Time-bound (SMART).

- Enhance performance by reducing server response times by at least 20%

- Reduce IT operational costs by 30% within one year post-migration

- Improve business agility by deploying new applications 50% faster

Selecting a Cloud Service Model

Based on the objectives, decide on the most suitable cloud service model. IaaS provides more control over the environment, whereas PaaS offers convenience by managing infrastructure, and SaaS delivers software as a service. The choice depends on organizational expertise, the need for customization, and management preferences.

180

Security and Compliance Evaluation

Before migration, evaluate the security policies, governance models, and compliance requirements. Identify the data laws applicable to the business sector and geographical location. This involves mapping existing controls to those provided by cloud providers and potentially implementing additional security measures as necessary.

- Review existing data encryption policies and compare with cloud provider offerings

- Determine the impact of cloud adoption on existing compliance certifications

- Assess the need for additional identity and access management controls

Designing the Migration Architecture

Plan the architecture of the solution in the cloud. This should include the blueprints for data storage, network design, and the interaction between different cloud services. Using diagramming tools can aid in visualizing and communicating the proposed architecture.

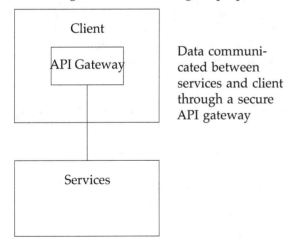

Data communicated between services and client through a secure API gateway

181

Migration Plan and Rollback Strategy

Develop a detailed migration plan stating the sequence of migrating resources. This plan should also include a clear rollback strategy should the migration face unexpected challenges or failures.

Algorithm 13: Migration and Rollback Plan

    Input: List of systems to migrate
    Output: Migration status report
1 initialization;
2 **for** *system in systems* **do**
3   attemptMigration(system);
4   **if** *success* **then**
5 | logSuccess(system);
6   **else**
7 | rollback(system);
8   logFailure(system);

Testing the Migration Plan

Validate the migration plan through comprehensive testing, including performance testing, integration testing, and user acceptance testing. Adjust the migration strategy based on the outcomes to ensure minimal business disruption during the actual migration.

The outcomes of this preparation are of paramount importance. They determine the efficiency and smoothness of transition to a cloud platform, ultimately influencing the organization's ability to leverage cloud technology effectively for business growth and improvement.

7.5   Lift-and-Shift vs. Cloud-Native Migration

When migrating to cloud platforms, organizations often choose between two primary strategies: *lift-and-shift* and *cloud-native* migration. Both strategies serve unique business needs and IT strategies, and decision-makers must understand the intricacies and implications of each to ensure a successful migration that aligns with organizational goals.

Lift-and-shift, also known as rehosting, involves moving applications and data from an on-premises environment to the cloud, without making extensive modifications to the applications' architecture. This approach is typically faster and less resource-intensive, as it avoids the complexities associated with modifying the existing software. Lift-and-shift is an attractive option for organizations that need to quickly exit data centers, reduce physical footprint, or comply with regulatory changes requiring data to be hosted in specific geographical locations without altering the functionalities of the legacy systems.

Here is a simple pseudocode that illustrates the basic steps involved in a lift-and-shift migration process:

Algorithm 14: Pseudocode for Lift-and-Shift Migration

Data: List of on-premise applications
Result: Applications running in the cloud environment

1 initialization()
2 **for** *each application in the list* **do**
3   replicate application data in cloud storage
4   deploy application on cloud provider's infrastructure
5   configure network settings to redirect traffic to the cloud instance
6   perform functional and performance tests
7   switch traffic to cloud environment completely
8 **end**

On the other hand, cloud-native migration involves redesigning and often rebuilding applications to fully exploit the advantages of cloud computing models. The cloud-native approach is oriented towards utilizing scalable, flexible, and fully managed services that cloud providers offer. This model leverages microservices architecture, serverless computing, and container orchestration technologies such as Kubernetes, which are inherently designed to enhance scalability, resilience, and maintenance.

A critical challenge in cloud-native migrations is addressing the complexity of breaking down monolithic applications into microservices. This process involves significant planning, skilled resources, and a robust testing strategy to ensure that the newly designed system aligns with business functionality and performance requirements. Here is an illustrative example of the transformation process in cloud-native migration:

Listing 7.1: Code Snippet for Containerizing an Application for Cloud-Native Migration

```
1   # Example: Dockerizing a Python Flask Application
2   from flask import Flask
3   app = Flask(__name__)
4
5   @app.route('/')
6   def home():
7       return 'Hello, World!'
8
9   if __name__ == '__main__':
10      app.run(debug=True, host='0.0.0.0', port=5000)
```

After containerization, the application can be managed using Kubernetes, which effectively handles scaling, self-healing, and load-balancing of containerized applications.

The selection between lift-and-shift and cloud-native migration depends on multiple factors including the strategic business objectives, budget constraints, timeline, system complexity, and readiness for organizational change. Lift-and-shift migration can serve as an intermediate step towards a more transformative cloud-adoption strategy. It allows an organization to rapidly gain cloud presence and subsequently evolve towards cloud-native approaches as they become more accustomed to cloud paradigms.

Typically, organizations might start with a lift-and-shift approach to quickly achieve cloud migration and then gradually refactor critical applications to a cloud-native architecture. This phased approach mitigates risk, provides immediate benefits from the cloud, and ensures a strategic transformation to increasingly efficient and innovative cloud-native technologies.

The decision between lift-and-shift and cloud-native migrations is crucial and hinges on thorough analysis and alignment with long-term business goals. Strategic planning, skilled resources, and effective deployment of technologies are indispensable to leveraging the full spectrum of cloud capabilities, ultimately enhancing the competitive edge and operational efficiency of the organization.

7.6   Automated Tools and Services for Cloud Migration

As enterprises embark on migrating applications to cloud platforms, the utilization of automated tools and services becomes indispensable.

These tools are designed to streamline the migration process, reduce the potential for human error, and accelerate the shift from on-premise systems to cloud environments.

Types of Cloud Migration Tools

The landscape of cloud migration tools is diverse, each catering to different aspects of the migration process. These tools can generally be categorized into:

- Assessment Tools: They perform preliminary analysis on the existing on-premise infrastructure to provide insights into the workload dependencies and the readiness for migration. These tools can help in identifying the parts of the infrastructure that should be migrated as is, re-platformed, or refactored.

- Migration Tools: These are tools specifically engineered to automate the actual transfer of applications, data, and configurations from the on-premise environment to the cloud.

- Monitoring Tools: Post-migration, these tools help in tracking the performance of applications in the cloud, ensuring that they meet the desired performance benchmarks and suggesting optimizations as necessary.

Examples of Popular Migration Tools

Here are some of the widely-used tools provided by major cloud service providers:

- **AWS Migration Tools**: Amazon Web Services offers a suite of tools such as AWS Migration Hub, AWS Database Migration Service (DMS), and AWS Server Migration Service (SMS). AWS Migration Hub provides a centralized location to monitor and manage migrations from on-premise to AWS. The Database Migration Service helps in migrating databases to AWS quickly and securely, while the SMS automates, schedules, and tracks incremental replications of live server volumes.

```
1  import aws_migration_services
2
3  # Setting up AWS Migration Hub
4  aws_migration_services.setup_migration_hub()
```

```
5
6   # Migrate database using AWS Database Migration Service
7   migration_status = aws_migration_services.migrate_database(source_db_config,
        target_aws_config)
```

- **Azure Migrate**: Microsoft's Azure Migrate offers a hub of tools that assess and migrate web apps, virtual machines, and databases to Azure. It encompasses a comprehensive discovery and assessment phase, allowing better planning and insights before the actual migration process begins.

```
1   import azure_migration_services
2
3   # Initial assessment using Azure Migrate
4   assessment_report = azure_migration_services.assess_infrastructure(
        assessment_params)
5
6   # Execute migration
7   migration_status = azure_migration_services.initiate_migration_plan(
        migration_plan_settings)
```

- **Google Cloud Migration Tools**: Including tools like the Velostrata and the Migrate for Compute Engine, Google offers services that facilitate quick migration of workloads to Google Cloud by enabling applications to start running in the cloud in minutes.

```
1   import gcp_migration_services
2
3   # Initialize Google Velostrata for workload migration
4   gcp_migration_services.setup_velostrata()
5
6   # Leverage Migrate for Compute Engine
7   migration_status = gcp_migration_services.migrate_to_compute_engine(
        source_vm_config, gcp_target_config)
```

Choosing the Right Tools

When selecting tools for migration, it's crucial to consider:

- Compatibility: Ensure the chosen tools support all legacy and current technologies used in the enterprises.

- Scalability: The tools must be scalable enough to manage the migration of large and complex environments.

- Security: Security features of the tools must align with the enterprise's compliance and security requirements.

186

- **Ease of Use:** The tools should have a user-friendly interface, with adequate support and documentation available.

Furthermore, it is advisable to engage in a pilot migration project using the selected tools. This can reveal unforeseen issues and provide practical insights into the effectiveness and efficiency of the tools in a controlled environment. This approach enables adjustments to be made before full-scale execution, thereby minimizing risks associated with downtime and data integrity.

Thus, the strategic selection and adept deployment of automated tools and services are pivotal in achieving a successful migration to cloud platforms. The right tools not only simplify the technical processes but also facilitate a more accurate and reliable migration workflow, ensuring that the cloud transition supports broader organizational goals concerning agility, performance, and cost-efficiency.

7.7 Managing Multi-Cloud and Hybrid Cloud Environments

With the evolution of cloud services and the diversification of organizational needs, enterprises often find themselves managing complex cloud environments comprising both multi-cloud and hybrid cloud models. This section delves into the strategies and best practices for effectively managing these environments, focusing on integration, cost control, security, and ensuring optimal performance.

Integration of Cloud Services

Integration in a multi-cloud or hybrid cloud environment is pivotal. It involves connecting various cloud services, both public and private, to function cohesively as a unified system. This can be challenging due to the varying APIs, standards, and protocols used by different cloud providers.

- Use of Hybrid Integration Platforms (HIPs): HIPs facilitate the integration of different cloud services and on-premise systems. They provide a common platform to manage APIs and data flows across systems.

- Implementation of Containers: Containers such as Docker and Kubernetes offer consistency across various infrastructures and simplify application deployment across different clouds.

- Adopting Enterprise Integration Patterns: These patterns help to address complex integration scenarios and ensure that different components can communicate effectively regardless of their deployment.

Example of Container Implementation:

```
1  # Dockerfile for deploying a simple Python application
2  FROM python:3.7
3  COPY . /app
4  WORKDIR /app
5  RUN pip install -r requirements.txt
6  EXPOSE 5000
7  CMD ["python", "app.py"]
```

Cost Control and Optimization

Managing costs is a critical aspect of operating in multi-cloud and hybrid environments. It is easy for costs to escalate unexpectedly due to the complex nature of services and varied pricing structures.

- Implementation of Cloud Cost Management Tools: Tools like AWS Cost Explorer, Azure Cost Management, and Google Cloud Platform's Cost Management tools help monitor and optimize expenditures.

- Adopting a Polycloud Approach: Use different cloud providers for different services based on the cost-efficiency of each service.

- Regular Audits and Adjustments: Periodic reviews of cloud usage and costs can help identify waste and optimize resource allocation.

Ensuring Security and Compliance

Security in multi-cloud and hybrid environments becomes complicated due to different security protocols and compliances required by various cloud providers.

- Centralized Security Management: Using tools like CASB (Cloud Access Security Broker) which provide a single pane of glass for managing security across all cloud services.

- Regular Security Assessments: Conduct assessments and penetration testing to identify and mitigate risks.

- Compliance Automation Tools: Implement tools that help in achieving and maintaining compliance with various regulations across different cloud platforms.

Performance Optimization

Performance management in diverse cloud environments requires continuous monitoring and fine-tuning of resources.

- Use of Performance Management Tools: Tools such as Dynatrace and New Relic provide insights into application performance across different clouds and help in proactive optimization.

- Implementing CDN Solutions: Content Delivery Networks (CDN) can reduce load-times and improve user experience in a globally distributed environment.

- Application Resource Allocation: Dynamically allocate and adjust resources based on performance metrics and predictive analysis.

```
1  # Example Python code for monitoring CPU usage
2  import psutil
3
4  # Get CPU percentage usage
5  cpu_usage = psutil.cpu_percent(interval=1)
6  print(f'Current CPU Usage: {cpu_usage}%')
```

Future Trends and Perspectives

Ongoing advancements in cloud technology will continue to influence strategies in managing multi-cloud and hybrid cloud setups. Future trends suggest greater reliance on Artificial Intelligence and Machine Learning for automated decision-making and more sophisticated integration frameworks to handle the increasing complexity of cloud ecosystems.

By embracing these evolving technologies and maintaining adherence to the outlined strategies, enterprises can effectively manage their multi-cloud and hybrid cloud environments to achieve optimal operation efficiency and strategic business advantage.

7.8   Data Migration Strategies for the Cloud

The transition of data to a cloud environment is a critical phase in cloud migration and necessitates a thoughtful approach to minimize the risks of data loss, corruption, or downtime. This section details several strategies and considerations essential for effective data migration to cloud platforms.

1. Assessment of Data and Identification of Dependencies: Before initiating any data migration, it is crucial to comprehensively assess the data corpus and identify all interdependencies. This step includes mapping data sources, their sizes, formats, and the relationships between them. Such detailed knowledge facilitates determining the most appropriate data migration strategy.

2. Choosing the Right Data Migration Strategy: Data migration strategies may vary significantly based on the organization's specific requirements, the type of data, and the involved cloud architecture. Commonly employed strategies include:

- *Rehosting (Lift and Shift):* This involves moving data in its current form to the cloud. It is typically quick and cost-effective but may not utilize cloud-native features optimally.

- *Replatforming:* Adjusting data formats or the relational database management system (RDBMS) to better suit cloud environments while keeping the core data architecture unchanged.

- *Refactoring/Re-architecting:* Involves significant changes to the data schema and application architecture to make full use of cloud-native technologies and capabilities, thereby improving performance and scalability.

Each strategy has its specific use cases and associated trade-offs in terms of cost, performance, complexity, and required time-frame which need rigorous evaluation.

3. Data Cleansing and Preparation: Before migration, data needs to be cleaned and prepared. This includes de-duplication, correcting inaccuracies, converting data formats, and partitioning data logically. These steps are essential to ensure that the migrated data is accurate, consistent, and optimally formatted for new cloud-based applications.

4. Migration Execution: Executing data migration involves:

- *Initial Transfer:* Moving a copy of the data to the cloud. Depending on the data size, this might involve physical shipment of data storage devices or high-speed network transfer.

- *Delta Synchronization:* After the initial transfer, any changes made to the data source during the migration process need to be synchronized with the cloud environment to ensure data integrity.

5. Use of Automation Tools: Automation tools can significantly enhance the efficiency and reliability of data migration. These tools often provide features like data validation, error logging, retry mechanisms, and real-time progress monitoring, which are indispensable for ensuring a smooth migration.

6. Ensuring Data Security: Securing data during its transfer and when at rest in the cloud is paramount. This may involve encryption, using secure protocols for data transfer, and implementing access controls and audit trails.

7. Post-Migration Activities: After migration, activities such as data verification, performance testing, and optimization are crucial. Verifying data integrity involves checking if all data was accurately transferred and is accessible. Performance testing is used to ensure that the cloud environment meets the required data access speed and latency expectations.

```
Example of post-migration verification command:
$ checksum source_data_folder destination_data_folder
```

8. Future Strategies and Cloud Data Management: Even after successful migration, continuous management and optimization of cloud-stored data are necessary. This involves regular backups, updates to security policies, and performance tuning to adapt to changing use patterns and business needs.

Adhering to these strategies ensures that data migration to cloud platforms is executed efficiently and effectively. Each step, right from the planning phase through post-migration adjustments, contributes significantly to leveraging the full potential of cloud environments, thus empowering organizations in their digital transformation initiatives.

7.9 Optimizing Costs and Resources in Cloud Migration

Achieving cost efficiency and optimal resource utilization during cloud migration necessitates a strategic approach to planning and executing the transition. One begins by thoroughly analyzing both the existing infrastructure and the anticipated needs within the cloud environment.

Understanding Usage Patterns and Resource Requirements: To effectively manage resources and thus optimize costs in cloud migration, an initial analysis of usage patterns and resource requirements is essential. This involves identifying peak data usage times, understanding the types of workloads (e.g., compute-intensive, memory-intensive), and forecasting potential scaling requirements.

- Assess workload performance metrics: Determine the average and peak CPU, memory, and storage usage to size the cloud resources correctly.

- Analyze traffic patterns: Understand intra-application and external traffic flows to optimize network architecture and associated costs.

- Evaluate compliance and security requirements: Certain data or applications may need enhanced security measures or specific geographic locations, impacting cost.

Strategies for Cost-Effective Resource Allocation: After mapping out the resource requirements, various strategies can be employed to ensure cost-effective resource allocation. Cloud providers usually offer a range of tools and services designed to aid in this process.

- Use of Reserved Instances or Savings Plans: Committing to certain levels of usage for one or three years can yield significant savings compared to on-demand pricing models.

- Implementation of Auto-Scaling: Auto-scaling features enable the system to automatically adjust resource allocation based on real-time demands, thus avoiding over-provisioning and minimizing waste.

- Right-sizing resources: Continuously monitor and adjust configurations to ensure that resources match requirements, avoiding under-utilization or over-provisioning.

Cost Monitoring and Management Tools: Modern cloud platforms provide comprehensive tools to monitor and manage costs. These tools offer dashboard views and detailed reports that break down costs by services, location, and time. For instance:

```
# Example code to extract cost data from a cloud provider API
import boto3

# Initialize a session using Amazon AWS credentials
client = boto3.client('ce', region_name='us-east-1')

# Define the time period for the cost exploration
time_period = {'Start': '2021-01-01', 'End': '2021-01-31'}

# Retrieve cost and usage data
response = client.get_cost_and_usage(
    TimePeriod=time_period,
    Granularity='DAILY',
    Metrics=['UnblendedCost', 'UsageQuantity'])

# Print the response dictionary
print(response)
```

```
{
    "Results": [
        {
            "TimePeriod": {"Start": "2021-01-01", "End": "2021-01-02"},
            "Total": {"UnblendedCost": {"Amount": "123.45", "Unit": "USD"}}
        },
        ...
    ]
}
```

Regular Optimization Reviews: To continually optimize cost and resource use, regular reviews of the cloud resources and their utilization should be conducted. This includes:

- Re-assessing resource needs and costs every quarter.

- Applying new features and discounts as they become available from the cloud provider.

- Adjusting to changing operational demands and scalability needs.

Through diligent planning, continuous monitoring, and effective management, organizations can optimize their cloud resource usage and realize significant cost savings. This, combined with an adjustment to shifting demands, ensures that the cloud infrastructure remains both efficient and cost-effective over time.

7.10 Security Considerations for Cloud Migration

Security represents a principal concern during the migration of services and data to a cloud environment. It is vital that enterprises adopt a series of stringent security protocols and strategies to safeguard their assets. This section elucidates various security threats and mitigative measures essential during cloud migration.

Common security threats during cloud migration include data breaches, loss of data integrity, inadequate data deletion, vulnerable APIs, and insider threats. To counter these threats, several security best practices and tools are adopted which are detailed below.

Firstly, the development and enforcement of comprehensive data security policies is crucial. These policies should outline acceptable usage and access control measures, data encryption guidelines, and incident response strategies. Prior to migration, a detailed audit of all data to be transferred should be conducted. This ensures sensitive data is adequately protected and identifies any compliance requirements for data handling and storage.

- Conduct a comprehensive risk assessment to identify vulnerabilities and prioritize their mitigation.

- Implement strong encryption protocols for both data at rest and data in transit. This can be achieved through technologies such as TLS (Transport Layer Security) and AES (Advanced Encryption Standard).

- Utilize identity and access management (IAM) solutions to enhance protection by ensuring that only authorized personnel can access certain data or application functionalities.

Furthermore, special attention must be paid to the selection and configuration of the cloud platform. The following listing shows an example snippet where security groups and roles are defined using Amazon Web Services (AWS) for restricting access:

```
1  import boto3
2
3  # Creating a new IAM role
4  iam = boto3.client('iam')
5  response = iam.create_role(
6      RoleName='MySecureRole',
```

```
7     AssumeRolePolicyDocument='...',
8     Description='Role with restricted access policies'
9   )
10
11  # Attaching a policy to the role
12  policy_response = iam.attach_role_policy(
13      RoleName='MySecureRole',
14      PolicyArn='arn:aws:iam::aws:policy/AmazonS3FullAccess'
15  )
```

Secure API endpoints are another critical aspect. The use of secure tokens and strict authentication methods reduces potential API vulnerabilities. Additionally, regular audits of API access logs help in detecting and responding to unauthorized access attempts swiftly.

Transitioning to a cloud environment often expands the attack surface. Therefore, continuous monitoring and real-time security systems are imperative. Deploying a Security Information and Event Management (SIEM) system can be an effective way to achieve continuous security monitoring. This system gathers and correlates data from various sources within cloud environments, providing comprehensive visibility and aiding in the early detection of potential security events.

Further ensure that the cloud provider complies with pertinent industry regulations such as GDPR for Europe, HIPAA for healthcare data in the United States, and CCPA for California residents. Compliance not only requires the cloud service providers to meet certain standards but also requires your migration process to be designed in such a way that compliance is maintained throughout the operation.

For example, the migration of applications dealing with protected health information (PHI) must consider HIPAA rules that protect patient data privacy. It is not just the cloud service provider but also your internal processes, access protocols, and migration strategies that must align with HIPAA requirements.

```
Compliance status: SUCCESS
Data migration completed with zero HIPAA violations reported.
Security logs indicate no unauthorized access attempts during migration.
```

To encapsulate, securing cloud migrations requires a multifaceted approach that involves not only technological solutions but also procedural and compliance mindfulness. By integrating strong encryption methods, robust identity management, continuous monitoring, and a deep understanding of compliance requirements, organizations can facilitate a secure and efficient migration to cloud platforms. Ensuring these practices are well-integrated and tuned to the specific risks associated with cloud migration enhances the security posture substantially and supports a successful transformation.

7.11 Compliance and Regulatory Challenges in Cloud Environments

Migrating operations to a cloud environment is not solely a technical endeavor but also a regulatory and compliance-driven process. Ensuring alignment with legal, regulatory, and compliance frameworks is critical to avoid substantial penalties and safeguard sensitive information. These frameworks can differ widely across industries and geographic locations. The sector-specific regulations like HIPAA for healthcare, PCI DSS for the payment card industry, and GDPR for data protection within the EU, involve very specific requirements that affect how data must be managed in the cloud.

The first step in navigating these challenges is to understand the regulatory requirements applicable to the specific industry and regions of operation. For example, if an application processes personal data from European citizens, it must comply with the General Data Protection Regulation (GDPR), which imposes duties on both data controllers and processors. Compliance implies adherence to principles such as data minimization, purpose limitation, and the integration of security from the initial design stages, commonly referred to as "privacy by design".

- Identify applicable regulations and understand specific compliance obligations.

- Evaluate how current compliance measures align with cloud environments.

- Develop a strategy to address gaps between existing practices and required cloud compliance measures.

Data localization norms pose considerable challenges as some countries mandate that certain types of data be stored within the country's borders. Migrating to a cloud environment often involves decentralizing data storage, which may conflict with these requirements. Consider creating hybrid cloud architectures or choosing cloud providers that

196

offer region-specific storage options as part of compliance strategy development.

Contractual agreements with cloud service providers (CSPs) must explicitly address compliance and regulatory needs. It is essential to ensure that such contracts have clear terms regarding responsibilities for data security, data breach notifications, and data handling practices. Additionally, the right to audit clauses in the contract will enable businesses to verify compliance through third parties, which is a requirement under several regulatory frameworks.

```
1   # Example of contract clause for data handling
2   contractual_clause = """
3   The CSP agrees to adhere to all applicable data protection and privacy laws
        relevant to the data provided by the Customer.
4   The CSP will permit independent audits by third-party auditors designated by the
        Customer, at least annually, to ensure compliance with the agreed standards
        and legal requirements.
5   """
```

Monitoring and maintaining compliance is an ongoing process, especially in dynamic cloud environments. Implementing robust governance frameworks and continuous compliance mechanisms, like automated compliance checks and real-time security audits, are crucial.

```
1   # Automated compliance check example
2   def compliance_check(rules, environment_status):
3       compliance_results = {}
4       for rule in rules:
5           compliance_results[rule] = rules[rule](environment_status)
6       return compliance_results
```

Cloud service providers often offer tools and services that aid in compliance and governance, such as AWS's Config, Google Cloud's Security Command Center, and Microsoft Azure's Compliance Manager. Utilizing these tools can help automate and simplify compliance processes.

- Contract negotiations with CSPs must incorporate compliance terms.

- Automated governance and compliance tools provided by CSPs should be implemented.

- Regular audits and real-time monitoring must be in place to maintain ongoing compliance.

Implementing an effective cloud compliance strategy requires comprehensive planning, a detailed understanding of applicable regulations, and strong coordination with selected cloud service providers.

Likewise, businesses must stay agile to adapt compliance strategies as regulations evolve and as their own cloud usage grows or changes. Continuous improvement and assessment led by a dedicated governance team can significantly reduce regulatory risks and enhance data protection efforts in cloud migrations.

7.12 Post-Migration Testing and Validation

Following the completion of a migration to a cloud platform, rigorous testing and validation are crucial to ensure that the newly migrated systems perform as expected, and to corroborate that data integrity is maintained. This step is fundamental to confirm the operational viability of the cloud infrastructure.

The first aspect to address in post-migration testing is the Validation of Data Integrity. Each piece of data needs to be verified to ensure that it has been accurately transferred from the legacy system to the cloud environment. This process includes checking for data completeness, correctness, and consistency. A common approach involves running queries on both the source and target systems and comparing the results. Automated scripts can be employed in this step to streamline the validation process.

```
Example output for data validation script:
Data records validated: 100,000
Data records in source system: 100,000
Data records in target system: 100,000
Validation status: SUCCESS
```

Subsequent to data validation, Functional Testing should be conducted. Functional testing involves testing the application in the cloud to ensure that all functionalities work as expected. This includes performing all operations that the application is expected to execute, from user transactions, data retrieval and processing, to backend operations. Each function is tested to verify that it performs according to the requirements and with the expected speed and accuracy.

```
1  def test_user_login():
2      user = UserFactory.create()
3      login_success = user.login('username', 'password')
4      assert login_success is True
```

Performance testing forms another critical component of post-migration assessment. It is essential to evaluate the performance of the cloud services to ensure they meet desired performance benchmarks and service level agreements (SLAs). Performance metrics such as response time, throughput, and system availability should be measured. Tools such as Apache JMeter or LoadRunner can be utilized to simulate a variety of real-world operating conditions and loads.

```
1  from locust import HttpUser, task, between
2
3  class WebsiteUser(HttpUser):
4      wait_time = between(1, 5)
5
6      @task
7      def index(self):
8          self.client.get("/")
```

Security validation is equally substantial. Post-migration, the security posture of the cloud environment needs to be tested to identify vulnerabilities and ensure compliance with security policies. Penetration testing and vulnerability assessments are critical to accomplish this task effectively.

```
1  import subprocess
2  def run_security_scan(target):
3      scanner_output = subprocess.run(["nmap", "-sV", target], capture_output=True,
                                        text=True)
4      print(scanner_output.stdout)
```

Load testing should also be carried out along with stress testing scenarios. These tests stress the cloud system to its breaking point, ensuring that it can handle peak loads especially during critical business operations or unusual surge in demand.

Integration testing in a cloud environment needs to ensure seamless interaction between different components and services, which might have dependencies across cloud providers in a multi-cloud or hybrid cloud setup. These tests are crucial for operations that involve integrations with APIs, external libraries, and services that were part of legacy systems but are now cloud-hosted.

Lastly, User Acceptance Testing (UAT) is employed to ensure that the cloud solution meets the business requirements and is user-ready. It involves real users who test the application in a production-like environment to validate the end-to-end business process, functionality, and performance.

The effectiveness of the cloud migration process largely depends on the thoroughness of the post-migration testing and validation phase. Ensuring the migrated applications not only function as intended but also leverage the advantages of the cloud infrastructure, is critical for achieving the migration objectives and for the system's long-term success. This phase helps in building confidence among stakeholders and signifies the readiness of the cloud environment for operational deployment.

Chapter 8

Testing Strategies for Microservices

Testing microservices effectively is essential due to their distributed nature and the complexity of interactions between services. This chapter introduces comprehensive testing strategies that cover unit testing for individual services, integration testing across multiple services, and end-to-end testing of entire systems. The focus is on ensuring functionality, performance, and reliability through various automated and manual testing techniques tailored specifically for microservices architectures.

8.1 Introduction to Testing in a Microservices Environment

Testing in a microservices architecture presents unique challenges that are not commonly encountered in monolithic applications. Due to the distributed nature of microservices, each service functions independently, communicating over a network which introduces variability and complexity in performance and functionality. This section details the foundational concepts and methodologies for testing within a microservices framework, aiming to encapsulate the core challenges and solutions in ensuring robustness and reliability in such systems.

The cornerstone of testing in a microservices environment is to address the independently deployable and scalable nature of microservices. Each microservice is typically a small, isolated piece of the overall application and focuses on executing one business capability. To effectively manage this, testers need to adopt a granular approach towards both functional and non-functional aspects of testing.

Isolation of Services: Initially, each microservice should be tested in isolation. Testing in isolation is crucial to ascertain that each service precisely fulfills its designated functionality. This involves focusing on unit testing each component with the use of stubs and mocks to simulate interactions with other services and external systems.

```
1  // Example of a simple unit test for a microservice
2  public void testUserServiceCreate() {
3      UserRepository mockRepo = mock(UserRepository.class);
4      UserService userService = new UserServiceImpl(mockRepo);
5      User user = new User("jdoe", "John Doe");
6      when(mockRepo.save(any(User.class))).thenReturn(user);
7      User result = userService.createUser("jdoe", "John Doe");
8      assertEquals("John Doe", result.getName());
9  }
```

Following successful unit testing, integration tests are employed to ensure that the microservices interact correctly with one another as well as with any databases, message brokers, or other resources. These tests are critical as they validate the communications and data flow between services which are pivotal for the operations of a microservices architecture.

```
1   // Example of an integration test between two microservices
2   public void testUserOrderCreation() {
3       User user = new User("jdoe", "John Doe");
4       Order order = new Order("001", "New Order for John Doe");
5       UserService userService = new UserServiceImpl(userRepository);
6       OrderService orderService = new OrderService(orderRepository);
7       when(userService.getUser("jdoe")).thenReturn(user);
8       when(orderService.createOrder("001", user.getId())).thenReturn(order);
9       Order result = orderService.getUserOrder("jdoe", "001");
10      assertEquals("New Order for John Doe", result.getDescription());
11  }
```

Microservices-specific challenges such as network latency, fault tolerance, and service discovery should also be addressed. These non-functional tests evaluate how the system performs under real-world conditions and are crucial for ensuring that the microservices architecture can handle expected load and stress.

- Load Testing: Simulates realistic user loads on the services to verify responsiveness and maximum load-bearing capacity.

202

- Stress Testing: Determines robustness and error handling under extreme conditions, typically beyond peak load.

- Network Failure Testing: Ensures that services can effectively handle network delays and failures.

To facilitate a comprehensive testing regime, automation plays a significant role. Automated tests improve not only speed but also contribute to the predictable and repeatable evaluation of complex microservices ecosystems. Tools and frameworks tailored for microservices, such as Docker for containerization, Jenkins for continuous integration, and Kubernetes for orchestration, are typically integrated into the testing process, offering robust capabilities to deploy, manage, and simulate various testing environments.

Example of automated test execution log output:

```
Running tests...
Test Suite: User Management Service Tests
    Test Case: User Creation - Passed
    Test Case: User Deletion - Passed
    Test Case: User Modification - Failed (Email validation error)
Completed Tests: 3, Passed: 2, Failed: 1
```

The introduction of automated monitoring tools also aids in the continuous assessment of microservices by providing real-time analytics on performance and operational status, which are invaluable for proactive troubleshooting and refining the testing strategies.

Thus, testing in a microservices environment necessitates a multi-faceted strategy involving detailed unit tests, comprehensive integration tests, and extensive testing of non-functional requirements, delivered through a combination of manual and automated processes to ensure system integrity, performance, and reliability. As microservices continue to evolve, so too must the strategies employed to test them, ensuring that these services meet the rigorous demands of modern software applications and infrastructure.

8.2 Unit Testing for Individual Microservices

Unit testing represents the first line of defense in ensuring the quality and reliability of microservices. Unlike traditional monolithic applications, microservices are characterized by their small, independent, and loosely coupled nature. This section meticulously outlines the strategies and methodologies for effectively conducting unit tests on individual microservices.

Definition of Unit Testing in Microservices Context: In microservices architectures, a unit is typically considered to be the smallest piece of the service that can be tested independently. This could be a single function, method, or even a class, depending on the service's design.

Best Practices for Writing Unit Tests:

- **Isolation:** Each test case should focus on testing only one function or method. This ensures that the tests are simple, straightforward, and easy to debug. It's crucial that dependencies such as data stores, network calls, or external services are properly mocked or stubbed to maintain isolation.

- **Repeatability:** The tests should be designed to produce the same results every time they are executed. This requires avoiding any reliance on external data or state that may change.

- **Automatability:** Unit tests should be executable in an automated environment without any manual intervention. This facilitates their integration into continuous integration pipelines.

- **Coverage:** Aim for high code coverage but prioritize testing the logic paths that are most critical to the operation of the microservice. Coverage tools can help identify untested parts of the microservice.

- **Performance:** Keep the tests fast to ensure they do not become a bottleneck during development or continuous integration.

Mocking and Stubbing:

When unit testing microservices, it is necessary to simulate the behavior of external dependencies via mocking or stubbing. This enables developers to verify the function or method logic without needing the actual services to be live or reachable. For example, if a microservice relies on a database, the database calls should be replaced with mocks that provide controlled responses pre-defined by the test.

Below is an example of a unit test in a Java-based microservice using JUnit and Mockito for mocking dependencies:

```
1  import static org.mockito.Mockito.*;
2  import static org.junit.Assert.*;
3  import org.junit.Before;
```

204

```
4   import org.junit.Test;
5   import org.mockito.Mock;
6   import org.mockito.MockitoAnnotations;
7
8   public class UserServiceTest {
9
10      @Mock
11      private Database databaseMock;
12
13      private UserService userService;
14
15      @Before
16      public void setUp() {
17          MockitoAnnotations.initMocks(this);
18          userService = new UserService(databaseMock);
19      }
20
21      @Test
22      public void testAddUserSuccess() {
23          when(databaseMock.addUser(any(User.class))).thenReturn(true);
24          boolean result = userService.addUser(new User("Alice", "alice@example.com"))
                ;
25          assertTrue("User should be added successfully", result);
26      }
27  }
```

This demonstrates the essential techniques of mocking where databaseMock simulates database interactions. UserServiceTest isolates the test to the UserService implementation, ensuring that the service behaves correctly when the database interface operates as expected.

Integration with Build Tools and CI/CD Pipelines:

To ensure that unit tests run automatically and consistently, they should be incorporated into the microservices' build tools. Most modern build tools such as Maven, Gradle, or Jenkins provide straightforward mechanisms for executing unit tests as part of the software build cycle. Here is an example of a Maven configuration snippet that includes the execution of unit tests:

```
1   <build>
2       <plugins>
3           <plugin>
4               <groupId>org.apache.maven.plugins</groupId>
5               <artifactId>maven-surefire-plugin</artifactId>
6               <version>2.22.2</version>
7               <configuration>
8                   <includes>
9                       <include>**/*Test.java</include>
10                  </includes>
11              </configuration>
12          </plugin>
13      </plugins>
14  </build>
```

205

By integrating unit tests in such a manner, they are executed automatically each time a build is triggered, thereby supporting continuous testing practices essential in DevOps approaches.

Understanding and implementing these methodologies will markedly increase the reliability of microservices by catching and addressing flaws early in the development lifecycle. This strategic approach helps manage complexity in microservices environments and provides solid groundwork for further stages in the testing lifecycle.

8.3 Integration Testing across Microservices

Integration testing is a critical phase in testing microservices architectures. It consists of validating the interactions between distinct service modules to ensure they work together as expected in a cohesive environment. In the context of microservices, integration tests verify the communication paths and interaction patterns between services which are isolated and maintained independently to each other. The primary goal is to detect interface defects and ensure correct data transmission between services.

To effectively orchestrate integration testing in microservices, one should create an integration testing environment that closely mirrors the production environment. This is essential as it encapsulates the service dependencies, network latencies, and configuration as they exist in a real-world scenario.

- Effective service stubbing and endpoint simulation are paramount. It ensures that services can interact with an initially controlled interface that mimics connected services, without the need to interface with actual live versions of those services.

- Utilize service virtualization to handle scenarios that are hard to replicate with conventional testing environments. Common examples include testing third-party integrations where significant constraints exist regarding rate limiting or data privacy.

To set up the integration tests, we use the following general approach:

Algorithm 15: Procedure to establish integration tests for microservices

---

Input: Services under test

1 **begin**
2   Identify all endpoints of each service
3   Define expected messages and formats to be sent/received
4   Construct stubs or mocking responses for each endpoint
5   Establish a testing suite that can send HTTP requests to these endpoints
6   Assert response integrity and HTTP status codes
7   Validate data persistence and rollback mechanisms
8   Analyze asynchronous services through callbacks or message queues

---

- Define clear boundaries for each microservice during testing. Each service should be able to independently resolve its respective responsibilities with minimal external impacts unless specifically designed for integration behaviors.

- Use tools for Continuous Integration (CI) to automate the deployment and testing sequences. This includes spinning up services and their dependent infrastructure, deploying integration tests, and reporting on outcomes.

To illustrate the process of verifying data integrity and communication efficacy, consider the following code snippet simulating an HTTP request to a microservice endpoint and assessing its response:

```
1   import requests
2
3   def test_service_integration():
4       # Simulated request to the payment microservice
5       response = requests.post('http://payment-service/api/pay', data={'amount': 150,
            'currency': 'USD'})
6
7       # Assert that the response status code is 200
8       assert response.status_code == 200
9
10      # Validate the response body
11      assert response.json() == {"status": "success", "transactionId": "xyz123"}
```

The corresponding API response can be mocked using service virtualization tools to facilitate such testing without reliance on the actual payment service being live during the test run:

207

```
{
    "status": "success",
    "transactionId": "xyz123"
}
```

This testing method ensures that each service correctly understands and processes incoming requests, and that data integrity is maintained throughout the process.

It is crucial to recognize that while integration testing aims to cover aspects between services, it must not replace unit tests for individual services nor end-to-end tests that simulate user interactions across the entire system.

Moreover, the adoption of a monitoring system that provides logs and metrics can also complement integration testing. Such tools help detect anomalies and performance issues that are often only observable under load, providing real-time insights that are invaluable during the integration testing phase.

Inherent in its design, integration testing for microservices is a complex endeavor, often evolving alongside changes in business requirements and service expansion. However, embedding a robust integration testing strategy early in development and maintaining its efficacy through automation and monitoring, significantly enhances the quality and reliability of microservices architectures.

8.4 Contract Testing for APIs and Services

Contract testing plays a crucial role in maintaining the reliability and stability of microservices-based applications, where services interact through complex chains of API calls. This type of testing is essential to ensure that each microservice accurately adheres to its advertised API contract. Each contract serves as an agreed-upon specification that the microservice promises to fulfill, which is critical in a distributed system where failure in one service could cascade to system-wide issues.

Definition and Importance of API Contracts: An API contract in the context of microservices is a formal specification that describes how services interact. It includes details such as request and response structures, endpoint URLs, expected error messages, and status codes. Ensuring that all services in a microservices architecture comply with their defined contracts prevents issues in service-to-service communication, which is a common source of errors in distributed systems.

Setting Up Contract Tests: The first step in contract testing is to define the expected behavior of the service interfaces. Using tools like Swagger or RAML can help automate this process by generating machine-readable API contracts that are both human-readable and executable. Once the contracts are established, they must be communicated to all teams involved, ensuring that both service providers and consumers operate with a unified understanding of the service definitions.

Benefits of Contract Testing: Contract testing isolates service dependencies by mocking out other services and focusing on the interactions as defined by the contracts. This approach offers several benefits:

- **Early detection of errors**: By testing that the API adheres to its contract, problems can be detected and corrected early in the development cycle.

- **Fast and reliable feedback**: Contract tests are generally quick to run, providing rapid feedback to developers.

- **Decreased integration issues**: Validating the interactions between services against a contract reduces the risk of defects cropping up during integration testing or production.

Tools and Frameworks for Contract Testing: To implement contract testing effectively, several tools and frameworks can be utilized:

- Pact: An open-source tool that allows testing interactions between service consumers and providers by checking HTTP requests and responses against a verified contract.

- Spring Cloud Contract: Designed for Spring applications, this tool supports the creation of executable contracts that can also be used to generate API stubs and tests.

- Postman: While primarily known for API exploration and manual testing, Postman can also be used to automate contract testing via scripting and test collections.

Implementing Contract Testing: To start with contract testing, the following steps are commonly undertaken:

1. Define the API contract using a tool that supports contract definitions and sharing.

2. Write consumer tests that use the contract to simulate calls to the service provider.

3. Implement provider tests that verify the service meets the agreed-upon contract.

4. Use a CI/CD pipeline to automate running these tests to ensure ongoing compliance.

Here is an example of setting up a basic contract test using `Pact`:

```
1   // Define consumer behavior
2   PactBuilder.createConsumer("OrderService")
3       .hasPactWith("InventoryService")
4       .uponReceiving("A request for inventory check")
5       .withMethod("GET")
6       .withPath("/inventory/check")
7       .willRespondWith()
8       .withStatus(200)
9       .withHeaders({"Content-Type": "application/json"})
10      .withBody("{\"status\": \"in-stock\"}");
11
12  // Mock provider setup
13  Provider provider = new Provider();
14  provider.given("item is in stock")
15      .expectsToReceive("A request for inventory check")
16      .with(thePactDefinedAbove())
17      .verify();
```

By ensuring all services in a microservices architecture faithfully adhere to their defined contracts through rigorous and ongoing contract testing, systems can maintain higher levels of stability and reliability. This process not only supports the technical needs of a multi-service environment but also enhances team collaboration by reinforcing clear and consistent communication around service functionalities and expectations.

8.5   End-to-End Testing Strategies

End-to-end testing for microservices involves a comprehensive validation of the entire system, simulating real-world scenarios to ensure all integrated components function collectively as expected. This type of testing validates not only the application but also its interaction with external systems, databases, and other services. Here, we outline the essential strategies, methodologies, and tools utilized to effectively undertake end-to-end testing in a microservices architecture.

The first step in end-to-end testing is to define clear and precise test cases that cover all critical user flows. These test cases should mimic real user behaviors that interact with the system at various levels. For example, consider a microservices-based e-commerce application where a typical user flow might involve searching for products, adding items to a cart, proceeding to checkout, entering payment information, and concluding with an order confirmation.

```
1   // Sample end-to-end test case (pseudocode)
2   1. Initialize the application environment.
3   2. Simulate user login.
4   3. Search for a specific product.
5   4. Add product to cart.
6   5. Proceed to checkout.
7   6. Perform payment operation.
8   7. Verify order confirmation details.
9   8. Log out.
```

For end-to-end testing to be effective, creating a staging environment that closely mirrors the production system is essential. This environment should include clones of all service dependencies, such as databases and external APIs, configured specifically for testing. It is also important that this environment supports scalable deployment of services to test load handling and failover mechanisms effectively.

End-to-end tests can be automated using tools such as Selenium, Cucumber, or Postman for API testing. Automation not only speeds up the process but also ensures consistency in test execution. However, because microservices are often developed and deployed independently, keeping test scripts synchronized with the current state of the services is a continuous challenge.

```
Example output of an automated end-to-end test:
[INFO] Test Case 1: User Login - Status: Passed
[INFO] Test Case 2: Search Product - Status: Passed
[INFO] Test Case 3: Add to Cart - Status: Passed
[INFO] Test Case 4: Checkout Process - Status: Passed
[INFO] Test Case 5: Payment Operation - Status: Failed
[ERROR] Payment gateway response timeout.
```

Handling data consistency and cleanup is another critical aspect of end-to-end testing. Since microservices often operate on different databases, ensuring that test data is consistent across these services and resetting the state for each test cycle is indispensable. Techniques like using transactional rollbacks, separate test databases, or containerized databases can help manage test data efficiently.

Additionally, end-to-end testing must include performance testing to validate the system under normal and peak load conditions. Using tools such as JMeter or LoadRunner, testers can simulate multiple users interacting with the application to understand the system's behavior under stress.

Finally, logging and monitoring play pivotal roles during end-to-end testing. They help in diagnosing failures and tracing steps that led to unexpected results. Centralized logging from all services could be gathered into a single system to facilitate comprehensive analysis.

End-to-end testing frameworks must be integrated into the continuous deployment pipeline. This means tests are run automatically whenever new versions of services are deployed in the test environment. This practice helps in identifying integration issues at early stages, thereby reducing the cost of bug fixes and speeding up the delivery process.

8.6   Mocking and Simulation Techniques for Microservices

Testing microservices effectively often requires the use of mocking and simulation techniques to isolate each service and test it in a controlled environment. Mocking refers to creating lightweight, simplified versions of external services or databases that behave like their real counterparts but are designed to return predictable and consistent results. Simulation, on the other hand, involves creating a more complex model that can mimic the behavior of external systems in a more realistic manner. Both techniques are crucial for achieving accurate and efficient tests in a microservices architecture.

Mocking Frameworks for Microservices

To facilitate mocking in microservices, several frameworks can be leveraged depending on the programming language used. For instance, in Java, Mockito and WireMock are popular choices. Mockito is primarily used for internal class-level mocking, whereas WireMock provides capabilities to mock external HTTP-based services.

```
1   // Example of using Mockito to mock a service class
2   import static org.mockito.Mockito.*;
3
4   public class InventoryServiceTest {
5       @Test
6       public void testInventoryCheck() {
7           InventoryService mockService = mock(InventoryService.class);
8           when(mockService.checkInventory("item100")).thenReturn(true);
9
```

```
10        // Conducting the test
11        assertTrue(mockService.checkInventory("item100"));
12      }
13    }
```

In the example above, Mockito is used to create a mock of InventoryService. This mock is programmed to return true when the method checkInventory is called with the argument "item100".

For mocking HTTP requests, WireMock can be an effective tool:

```
1  // Example of using WireMock for HTTP service mocking
2  import com.github.tomakehurst.wiremock.WireMockServer;
3  import static com.github.tomakehurst.wiremock.client.WireMock.*;
4
5  public class PaymentServiceTest {
6      private WireMockServer server;
7
8      @Before
9      public void setup() {
10         server = new WireMockServer(8080);
11         server.start();
12         configureFor("localhost", 8080);
13         stubFor(get(urlEqualTo("/payment-status"))
14                 .willReturn(aResponse()
15                     .withBody("Accepted")
16                     .withStatus(200)));
17     }
18
19     @After
20     public void teardown() {
21         server.stop();
22     }
23
24     @Test
25     public void testPaymentStatus() {
26         // Code to make HTTP call to /payment-status and assert response
27     }
28 }
```

In this example, WireMock starts a local server at port 8080, and configures a stub response for HTTP GET requests to /payment-status. With this setup, any HTTP client in the test can query this URL and will receive a mock response, simulating an external payment service's accepted transaction.

Simulation Environments

Simulation takes mocking a step further by creating an environment that replicates the functionalities and possible states of external systems

213

or services. With proper tools, developers and QA engineers can simulate the entire network of microservices, individual or collectively, to observe behaviors and interactions under different conditions.

Containerization technologies such as Docker and orchestration systems like Kubernetes can aid in setting up simulation environments by containerizing mock or stub services. These containers can be deployed and managed isolatedly or collectively, allowing for scalable simulations that mimic real-world scenarios more closely.

```
Simulated response from a containerized mock service:
{
    "transactionId": "12345",
    "status": "success"
}
```

Using Docker, simulation can be configured as follows:

```
1   # Dockerfile example for a simulated microservice
2   FROM python:3.8-slim
3   COPY . /app
4   WORKDIR /app
5   RUN pip install -r requirements.txt
6   CMD ["python", "simulated_service.py"]
```

The Dockerfile above prepares an image for a Python-based simulation service, which could be part of a broader simulation test to understand the impact of different request patterns or system failures.

All these tools and strategies, by isolating the units under test and controlling their interactions and environment, not only make it feasible to manage the complexity inherent in testing microservices but also provide a robust groundwork for ensuring that these complex distributed systems function as intended. Through mocking and simulation, developers can predict service behavior in a production-like environment, thus significantly enhancing the service's reliability and performance.

8.7   Testing for Database Interactions and Data Integrity

Testing database interactions and ensuring data integrity are crucial aspects of validating microservices, especially given their often complex and dynamic data requirements. Effective testing strategies here not only confirm the correctness of the data but also its robustness across distributed systems.

The first step in database testing within a microservices architecture is to understand the specific responsibilities of each service concerning data management. Services in a microservice architecture typically manage their database, isolated from others, leading to challenges in ensuring data consistency and integrity across services.

Isolated Unit Testing of Database Layers: Begin with unit tests that verify the functionalities of the database layers within each microservice. These tests involve interactions with the database, validating SQL queries, schema validations, and operations such as insert, update, delete, and retrieval.

```
1  // Example of a unit test for a database retrieval function
2  const db = require('service-db');
3  test('retrieveData returns correct data from database', async () => {
4    const expected = { id: 1, name: 'Test Data' };
5    db.query.mockResolvedValueOnce(expected);
6    const result = await db.retrieveData(1);
7    expect(result).toEqual(expected);
8  });
```

Integration Testing: Once unit testing is adequately covered, integration tests should be conducted. These tests will check data flow across different services and the entire system's responses to database state changes. This involves deploying all microservices that share interfaces with the database and testing typical workflows to monitor data integrity and error handling capabilities.

Contract Testing for Database Schemas: Contract testing can be implemented to ensure that the database schema adheres to agreed-upon formats expected by various services. This is crucial for maintaining data consistency across services that are being developed by different teams, often in larger organizations.

```
1  // Example of a schema contract test
2  const schema = require('microservice-schema');
3  describe('Database schema contract test', () => {
4    it('validates user data schema', () => {
5      const userData = { id: 123, name: 'John Doe', email: 'john.doe@example.com' };
6      expect(schema.validate(userData)).toBe(true);
7    });
8  });
```

Testing Data Integrity: Data integrity tests ensure that across various operations—amidst possible failures—data remains accurate and reliable. This involves testing scenarios such as network failures, concurrent database accesses, and rollbacks after transaction failures.

```
Output example after a simulated network failure:
Transaction Error: Network failure detected. Rolling back transaction.
```

215

Performance Testing of Database Operations: Performance tests should be applied to measure the throughput and latency of database operations, especially under load. This testing ensures that database interactions do not become bottlenecks, particularly when services scale out during peak loads.

```
1  // Performance test snippet using JMeter or similar tool
2  public class DatabaseLoadTest {
3    @Test
4    public void testDatabaseUnderLoad() {
5      int numberOfThreads = 50;
6      runLoadTest(numberOfThreads);
7      assertTrue(responseTimesUnderThreshold());
8    }
9  }
```

Each of these testing techniques plays an integral role in overall service reliability and functionality. By assuring comprehensive coverage of scenarios through a combination of isolated, integration, and performance tests, teams can deliver microservices capable of robust and scalable database interactions. This ensures that users experience consistent, reliable, and efficient services regardless of the underlying interactions and complexities of distributed database management.

8.8 Performance and Load Testing for Microservices

Performance and load testing are critical components in evaluating the robustness and efficiency of microservices. These testing regimes simulate user activity and traffic to measure system responses and behavior under various conditions. The objective is to identify performance bottlenecks, ensure the system meets required service level agreements (SLAs), and validate the system's capacity planning assumptions. This section delineates methodologies and tools specifically designed for performance and load testing in microservices architectures.

Defining Performance Metrics

Critical performance metrics for microservices include:

- Response Time: The time taken for a microservice to return a response to a request.

216

- `Throughput`: The number of requests a system can handle per unit of time.

- `Resource Utilization`: The amount of system resources (CPU, memory, disk I/O, network I/O) used when a microservice is under load.

- `Error Rate`: Percentage of requests that result in errors during the test.

These metrics provide indicators of a microservice's performance and help in identifying areas that require optimization.

Selecting the Right Tools

Numerous off-the-shelf tools are available for performance testing of microservices. Popular choices include:

- `JMeter` – An open-source tool capable of load and performance testing for analyzing and measuring the performance of a variety of services.

- `Gatling` – Another open-source tool, which is widely used due to its high-performance capabilities and detailed performance metrics graphical representation.

- `Locust` – A user-friendly, scalable tool written in Python that allows writing test scenarios in simple Python code.

These tools enable testers to craft customized testing scenarios that replicate vast and varied real-life loads on microservices, thereby providing an insight into how the services would perform in production environments.

Techniques for Effective Load Testing

Efficient performance and load testing of microservices require strategic planning. Below outlined are some of the prolific techniques:

- *Baseline Testing:* Start by establishing a performance baseline for individual microservices, which serves as a reference to measure against as changes are made to the application.

- *Stress Testing:* This involves testing beyond normal operational capacity, often to a breaking point, to determine the microservices' robustness.

- *Soak Testing:* Running a system under significant load for a prolonged period to identify performance issues that might develop over time such as memory leaks and degradation.

- *Spike Testing:* Quickly ramping up the users or load generated to test how the system handles large variations in load.

It is essential to integrate these testing techniques within the Continuous Integration/Continuous Deployment (CI/CD) pipelines to ensure performance benchmarks are consistently met.

Simulating Real-World Scenarios

Real-world user behavior poses unpredictable patterns and peak load situations. To recreate these, scripts can be used that simulate typical user interactions with the microservices. Data from production environments can also be used to model these scenarios accurately. Additionally, using container orchestration platforms like Kubernetes allows for dynamically scaling the microservice under test to see how the scaling affects performance.

Analyzing the Results

The outputs from the testing tools typically include a multitude of data points. Efficient analysis involves:

- Identifying trends from the data – for example, at what load levels do the response times and error rates start to spike?

- Comparing the results with the performance objectives defined in the microservice specifications.

- Utilizing automated tools to derive actionable insights from the data to guide performance optimization efforts.

Visualization tools can also be instrumental in representing data through graphs and charts that depict performance metrics effectively,

218

providing a clear visual understanding of any potential bottlenecks or performance issues.

This section has comprehensively covered techniques and strategic insights for conducting effective performance and load testing in a microservices architecture. Carrying out such tests will lead to the identification of potential bottlenecks and provide an assurance that the microservices will perform as expected under varying conditions, thereby ensuring a robust architecture ready to handle real-world demands efficiently.

8.9 Security Testing in Microservices Architectures

Security testing in microservices architectures is critical in identifying and mitigating vulnerabilities that could lead to security breaches. Given the distributed nature of microservices, where different services may be developed and maintained by separate teams, consistency in security practices is challenging yet essential.

The first aspect of security testing involves identifying the specific requirements and potential threats for each microservice. It is recommended to adopt a threat modeling approach, which systematically reviews what could go wrong in terms of security threats. Consider common security pitfalls such as unauthorized data access, data leaks, or denial of service attacks.

- Authentication and Authorization checks: Ensure that all endpoints are protected with the correct authentication mechanisms and that authorization is appropriately enforced at each service level.

- Secure Communication: Verify that communication channels between services utilize TLS to encrypt data in transit. Opportunistically employ Mutual TLS (mTLS) where possible to enhance security.

- Input Validation: Regularly test all input points to the microservices (e.g., APIs, service endpoints) to ensure they appropriately reject malformed or malicious content.

219

In regards to the actual process of testing, the following methodologies can be employed:

Static Application Security Testing (SAST) tools can be used to scan the source code of the microservices for known vulnerability patterns. These tools are capable of identifying issues such as SQL injections, XSS vulnerabilities, and insecure API usage before the application is run.

Dynamic Application Security Testing (DAST) tools are employed post-deployment to attack the microservices using real-world attack vectors to identify runtime vulnerabilities. This can often surface security issues that are not visible through static analysis alone.

```
Typical outputs from DAST tools might report:
- Endpoints susceptible to SQL injection.
- Services that disclose sensitive information in error messages.
- Endpoints vulnerable to XSS attacks.
```

Another tactical measure in security testing is the use of Penetration Testing, where skilled security professionals simulate attacks to identify hard-to-detect vulnerabilities. Such tests may cover areas such as:

```
1    - Testing of authentication mechanisms.
2    - Simulating DoS attacks on service endpoints.
3    - Checking for encryption schema weaknesses.
```

Furthermore, the adoption of Security as Code practices where security configurations (like firewall rules, security groups) are treated and managed as code, can also benefit the security testing by automatically applying and verifying security policies across all environments consistently.

To handle potential vulnerabilities effectively, immediate and automated feedback to the development teams is crucial. Continuous Integration (CI) pipelines should be configured to include security tests as part of the regular build process. This could be set up to ensure that builds are only promoted once they pass all the security checks.

Lastly, security tests should be updated regularly to adapt to new security threats. Regular audits and updates to the test suite are necessary to cover recent vulnerabilities and newly discovered security flaws.

These tests provide confidence in the security posture of your microservices architecture but should be viewed as part of a broader security strategy, which includes regular reviews and updates to security practices and protocols. As microservices continue to evolve with new features and updates, so too should the approach to their security, ensuring a resilient and robust system against evolving threats.

8.10 Testing for Fault Tolerance and Resilience

Testing for fault tolerance and resilience in microservices involves verifying the system's capacity to continue operating in the face of faults or failures within its components. This type of testing is critical as it ensures that the system can encounter failures gracefully and continue to provide service, albeit possibly at a reduced capacity, without complete system failure.

Defining Fault Tolerance and Resilience in Microservices

Fault tolerance pertains to the ability of a system to continue functioning in the event of a failure of some of its components. Resilience refers to the system's ability to recover quickly and return to its full operational status after the failure has been resolved. For microservices architectures, these characteristics are crucial due to the distributed nature of the systems and their dynamic scaling capacities.

Techniques for Testing Fault Tolerance

Testing microservices for fault tolerance involves introducing faults into the system and observing how it reacts. This can be done through a variety of methods:

- **Chaos Engineering:** This involves intentionally injecting failures into the system to test how the rest of the system compensates for the failure. This can include killing processes, simulating network latencies, and creating resource bottlenecks.

- **Failover Testing:** This test verifies that the system automatically redirects the failed service's tasks to a backup or standby service without human intervention.

- **Disaster Recovery Testing:** This simulates a severe incident that affects not just discrete components, but entire regions or data centers. The aim is to test the system's recovery protocols and backup systems.

221

Implementing Resilience Testing

Resilience testing evaluates the system's ability to recover from crashes, failures, or errors. Key aspects include:

- **Recovery Time Objective (RTO):** Measure how quickly the system can recover to its normal functioning after a disruption.

- **Recovery Point Objective (RPO):** Measure the maximum acceptable amount of data loss measured in time.

These metrics are crucial for understanding the impact of a downtime or failure on the business operations and are typically defined during the Service Level Agreement (SLA) formulation.

Practical Implementation of Fault Tolerance and Resilience Testing

One practical approach to implementing fault tolerance and resilience testing is through the use of tools and frameworks designed for chaos engineering. Tools such as Chaos Monkey by Netflix are designed to randomly disable instances in production to ensure that the system can sustain any level of failure.

```
1   // Example of a basic chaos tool configuration
2   {
3       "service": "microservice-a",
4       "type": "shutdown",
5       "instanceCount": 2,
6       "region": "us-west-2"
7   }
```

The configuration above instructs the tool to randomly shut down two instances of "microservice-a" in the "us-west-2" region. It is essential to observe how the remaining instances of the microservice and its related services respond to this disruption.

The outcome of this test should be meticulously recorded to identify response times, the behavior of dependent services, error handling, and system recovery processes.

Best Practices for Continuous Resilience Testing

For microservices, the following practices are recommended to ensure ongoing resilience and fault tolerance:

222

- **Regularly Schedule Chaos Experiments:** As the system evolves, it's important to continuously test and update your understanding of its resilience.

- **Automate Response Mechanisms:** Implement automated recovery processes such as restarting failed instances or rerouting traffic.

- **Monitor and Alert:** Effective monitoring and alerting systems are crucial to detect and respond to failures as quickly as possible.

By incorporating these testing strategies, organizations can mitigate the risks associated with failures and ensure that their microservices architectures are both resilient and fault-tolerant. The integration of such tests into the development lifecycle not only reduces the potential impact of failures but also enhances the stability and reliability of the entire system. This systematic approach to testing will align closely with the dynamic and evolving nature of microservices, thus providing a robust foundation for building scalable and dependable systems.

8.11 Continuous Integration and Continuous Testing in DevOps

To attain a high efficacy in microservices architectures, the integration of continuous integration (CI) and continuous testing (CT) within the DevOps pipeline is crucial. These practices are pivotal in ensuring a robust, efficient, and dynamic development environment, providing quick feedback loops and early defect detection. Employing CI and CT optimally requires the orchestration of various tools and platforms' integration, test automation strategies, and monitoring techniques.

Integration of Tools in CI/CT Pipelines   The success of CI in a microservices setup heavily relies on the seamless integration of development tools with CI servers. Tools such as Jenkins, GitLab CI, and CircleCI are commonly employed to automate the merging and testing of code. These tools monitor the main repository and execute predefined test suites upon any new code commits or during scheduled maintenance windows.

For instance, configuring a Jenkins pipeline involves setting up project-specific parameters including build triggers, environment configurations, and test scripts. This setup can be represented as follows:

```
 1  pipeline {
 2      agent any
 3      stages {
 4          stage('Build') {
 5              steps {
 6                  sh 'make'
 7              }
 8          }
 9          stage('Test') {
10              steps {
11                  sh 'make test'
12              }
13          }
14      }
15  }
```

This script configures Jenkins to execute a build and test stage whenever changes are pushed to the repository. Each stage is clearly defined, ensuring that changes are not only built but also subjected to rigorous tests, which are crucial for early detection of potential release blockers.

Automated Testing Strategy Continuous Testing as part of CI/CD pipeline requires a well-thought-through strategy aligning with microservices' decoupled nature. To this end, automated testing should include a range of test types such as unit tests, service integration tests, and end-to-end tests.

- Unit tests are used to validate the functionality of individual units of code in isolation. In microservices, each service can be considered as a unit, and its business logic must be tested without external dependencies.

- Integration tests validate the interaction between services and are crucial for uncovering issues in the network calls, data format, and shared databases/events.

- End-to-end tests simulate user behavior across the entire system to validate the complete path of data through multiple services.

For a microservice handling user data processing, the testing scripts might appear as follows:

```
1  import requests
2  def test_user_creation():
```

```
3    response = requests.post("http://user-service/create", json={"name": "John Doe"
        })
4    assert response.status_code == 200
```

The above Python test verifies the user creation functionality of a microservice by making an HTTP POST request and asserting the response status code.

Monitoring and Feedback Loops   Effective continuous testing is not complete without appropriate monitoring and feedback mechanisms in place. These tools help in identifying problems early, facilitating quick corrective actions, and sustaining high availability and reliability.

Tools such as Prometheus and Grafana are widely adopted for monitoring microservices. They provide real-time metrics visualization and alerting for conditions that might affect the performance or reliability of services.

```
1    # Example Prometheus monitoring configuration
2    global
3      scrape_interval 15s
4      external_labels
5        monitor 'microservice-monitor'
6    \end{
```

By integrating such monitoring configurations, teams can visualize throughput, latency, error rates, and resource usage metrics, which are essential for understanding the health of microservices.

The constant feedback from monitoring tools should inform ongoing development and testing phases, ensuring that each iteration of the software is better tuned for its operational environment, thus effectively harnessing the power of continuous testing and integration within a DevOps framework. By incorporating these methodologies strategically, development teams can significantly enhance deployment frequency and predictability, improve defect detection rates, and reduce the time to market for new features and updates.

8.12 Monitoring and Logging to Inform Testing

Effective testing of microservices is not only about executing test cases but also about capturing and analyzing detailed logs and monitor metrics that can provide insight into the system's behavior under various conditions. Monitoring and logging serve as critical components in understanding the dynamic interactions and states within the microservices architecture. Properly implemented, they yield valuable data that can guide the improvement and reliability of test strategies.

Importance of Logging

A meticulously designed logging strategy ensures that logs contain relevant information, which assists developers and quality assurance teams in identifying issues that might not manifest clearly through outward system behavior alone. When implementing logging within microservices, it is crucial to standardize the format of log files across services and to include identifiers that correlate logs from various sources.

Logs should capture both normal and abnormal behaviors, including:

- Time-stamped entries of internal state changes and access logs,

- Errors and exception handling,

- Requests and responses, including their source and destination, and

- System events relevant to business transactions.

Consider using structured logging formats like JSON, which facilitate automated analysis tools to filter, sort, and aggregate logs without requiring complex parsing logic. Below is an example configuration snippet for a microservice written in Python using the logging library:

```
1  import logging
2  import json_log_formatter
3
4  formatter = json_log_formatter.JSONFormatter()
5
6  file_handler = logging.FileHandler('micorservice.log')
7  file_handler.setFormatter(formatter)
8
```

```
9   logger = logging.Logger('microserviceLogger')
10  logger.addHandler(file_handler)
11
12  logger.info('Service has started')
```

Monitoring Techniques

Monitoring, on the other hand, involves collecting data about the operational aspects of microservices. This includes metrics like throughput, latency, error rates, and system resource utilization. Real-time monitoring tools such as Prometheus or Grafana provide visual representations of these metrics, which help in quick identification of outliers or anomalies.

The architecture for monitoring should include:

- Time series databases for storing metrics,

- Alerting mechanisms for automated notification of potential issues, and

- Health check endpoints for continuous service status verification.

Consider the following data collection from a node in a microservice environment using Prometheus:

```
1   # Configuration to scrape metrics from microservices
2   scrape_configs:
3     - job_name: 'microservice'
4       static_configs:
5         - targets: ['localhost:9090']
```

Combining Monitoring and Logging for Comprehensive Testing

The integration of logs and monitoring data makes it possible to trace issues not just to specific services but to particular transactions or even code paths. Advanced monitoring systems are capable of capturing traces, which provide a sequential breakdown of service interactions. This is particularly useful when analyzing the propagation of a fault across service boundaries.

For example, consider a scenario where a spike in latency is detected in a critical microservice. The corresponding logs can be scrutinized to

227

identify the operations that were executed around the time of the spike, possibly revealing an inefficient database query or an external API call delay.

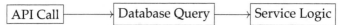

In an effective DevOps environment, this integrated information provides a feedback loop to developers, allowing continuous refinement and verification of both the software itself and its surrounding testing practices. This approach not only localizes problems faster but also helps in assessing the impact of issues in terms of real user experience, thereby aligning testing efforts more closely with user requirements and system expectations.

Chapter 9

Monitoring and Maintenance in a Cloud-Native Environment

Monitoring and maintenance are pivotal for sustaining the efficiency and reliability of applications in cloud-native environments. This chapter covers the strategies and tools necessary for effective monitoring, which enable real-time visibility into operations and help preempt issues before they escalate. It also delves into maintenance practices that ensure applications remain up-to-date, secure, and performing optimally, taking advantage of the dynamic and scalable nature of cloud-native infrastructure.

9.1 Essentials of Monitoring in a Cloud-Native Environment

Effective monitoring within a cloud-native environment is crucial for the assessment of both the operational health and the performance-related aspects of such systems. Cloud-native applications often consist of a complex mix of services and components, deployed over dynamic and scalable infrastructure. This requires a monitoring approach that can cope with rapid changes in the environment and provide continuous insights.

The first step in setting up an adequate monitoring system in cloud-native architectures is the identification of key application and infrastructure metrics. Performance metrics such as latency, error rates, and throughput need to be recorded alongside infrastructure utilization stats, including CPU usage, memory consumption, and disk I/O. These metrics provide a primary dataset to understand the system behaviors under normal and peak conditions.

- Latency measures the time taken to process a request within the system.

- Error rate refers to the percentage of all requests that result in an error.

- Throughput is the number of requests that can be handled by the system within a certain time period.

To facilitate real-time monitoring, it is essential to leverage specialized monitoring tools and software that are capable of handling the high volume and velocity of data generated by cloud-native systems. Tools such as Prometheus, Grafana, and Elastic Stack are frequently used for this purpose. These tools support the extraction, visualization, and analysis of metrics across the distributed components, ensuring that the teams have visibility into every aspect of the environment.

```
1   # Example configuration snippet for Prometheus monitoring
2   global:
3     scrape_interval: 15s # Set the scrape interval to every 15 seconds.
4     external_labels:
5       monitor: 'cloud-native-app'
6
7   scrape_configs:
8     - job_name: 'kubernetes-pods'
9       kubernetes_sd_configs:
10        - role: pod
```

230

```
# Example Prometheus query output
up{job="kubernetes-pods"}    1
```

Continual monitoring necessitates not only collecting metrics but also setting up thresholds and alerts to ensure that anomalies and potential issues are detected early. This is usually accomplished through the configuration of alerting rules within the monitoring tools.

```
1   # Example alerting rule in Prometheus
2   groups:
3   - name: example-rules
4     rules:
5     - alert: HighErrorRate
6       expr: rate(http_requests_total{status="500"}[5m]) > 1
7       for: 10m
8       labels:
9         severity: critical
10      annotations:
11        summary: High request error rate
```

Another aspect of cloud-native monitoring involves tracing and log aggregation. Distributed tracing provides insights into the flow of requests through the various components and services, helping to pinpoint causes of delays or failures in complex transactions. Tools like Jaeger and Zipkin are popular choices for this.

Client $\longrightarrow$ Service 1 $\rightarrow$ Service 2 $\rightarrow$ Database

Logs, on the other hand, provide detailed textual records of events within the system. The aggregation of logs in a central location, often achieved using solutions like Fluentd, Logstash or AWS CloudWatch, enables the in-depth analysis and correlation of events across services. This is invaluable for diagnostic purposes and post-mortem analyses. Setting up efficient logging practices is further discussed in the subsequent sections of this chapter.

These primary elements — metric collection, tracing, and robust logging — constitute the core framework needed for effective monitoring in a cloud-native environment. Employing this diversified approach is essential for gaining the comprehensive visibility required to manage these modern, dynamic systems. As these environments continue to grow in complexity, the tools and practices around monitoring must also evolve to support the demands of cloud-native operations.

9.2 Key Metrics and Indicators to Monitor

Effective cloud-native monitoring relies heavily on identifying and tracking the appropriate metrics and indicators that reflect the health, performance, and availability of both applications and the underlying infrastructure. Focusing on the right metrics is crucial for gaining actionable insights and efficiently tackling potential issues. This section details the essential metrics for monitoring cloud-native applications and systems, outlining their relevance and mechanisms for collection.

Application Performance Metrics

Application performance metrics are vital for ensuring applications meet expected service level agreements (SLAs) and provide a good user experience.

- **Response Time**: The time it takes for a system to respond to a request. It is crucial for assessing user satisfaction and the responsiveness of the application.

- **Error Rates**: The frequency of failed requests compared to total requests. Monitoring error rates helps in identifying the stability and reliability of applications.

- **Throughput**: The number of requests an application can handle within a certain timeframe. This metric is useful for planning capacity and scaling resources effectively.

- **System Utilization**: This includes CPU usage, memory consumption, and disk I/O operations, which are indicative of the resource needs and efficiency of the application.

System Availability Metrics

Ensuring high availability is a core objective in cloud-native environments. The following metrics help monitor this aspect:

- **Uptime/Downtime**: Tracks the time the application or service is available/unavailable. This metric is crucial for availability calculations and SLA compliance.

- **Health Checks**: Regular checks on services and databases to ensure they are operational. These metrics are essential for proactive maintenance and immediate fault detection.

Network Performance Metrics

Network performance is integral to service delivery, especially in distributed systems. Key network metrics to monitor include:

- **Latency**: The delay before a transfer of data begins following an instruction for its transfer. High latency can significantly impact user experience and application performance.

- **Traffic Volume**: Measures the amount of data moving across the network. This metric helps in understanding demand and potential bottlenecks.

- **Packet Loss**: Represents the packets of data that never reach their destination. High packet loss can indicate network issues that could degrade application performance.

Business-Specific Metrics

Apart from technical metrics, it is imperative to monitor business-specific metrics that directly affect business outcomes and objectives.

- **User Engagement**: Includes active sessions, session duration, and user actions per session. These metrics provide insights into user behavior and application effectiveness.

- **Conversion Rates**: The percentage of users who complete a desired action, such as making a purchase or registering. This metric is essential for measuring business success.

Security Metrics

In cloud-native environments, security is paramount. Relevant security metrics include:

- **Number of Security Incidents**: Tracks the frequency of detected security incidents which could potentially threaten system integrity.

233

- **Patch Status Metrics**: Ensures that all components of the system are up-to-date with the latest security patches.

```
Sample Security Incident Alert:
    Alert Type: Unauthorized Access Attempt
    Severity: High
    Detected At: 03:45 UTC
    Location: EU-West Server Cluster
    Action Required: Immediate Investigation
```

Monitoring these metrics involves a combination of automated tools and manual oversight to ensure that all aspects of system performance and health are within acceptable boundaries. Tools implemented should have capabilities to customize metric thresholds and alerts based on the specific needs and priorities of the business. This targeted approach helps in quickly identifying and mitigating issues before they escalate, thus maintaining system reliability and performance.

9.3 Implementing Effective Logging Practices

Effective logging practices in a cloud-native environment are crucial for providing insights into application behavior, aiding in debugging, and ensuring compliance with governance policies. Understanding what to log, how to manage log data, and how to analyze this information is essential for maintaining the health and performance of cloud-native applications.

What to Log: Deciding the scope of logging is the first and most critical step. It is important to capture not only errors and exceptions but also significant state changes and business events. Here is a clear guideline on critical loggable events:

- **Errors and Exceptions:** All exceptions and software errors should be logged with their stack traces to aid in diagnosing problems.

- **System State Changes:** Modifications in the system's state that may affect its operations should be recorded.

- **User Actions:** Activities performed by users, especially those that alter data or system configurations.

- **Transaction Events:** Start and end of transactions, especially in services where multiple components interact, should be logged to trace the flow of data.

- **Performance Metrics:** Response times and other performance-related metrics should be captured at regular intervals to monitor trends and detect anomalies.

How to Manage Log Data: Proper management of log data is essential to ensure its usefulness. The management involves structured logging, centralized logging, and log rotation.

Structured Logging: Structured logging is the practice of writing logs in a structured format, usually as key-value pairs or encoded in JSON. This format makes logs easier to analyze and query. Here is an example of structured logging in Python using the standard logging library:

```
1   import logging
2   import json
3
4   logging.basicConfig(level=logging.INFO)
5   logger = logging.getLogger(__name__)
6
7   def log_event(action, description):
8       log_entry = {'action': action, 'description': description}
9       logger.info(json.dumps(log_entry))
10
11  log_event('login_attempt', 'User logged in successfully.')
```

The output generated by this logging method is structured and easily parsed by log management tools:

```
{"action": "login_attempt", "description": "User logged in successfully."}
```

Centralized Logging: In cloud-native architectures, applications are often distributed across multiple services and nodes. Centralized logging provides a single point where all logs are aggregated, making monitoring and analysis more effective. Technologies such as Elasticsearch, Logstash, and Kibana (ELK stack) or Fluentd provide robust solutions for implementing centralized logging. Centralized logging ensures that logs from all services and components are collected in a consistent format in a central location.

Log Rotation: Log files can grow rapidly, especially in a high-volume transaction environment. Implementing log rotation is critical to manage disk space and maintain log file performance. Log rotation involves creating new log files periodically and archiving the old ones. Most operating systems and log management solutions support log rotation out-of-the-box.

Analyzing Log Data: Once logs are collected and well-managed, the analysis phase can begin. Real-time log analysis tools can detect anomalies, generate alerts, and provide dashboards for a visual overview of the system's health and activity. This real-time analysis enables teams to react quickly to potential issues before they affect users.

For effective real-time analysis, you can implement tools like Splunk or use the ELK Stack's capabilities to monitor logs and trigger alerts based on predefined rules concerning error rates, performance benchmarks, or unexpected behavior.

Utilizing advanced machine learning algorithms can further enhance capability by predicting potential system failures or detecting unusual patterns that could indicate security breaches.

Employing these effective logging practices helps in transforming raw data into actionable insights, facilitating proactive management and rapid response to events within a cloud-native environment. Moreover, integrating monitoring tools within Continuous Integration/Continuous Deployment (CI/CD) pipelines ensures ongoing scrutiny and immediate feedback on system performance throughout the development lifecycle.

9.4   Using APM Tools for Performance Monitoring

Application Performance Management (APM) tools are integral to monitoring and enhancing the performance of applications in a cloud-native environment. These tools provide detailed insights into the runtime behavior of applications, enabling developers and operational teams to detect, diagnose, and resolve performance bottlenecks effectively. APM tools accomplish this by collecting, aggregating, and analyzing data to provide real-time performance metrics and transaction details.

The core functionalities of APM tools include user experience monitoring, application topology discovery, transaction profiling, and performance bottleneck analysis. User experience monitoring allows teams to see application responsiveness and behavior from the user's perspective. Application topology discovery helps in visualizing the complex interactions between various components and services within the cloud architecture. Transaction profiling traces individual user requests as they flow through various application components, identifying slow or failed transactions. Lastly, performance bottleneck analysis identifies specific code blocks or database queries causing delays.

To integrate an APM tool into a cloud-native system, one must follow several strategic steps. First, identify the key performance indicators (KPIs) that are crucial for the cloud applications' operating environment. Common KPIs include response time, error rate, system throughput, and database transaction time.

Next, select an APM tool that aligns with the organization's technological stack and monitoring objectives. Some popular APM tools include Datadog, New Relic, and Dynatrace. These tools support a wide range of programming languages and frameworks, making them versatile options for diverse cloud-native applications.

```
1   # Sample integration code for inserting APM tool monitoring within an application
2   import apm_module
3
4   # Initialize APM monitoring
5   apm_module.initialize(APM_CONFIG)
6
7   # Function to monitor
8   def process_transaction(transaction):
9       transaction.start_monitoring()
10      # Transaction processing logic
11      transaction.end_monitoring()
```

Once the APM tool is selected, it needs to be seamlessly integrated into the application's deployment pipeline. This integration often involves adding APM agents or SDKs into the application's codebase, as shown above, which collect and send performance data to the APM servers.

```
Transaction Started
Transaction Executed in: 200ms
APM Data Collected
```

Following the integration, it is essential to configure the APM tool according to specific monitoring needs. This involves setting thresholds for alarms, defining alerts, and configuring data capture levels to balance detail with performance overhead.

- Configure alert thresholds for response times and error rates.

- Set up customized dashboards to visualize application performance in real-time.

- Define automated reactions, such as scaling up instances when throughput increases.

APM tools also offer capabilities for anomaly detection and root cause analysis, leveraging machine learning algorithms to predict potential issues before they affect users. By continually monitoring application health and trends over time, these tools help in proactively managing the application performance, ensuring optimal user experiences.

Integration of APM into CI/CD pipelines ensures that monitoring is an integral part of the development process, not just an afterthought. By automating performance tests and incorporating APM metrics as part of the software release process, teams can ensure that no degradation occurs as new versions are deployed.

Performance monitoring with APM tools in cloud-native environments is not merely about detecting problems after they happen but preventing them in the first place. By strategically deploying APM tools and leveraging their extensive capabilities, organizations can capitalize on the dynamic and scalable nature of cloud computing to maintain robust, high-performing applications that meet user expectations consistently.

9.5 Infrastructure Monitoring and Management

Infrastructure Monitoring and Management in a cloud-native environment is a complex but crucial aspect that involves observing and controlling the infrastructure components such as servers, databases, and networks to ensure they perform optimally. The dynamic nature of cloud-native environments, where services are often scaled up and down automatically, necessitates robust monitoring and active management strategies to prevent downtimes and performance lags. This involves several components and strategies, which will be dissected in this section.

Firstly, the scope of infrastructure monitoring must encompass both hardware and virtual resources. Monitoring these resources involves collecting data about their performance, availability, and health status. This is typically achieved through the use of monitoring tools that can provide real-time analytics. Tools such as Prometheus, Grafana, and Zabbix are popular choices in the industry due to their flexibility and comprehensive monitoring capabilities. For example, Prometheus can be configured to scrape various metrics from multiple sources, and Grafana can be used to visualize these metrics. Here is a typical configuration snippet using Prometheus:

```
1   # A minimal Prometheus configuration example
2   global:
3     scrape_interval: 15s # Set the scrape interval to every 15 seconds
4
5   scrape_configs:
6     - job_name: 'prometheus' # Defining a job named 'prometheus'
7       static_configs:
8         - targets: ['localhost:9090'] # Specifying target to scrape
```

Once the data is collected, it must be efficiently managed and analyzed to be useful. Logging this data allows historical performance metrics to be reviewed for insights and patterns. This step is crucial for the proactive mitigation of potential issues. Furthermore, using machine learning techniques with time-series data can automate the recognition of anomalous patterns which deviate from the baseline. Such capabilities enable predictive maintenance by identifying potential failures before they occur.

Managing this infrastructure goes beyond passive monitoring. It involves actively ensuring that configuration changes, updates, and patches are carried out promptly and consistently across the entire ecosystem. Configuration management tools such as Ansible, Puppet, or Chef automate the process of rolling out changes, enhancing both efficiency and reliability. Here is an example where Ansible is utilized to ensure that a package is installed and a service is running:

```
1    # Example Ansible playbook to ensure nginx is installed and running
2    - hosts: all
3      tasks:
4        - name: Ensure nginx is at the latest version
5          apt:
6            name: nginx
7            state: latest
8          become: true
9
10       - name: Start nginx service
11         service:
12           name: nginx
13           state: started
14           enabled: yes
15         become: true
```

Moreover, to optimize the response to infrastructure incidents, automated health checks and alerts must be implemented. These facilitate real-time response and resolution through automated scaling, resource allocation, or restarting failed services without human intervention. These automated processes are critical in maintaining the reliability

239

and availability of cloud-native applications, especially in high-traffic scenarios.

Lastly, monitoring network traffic and ensuring security compliance are also integral components of infrastructure management. Effective traffic monitoring can identify patterns that may indicate a security breach or a bottleneck impacting application performance. Coupling this with strong security practices such as regular audits and adherence to compliance frameworks ensures the integrity and availability of the cloud-native ecosystem.

Through the integration of these monitoring and management strategies, a cloud-native infrastructure can not only sustain but also enhance its performance and reliability, thereby supporting the overarching objectives of the organization's IT strategy. The sophistication deployed in monitoring and the proactive steps taken in management together forge a robust framework that underpins the operational excellence of cloud-native applications.

9.6 Configuration Management in Cloud-Native Systems

Configuration management in cloud-native systems is a crucial aspect that ensures all software running across multiple deployment environments behaves as expected. It involves the maintenance and coordination of underlying infrastructure, software services, and application configurations, thereby aligning them consistently across all environments from development through to production.

Cloud-native configuration management incorporates dynamically controlling system configurations to maintain the availability, performance, and security required in a continuously evolving cloud environment. It leverages tools and practices that enable configurations to be versioned and treated as code which can be automated, replicated, and rolled back if necessary. This practice, often referred to as "Infrastructure as Code (IaC)," is essential for supporting the scalability and automation that cloud-native architectures demand.

Tools for Configuration Management: Several tools exist for managing configurations in a cloud-native setup:

240

- *Ansible* provides a simple and declarative language named YAML for infrastructure automation.

- *Terraform*, by HashiCorp, enables the provisioning of infrastructure using a declarative configuration language.

- *Chef* and *Puppet* offer mature solutions with a focus on providing powerful automation capabilities across complex infrastructures.

- *Kubernetes ConfigMaps* and *Secrets* manage containerized application configuration data and sensitive information separately from the container image, enhancing both application portability and security.

Versioning of Configuration Files: The use of version control systems (VCS) in cloud-native configuration management ensures that changes are trackable, auditable, and reversible. This involves storing all environment and application configurations as code in repositories. Below is an example of storing an application configuration using Git:

```
1   # Clone the configuration repository
2   git clone https://github.com/exampleOrg/config-repo.git
3
4   # Change into the repository directory
5   cd config-repo
6
7   # Make changes to configuration
8   nano application.yml
9
10  # Commit and push the changes
11  git add .
12  git commit -m "Update application configuration"
13  git push origin master
```

Through version control, teams can manage the environment-specific configurations for development, testing, staging, and production separately while keeping the integrity and consistency of configurations across these environments.

Automation Through Continuous Integration/Continuous Deployment (CI/CD): Integrating configuration management into CI/CD pipelines is essential for automating the deployment process. This integration allows updates in configuration to trigger rebuilds, tests, and deployment suits automatically, reducing manual work and human errors.

Below is a pseudo code representation incorporating configuration updates into a CI/CD workflow:

241

---

output : automated deployment on configuration change
input : configuration file update

```
1  triggerBuildAndTest:
2     checkForConfigurationChanges()
3     if changes detected then
4        runTests()
5        if tests pass then
6           deployToStaging()
7           runIntegrationTests()
8           if integration tests pass then
9              deployToProduction()
10          end
11       end
12    end
```

Such automation exemplifies how cloud-native systems utilize advancements in technology and process orchestration to maintain a rapid and reliable delivery cycle.

Furthermore, automating configuration changes can not only aid in upholding system functionality but also serve in adherence to compliance and security standards by ensuring that only verified and approved changes are propagated across the operational environments.

Ultimately, integrating comprehensive configuration management practices into cloud-native systems enhances operational resilience, expedites product iterations, and maintains a stringent security posture in dynamic and potentially volatile deployment environments. The cascading effects of well-implemented configuration management strategies naturally lead to improved software delivery timelines and reduced rollback frequency, reinforcing the effectiveness and efficiency of cloud-native solutions.

9.7 Automating Health Checks and Alerts

Automating health checks and alerts is a crucial strategy for maintaining the robustness and reliability of cloud-native applications. This section elucidates the methods and technologies employed to automate these processes and how they contribute to a proactive monitoring framework.

Health checks are operations that assess the operational aspects of a system to ensure they are functioning correctly at any given moment. Effective health checks should be comprehensive, encompassing various components from databases to individual microservices that make up the application architecture. Automation of these checks is essential in a cloud-native environment due to the dynamic and distributed nature of services.

Designing Automated Health Checks

When designing automated health checks, it is crucial to define what constitutes a healthy state for each component. The checks are typically HTTP endpoints that return a status code: a 200 OK status indicates health, whereas any other status might indicate issues. These endpoints should perform quick, stateless checks to determine the immediate health of the application. For microservices, a common practice is to implement a '/health' endpoint which performs several sub-checks, such as:

- Database connectivity and latency checks.

- External service dependency verification.

- Local system resource utilization, like CPU and memory usage.

- Application-specific checks, such as queue lengths or internal job completions statuses.

Below is an example of a simple health check implementation for a microservice in Python using a popular web framework, Flask:

```
1   from flask import Flask, jsonify
2   app = Flask(__name__)
3
4   @app.route('/health', methods=['GET'])
5   def health_check():
6       # Example check to verify database connectivity
7       if not check_database_connection():
8           return jsonify({'status': 'unhealthy'}), 500
9       return jsonify({'status': 'healthy'}), 200
10
11  def check_database_connection():
12      # Function to check database connectivity
13      # Implement actual database check here
14      return True
```

243

```
15
16   if __name__ == '__main__':
17       app.run(port=5000)
```

In the listing above, the microservice exposes a '/health' endpoint which internally calls a hypothetical check_database_connection function designed to verify database connectivity.

Automating Alerts Based on Health Check Failures

Once health checks are implemented, the next step involves setting up automated alerts to notify relevant personnel or automated systems when a check fails. This responsiveness is critical to mitigate issues before they escalate to affect the customer experience. Automation of alerts typically involves integrating with monitoring tools that support alerting features, such as Prometheus or Datadog.

Here is an example of how one might configure such alerts using Prometheus:

```
alert: ServiceHealthFailure
expr: up{job="my_microservice_health"} == 0
for: 5m
labels:
    severity: critical
annotations:
    summary: "Health check failed for microservice"
    description: "This alert fires when the health checks for the microservice have been failing for more than 5 minutes."
```

The configuration defines an alert ServiceHealthFailure that triggers if the health check metric up for the job labeled 'my_microservice_health' is zero for more than 5 minutes, suggesting the service is not healthy.

Lastly, integrating these alerts with notification systems like Slack, emails, or even automated ticketing systems ensures that the right teams are informed promptly to take necessary actions. In addition, the alerts can trigger automated workflows designed to mitigate known issues without human intervention, enhancing the system's resilience and availability. The automation of health checks and alerts not only decreases the time to detect and resolve incidents but also significantly reduces the probability of downtimes in cloud-native architectures.

9.8   Monitoring Network Traffic and Security

Monitoring network traffic and ensuring security in a cloud-native environment is essential due to the intrinsic complexity and dynamic nature of modern distributed systems. Effective network monitoring enables administrators to identify potential bottlenecks, malicious activities, and failures in real-time, thereby maintaining optimal performance and robust security posture.

Network Traffic Analysis

Network traffic analysis in a cloud-native environment involves the examination of the data packets flowing through the network to identify patterns, anomalies, and performance issues. This is achieved by capturing and analyzing metadata from the packets, such as source and destination IP addresses, port numbers, and protocol types.

To efficiently perform network traffic analysis, tools such as Wireshark or Tcpdump are commonly used. These tools help in capturing network packets, which can then be analyzed to detect anomalies or misconfigurations. The following lstlisting demonstrates a simple command to capture traffic using Tcpdump:

```
1   tcpdump -i eth0 -n 'port 80'
```

This command captures packets on interface eth0 that are destined for or originating from port 80, typically used for HTTP traffic. Analyzing this traffic can provide insights into the volume and type of HTTP requests, which is crucial for troubleshooting issues or detecting potential security threats.

The captured data can be further analyzed using network monitoring tools to generate reports and visualizations, providing a clear view of network health and activities. This approach allows IT teams to make informed decisions regarding network management and security policies.

Security Measures

In the context of security, monitoring network traffic becomes a vital component to ensure that the environment is free from unauthorized access and vulnerabilities. Implementing comprehensive security measures such as intrusion detection systems (IDS) and intrusion prevention systems (IPS) can help mitigate risks. These tools function by analyzing network traffic patterns and comparing them against a database of known attack signatures or anomalies.

The implementation of a typical IDS involves setting up sensors throughout the network, which report back to a central management console where the data is analyzed. Below is a pseudocode representation using `algorithm` that depicts the general workflow of an IDS:

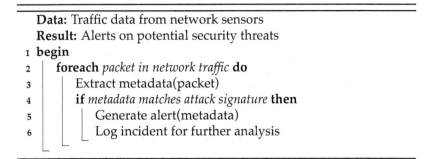

This algorithm highlights the process of metadata extraction from each packet and checks against predefined attack signatures. Alerts are generated for matched patterns, and incidents are logged for further investigation.

Enhancing Security Posture with Continuous Monitoring

Continuous monitoring of network traffic is paramount in handling evolving security threats. Tools like Network Performance Monitoring (NPM) and Security Information and Event Management (SIEM) systems can automate the monitoring processes and provide real-time analysis of security logs and network performance.

Integration of machine learning techniques with these tools can further enhance their capabilities by identifying new patterns and unknown threats based on behavioral analysis. For example, an abnormal increase in outbound traffic could indicate a data breach or exfiltration attempt, which can be quickly addressed by automated responses configured within the SIEM system.

Implementing a robust monitoring strategy for network traffic and security in cloud-native systems not only assists in maintaining operational continuity but also supports compliance with regulatory standards and best practices. This is essential as organizations increasingly rely on cloud technologies to drive business processes. The depth of visibility gained into network and security operations empowers organizations to preemptively resolve issues, minimizing potential downtime and loss while fortifying their defenses against cyber threats.

9.9 Maintenance Strategies for Cloud-Native Applications

Maintaining cloud-native applications involves a continuous observance and enhancement cycle to ensure they not only align with business needs but also take advantage of evolving cloud capabilities. This section outlines various strategies critical for maintaining the robustness, responsiveness, and efficiency of these applications.

The cornerstone of effective maintenance in cloud-native environments is the application of strategies that recognize and embrace the dynamic and distributed nature of cloud computing platforms. This includes adopting practices like immutable infrastructure, automated rollbacks, canary releases, and blue-green deployments.

- **Immutable Infrastructure**: Using immutable infrastructure where any changes needed require deploying a new version of infrastructure rather than altering the existing one. This approach avoids configuration drift issues and contributes to more reliable systems. For application updates, a new container or server instance is created, fully configured and ready to deploy. Once validated, traffic is shifted to the new instances, promoting a seamless upgrade process.

```
1  # Example of deploying updated container image in an immutable infrastructure
2  kubectl set image deployment/myapp myapp=myapp:new_version --record
```

```
deployment "myapp" image updated
```

- **Automated Rollbacks**: Setting up automated rollbacks to previous application versions if critical errors are detected post-deployment. This ensures service continuity by minimizing downtime and negative user experience. Implementation involves monitoring key performance indicators post-deployment and triggering a rollback if they deviate from established thresholds.

```
1  # Example of automated rollback using monitoring scripts to monitor service
     health
```

247

```
2  if ! check_service_health(service_url):
3      rollback_version("myapp")
```

Rolling back to previous stable version.

- **Canary Releases**: Partially rolling out new features to a small subset of users to gauge impact and functionality before full deployment. This mitigates risk by providing an environment to capture unanticipated bugs or issues without affecting the entire user base.

- **Blue-Green Deployments**: Maintaining two identical production environments, only one of which is live at any given time. When deploying a new version, the new release is done in the 'green' environment. After testing and validation, traffic is switched from the 'blue' to the 'green' environment, effectively reducing downtime and rollback complications.

```
1  # Command to switch traffic in a cloud environment
2  shift_traffic --source blue --target green
```

Traffic successfully shifted to green environment.

In addition to these strategic practices, the use of A/B testing enhances maintenance by allowing developers to present multiple variants of an application feature to different user segments, thereby comparing performance, usability, and user engagement metrics directly derived from real-world usage.

Moreover, the integration of comprehensive monitoring tools plays a substantial role in maintenance. These tools facilitate immediate detection and correction of issues, ensuring that applications remain healthy and perform optimally across all deployment stages. To illustrate, consider the impact of incorporating Application Performance Monitoring (APM) tools and logging frameworks, which continuously track application performance and log data respectively, aiding in swift remediation of any emerging issues.

Operational excellence in maintenance for cloud-native applications is achieved through consistent evaluation of these strategies, and refinement based on insights gained from ongoing operations. This continual adaptation not only aligns the application more closely with changing business requirements but also harnesses advancements in cloud technologies to improve scalability, reliability, and overall performance.

9.10 Implementing Auto-Scaling and Resource Optimization

Auto-scaling is a fundamental feature in cloud-native architectures that ensures applications dynamically scale resources based on real-time demand. This capacity not only enhances the efficiency of resource use but also maintains performance stability during variable workload conditions. The implementation of auto-scaling and resource optimization requires a thorough understanding of the underlying infrastructure, specific workload patterns, and understanding integration points with cloud-native monitoring tools.

Auto-Scaling Mechanisms

Auto-scaling can be implemented through two primary mechanisms: horizontal scaling and vertical scaling. Horizontal scaling, also known as scaling out and in, involves adding or removing instances of an application to match demand. Vertical scaling, or scaling up and down, on the other hand, adjusts the resources of an existing instance, such as CPU or memory.

For horizontal auto-scaling, cloud-native platforms like Kubernetes utilize controllers that monitor the performance of pods against predefined metrics such as CPU usage or custom metrics that an application emits. An example is shown below in Kubernetes configuration that scales based on CPU usage:

```
1   apiVersion: autoscaling/v1
2   kind: HorizontalPodAutoscaler
3   metadata:
4     name: example-autoscaler
5   spec:
6     scaleTargetRef:
7       apiVersion: apps/v1
8       kind: Deployment
9       name: example-application
10    minReplicas: 1
11    maxReplicas: 10
12    targetCPUUtilizationPercentage: 50
```

This configuration ensures that the number of pods of 'example-application' will increase when the CPU utilization exceeds 50%, ensuring that performance is not compromised due to insufficient resources.

Metrics for Auto-Scaling

Selecting the right metrics is crucial for effective auto-scaling. Essential metrics typically include CPU usage, memory usage, request rate, and response time. However, depending on the application's nature, custom metrics might be necessary to capture specific performance aspects that typical metrics do not cover.

For instance, an e-commerce website might want to scale based on the number of simultaneous users or shopping cart operations per second. Implementing custom metrics usually involves instrumenting the application's code with monitoring hooks:

```
1  from prometheus_client import Counter
2  c = Counter('shopping_cart_operations', 'Number of operations on shopping cart')
3  def add_to_cart(item):
4      c.inc() # Increment the counter
5      # Logic to add item to the shopping cart
```

Resource Optimization Strategies

Optimizing resources in a cloud-native environment not only conserves financial costs but also improves the application's ecological footprint. Techniques such as bin packing—where instances are packed efficiently into the fewest number of servers—can significantly reduce resource wastage. On cloud platforms, policies such as 'Preemptible VMs' or 'Spot Instances' offer further cost optimizations by utilizing unused capacity at lower prices.

Integration of predictive scaling can enhance resources' optimization by learning the application's demand patterns and preparing the environment ahead of anticipated load increases, using techniques from predictive analytics and machine learning. Here, historical data is utilized to forecast demand, which guides the scaling actions:

```
1  import numpy as np
2  import pandas as pd
3  from sklearn.linear_model import LinearRegression
4
5  # Load historical data
6  data = pd.read_csv('historical_data.csv')
7  X = data[['time_of_day']].values
8  y = data['demand'].values
9
10 # Create and train a linear regression model
11 model = LinearRegression()
12 model.fit(X, y)
13
14 # Predict demand for future time points
```

250

```
15   predicted_demand = model.predict(np.array([[12]]))  # Predict demand at noon
```

The synergy between real-time metrics and predictive models ensures that resources are optimally utilized, adapting promptly to both expected and unexpected changes in the workload.

By leveraging detailed metrics, effective scaling strategies, and predictive analytics, cloud-native systems can achieve both automated scaling and resource optimization—critical components in maintaining performance efficiently and cost-effectively. This approach not only reflects advanced resource management practices but also aligns with the dynamic, resilient nature of cloud-native environments.

9.11 Using Predictive Analysis for Proactive Maintenance

Predictive analysis within the framework of maintenance for cloud-native applications fundamentally transforms reactive maintenance strategies into a proactive approach. This method relies heavily on machine learning algorithms and data analysis techniques that forecast potential failures or issues before they impact the system's performance.

First, it is essential to distinguish between traditional monitoring and predictive analytics. While traditional methods focus on alerting the system administrators about issues as they occur, predictive analytics endeavors to predict and mitigate those issues beforehand. The core of predictive analysis involves the accumulation and examination of historical data to identify patterns or trends that could signify impending problems.

To implement predictive analysis in a cloud-native environment, the initial step involves data collection. Data from various sources such as logs, performance metrics, and other monitoring tools needs to be aggregated. This collected data serves as the training set for machine learning models. Here is an example of how you might collect system logs and performance data using a hypothetical logging tool:

```
1   # Example Python code for collecting logs and performance data
2   import logging
3   from system_monitor import fetch_performance_data
4
5   # Setup logging
6   logging.basicConfig(level=logging.INFO)
7
8   # Collect and log performance data
```

251

```
9   performance_data = fetch_performance_data()
10  logging.info("Performance Data Collected: %s", performance_data)
```

Once data collection is established, the next pivotal step is data pre-processing. This involves cleaning the data, handling missing values, normalizing datasets, and potentially transforming features to be more suitable for machine learning models.

```
1   import pandas as pd
2
3   # Example dataset
4   data = pd.read_csv('system_performance_logs.csv')
5
6   # Preprocessing steps
7   data = data.fillna(method='ffill') # Forward fill to handle missing values
8   normalized_data = (data - data.mean()) / data.std() # Normalization
```

After preprocessing, selecting a suitable model for analysis is crucial. Various algorithms can be employed, such as regression models, neural networks, or ensemble methods, depending on the complexity and nature of the data. The model is trained on the historical data to learn the patterns of failures or degradations.

Here is an example pseudocode for a machine learning model training process:

Algorithm 16: Example of using pseudocode in LaTeX

Data: YourInput
Result: How to write hello World!
1 initialization
2 **while** *Not at end of this document* **do**
3   read current
4   **if** *understand* **then**
5   go to next section
6   current section becomes this one
7   **else**
8   go back to the beginning of current section

Monitoring and analysis are continuous processes, where the trained model is applied to new, incoming data to predict potential issues. When the model predicts a failure or a degradation, alerts can be configured to notify the operations team, ensuring that they can act before users are impacted.

```
Example output from a predictive maintenance system:
WARNING: Potential degradation detected in module XYZ, predicted failure in 24 hours.
```

Utilizing predictive analysis shifts the maintenance paradigm from a reactive to a proactive stance, allowing for smarter resource allocation and more efficient system operation. Leveraging these techniques effectively increases the reliability of cloud-native applications and enhances overall operational efficiency. Continuous refinement of the models, together with regular updates based on new data and feedback, ensures that the predictive maintenance system evolves in alignment with the system it is monitoring.

9.12 Integrating Monitoring Tools with CI/CD Pipelines

Integrating monitoring tools within Continuous Integration/Continuous Deployment (CI/CD) pipelines is fundamental for enhancing the operational visibility and responsiveness of cloud-native applications. This integration facilitates early detection of issues during the deployment cycle, thereby reducing downtime and improving the reliability of releases. This section explores strategic approaches to this integration, with a focus on practical implementation.

CI/CD pipelines automate steps in software delivery, such as building code, running tests, and deploying to production environments. By embedding monitoring tools into these pipelines, teams can gain instant feedback on the impact of recent changes, enabling a more proactive approach to quality assurance and system stability.

Selection of Monitoring Tools: The first step in integration is the selection of appropriate monitoring tools that align with the organization's technology stack and operational goals. Tools such as Prometheus, Grafana, and ELK Stack are commonly used for monitoring various aspects of cloud-native applications. These tools can be configured to collect metrics, logs, and traces that provide insights into the application's performance and health.

- Prometheus is suitable for gathering time-series data about the application's operations.

- Grafana serves as a visualization platform for the data collected by Prometheus.

- ELK Stack (Elasticsearch, Logstash, Kibana) is effective for log data management and analysis.

253

Embedding Monitoring as a Pipeline Stage: Once the tools are selected, the next step is to embed monitoring as a distinct stage within the CI/CD pipeline. This involves setting up scripts or configuration files that trigger metrics collection and analysis during different pipeline stages.

```
1   # Example Jenkins pipeline script integrating Prometheus
2   pipeline {
3     agent any
4     stages {
5       stage('Build') {
6         steps {
7           sh 'make build'
8           post {
9             success {
10              script {
11                // Triggering Prometheus metrics collection
12                sh 'collect_metrics.sh'
13              }
14            }
15          }
16        }
17      }
18      stage('Test') {
19        steps {
20          sh 'make test'
21        }
22      }
23      stage('Deploy') {
24        steps {
25          sh 'make deploy'
26        }
27      }
28    }
29  }
```

Analyzing and Acting on Monitoring Data: Integrating monitoring tools is not solely about data collection. The real value lies in analyzing this data and acting upon it to improve the system. Configuration of alerts based on thresholds for performance metrics ensures that any anomalies are promptly addressed. Additionally, visualizing the performance trends over time assists in identifying patterns that might indicate deeper systemic issues.

```
Alert: CPU Usage Exceeded
Description: The CPU usage has exceeded the threshold of 85% for over 10 minutes.
Severity: High
Action: Investigate the high CPU usage and optimize the application performance.
```

Continuous Feedback Loop: Finally, it is crucial to establish a continuous feedback loop where insights gained from monitoring tools are used to refine the CI/CD process. This may involve adjusting pipeline configurations, updating application code, or tuning the operational environment. The goal is to evolve both the application and

254

the deployment process incrementally to achieve higher resilience and performance standards.

Integrating monitoring tools into CI/CD pipelines blends operational management with development processes, providing a holistic view of system performance throughout the application lifecycle. This approach not only speeds up issue detection and resolution but also drives a culture of continuous improvement within development teams. Achieving this integration effectively ensures that cloud-native applications operate efficiently and reliably in dynamic environments, maintaining high performance standards and adapting quickly to changes.

Chapter 10

Security Considerations in Microservices and Cloud-Native Systems

Security in microservices and cloud-native systems is critically important due to their distributed architecture and the extensive use of internet-facing services. This chapter explores the unique security challenges posed by these architectures, discussing strategies for securing inter-service communications, managing sensitive data, and implementing robust access controls. It also addresses the necessity of incorporating security into the development lifecycle to prevent breaches and ensure compliance with industry standards and regulations.

10.1 Understanding the Security Landscape in Microservices and Cloud-Native Systems

The move from monolithic to microservices and cloud-native architectures has introduced both new opportunities and challenges concerning security. Unlike monolithic systems where components are tightly integrated, microservices are decentralized and distributed. This distribution, though beneficial for scalability and flexibility, multiplies the potential vectors for security threats due to the increased number of services and communication points.

Increased Surface Area for Attacks

In microservices architectures, each service is a potential entry point for attacks. The inter-service communications typically occur over a network, which exposes services to network-related security threats such as man-in-the-middle attacks, eavesdropping, and session hijacking.

- The network layer must enforce Transport Layer Security (TLS) to secure these communications.

- Proper authentication and authorization mechanisms must be instituted for both users and services.

Furthermore, each microservice might be developed using different frameworks and languages which can lead to inconsistencies in security implementations and increased maintenance complexity.

Increased Configuration and Secret Management Complexity

The autonomous nature of microservices requires each service to manage its configuration and secrets (such as API keys and database passwords). The multiplicity and distribution of these secrets elevate the risks related to secret management:

- Secrets must be encrypted both at rest and in transit.

- Access to secrets must be securely controlled and regularly audited.

Failure in effective configuration and secrets management can lead to severe security breaches, making it essential for organizations to utilize robust tools and practices such as centralized secret managers that offer encryption, rotation, and fine-grained access controls.

Dependencies and External Services

Microservices often depend on external libraries and third-party services, which can introduce vulnerabilities if not properly managed:

- Regular scanning for vulnerabilities in third-party dependencies should be carried out.

- Employ automated tools to track and update these dependencies.

Such practices help in mitigating the risks from vulnerabilities that can be exploited via outdated software components.

Dynamic and Ephemeral Nature of Cloud-native Environments

Cloud-native environments are characterized by their dynamic and often ephemeral nature. Components such as containers can be spun up and down in response to demand, which introduces challenges for traditional security monitoring and management tools that expect more static deployments. Consequently:

- Security tools must be capable of handling rapidly changing environments.

- Implementations should ensure that even short-lived components are secured and monitored.

Moreover, the adoption of Infrastructure as Code (IaC) practices in these environments further necessitates rigorous security assessments of the code managing the infrastructure, to ensure that security standards are embedded from the beginning.

Regulatory Compliance and Data Governance

Compliance with industry standards and regulations becomes more complex in distributed systems. The system's wide geographical spread can interact with various jurisdictional requirements on data privacy such as GDPR, HIPAA, or CCPA.

- Data must be classified and handled according to its sensitivity.

- Audit trails must be maintained to track access and usage of sensitive data.

These controls are critical not only to comply with regulatory requirements but also to maintain the integrity and confidentiality of the data being handled.

The security landscape in microservices and cloud-native systems presents a complex array of challenges due to the increased attack surface, dependence on a plethora of external entities, dynamic operational models, and stringent compliance requirements. As these systems continue to evolve, a well-thought-out strategy encompassing dynamic security solutions, comprehensive management practices, and continuous compliance enforcement becomes indispensable for maintaining the confidentiality, integrity, and availability of systems and data.

10.2 Principles of Security in Distributed Systems

Distributed systems, particularly in the context of microservices and cloud-native architectures, must adhere to rigorous security protocols to mitigate risks associated with their expansive and decentralized nature. This section outlines fundamental security principles essential for maintaining robust security measures in these systems.

The Principle of Least Privilege

The principle of least privilege (PoLP) is a critical security strategy in distributed systems. It stipulates that a user, program, or system should have no more privilege than is necessary to perform its function. Applying PoLP minimizes the potential damage from accidents or attacks by limiting access rights for users, applications, and systems to the bare minimum necessary to perform their duties.

```
Example: A database management system that only has
the permissions necessary to read from and write to the database,
but not to alter its schemas or underlying system configurations.
```

Fail-Safe Defaults

In the context of security, fail-safe defaults ensure that, in the absence of explicit access granting, default configurations deny access. This principle defends against oversights in security configurations that could otherwise provide unintended access.

```
Example: A newly deployed microservice is by default not reachable
until access permissions are explicitly defined.
```

Economy of Mechanism

This principle suggests that simplicity in security mechanisms facilitates security. Complex designs introduce multiple attack surfaces and misconfigurations. Hence, security systems should be as simple as possible, making them easier to scrutinize and less error-prone.

```
Example: Using a single, well-reviewed authentication library
instead of multiple, potentially conflicting, security frameworks.
```

Complete Mediation

Complete mediation requires that every access to a resource must be checked for authorization. This prevents unauthorized access that might occur if an initial authentication step is bypassed or circumvented.

```
Example: Each API request is authenticated and authorized independently,
ensuring that changing conditions or context does not compromise security.
```

Open Design

Security through obscurity is a discouraged practice in security engineering. The open design principle advocates that the security of a system should not depend on the secrecy of its implementation or operation. Security measures should remain secure even if the attackers are aware of the security mechanisms and their implementation details.

```
Example: Encryption algorithms are public, and their security
does not rely on their implementation remaining opaque to outsiders.
```

Separation of Privileges

The separation of privileges principle dictates that a system should not rely on a single condition for privileges granting. By requiring multiple conditions, the security model ensures greater resistance against unauthorized actions or breaches.

```
Example: A user needs to both authenticate through a password and a biometric
input to access sensitive system components.
```

Least Common Mechanism

Minimizing the amount of mechanisms shared across different users or processes prevents accidental or malicious breaches of security. Shared mechanisms could lead to unintended privilege escalation or data leakage between processes that should be isolated.

```
Example: Separate database servers are used for application data and sensitive
user data, thereby limiting the common points of interaction.
```

Psychological Acceptability

Security mechanisms should not make the system cumbersome to users. If security measures are too restrictive or convoluted, users might seek ways to circumvent them, thus jeopardizing system security.

```
Example: Single Sign-On (SSO) capabilities allow users to access multiple
services through one set of login credentials, balancing security needs
with usability.
```

- Incorporating these principles requires vigilant adherence throughout the application's lifecycle, from design through deployment and maintenance.

- Ensuring that these principles are deeply embedded can help protect the infrastructure from a diverse array of threats while maintaining operational efficiency and compliance with regulatory frameworks.

These principles form the foundation of a secure distributed system and provide guidelines that help in designing, implementing, and maintaining security controls. It is essential that security measures and policies are continuously reviewed and adapted to the evolving threat landscape and technological advancements to maintain the integrity and confidentiality of the system.

10.3 Authentication and Authorization Strategies

Authentication and authorization form the backbone for secure access control in microservices and cloud-native architectures. Correct implementation of these strategies ensures that only legitimate users and services can access sensitive resources. This section delves into effective methods to implement both authentication and authorization in distributed systems.

Authentication Mechanisms

Authentication is the process of verifying the identities of users, computing entities, or services requesting access to resources. There are several standard authentication mechanisms suitable for microservices ecosystems:

- **Basic Authentication:** Involves sending a user name and password with each request. Although simple, this method is less secure and typically recommended to be used with SSL/TLS.

- **Token-based Authentication:** Uses security tokens (e.g., JSON Web Tokens - JWTs) that contain all necessary user data. This method is stateless and scales well with microservices architectures.

- **OAuth 2.0:** An open standard for access delegation commonly used as a way to authorize web and mobile applications by providing tokens instead of credentials.

- **OpenID Connect:** Built atop OAuth 2.0, this layer adds authentication on top of OAuth's authorization framework, enabling clients to verify the identity of the end user.

For practical application, consider the following example using JWTs for secure token-based authentication:

```
# Sample Python function to generate a JWT
import jwt
import datetime

def generate_jwt(user_id):
    payload = {
        'exp': datetime.datetime.utcnow() + datetime.timedelta(days=1),
```

```
8      'iat': datetime.datetime.utcnow(),
9      'sub': user_id
10  }
11  return jwt.encode(payload, 'SECRET_KEY', algorithm='HS256')
```

Authorization Techniques

Authorization, the process of determining if a specific authenticated
entity has the right to access a resource, can be implemented using
various models:

- **Role-Based Access Control (RBAC):** Entities are assigned to
roles, and access rights are set based on these roles. This model
is widely used due to its simplicity and effectiveness.

- **Attribute-Based Access Control (ABAC):** Decisions are based on
attributes of the user, resource, and environment. This model
offers finer-grained control and flexibility compared to RBAC.

- **Policy-Based Access Control (PBAC):** Utilizes policies that are
evaluated at runtime to make authorization decisions. This can
integrate with ABAC for dynamic scenarios.

Implementing RBAC in a microservices architecture can be exemplified
as follows:

```
1   # Example Python function for authorization using RBAC
2   def authorize(user_role, action, resource):
3       permissions = {
4           'admin': {'read': ['*'], 'write': ['*']},
5           'editor': {'read': ['*'], 'write': ['articles']},
6           'subscriber': {'read': ['articles']}
7       }
8
9       allowed_resources = permissions.get(user_role, {}).get(action, [])
10      return resource in allowed_resources or '*' in allowed_resources
```

Integrating Authentication and Authorization

Integrating authentication and authorization strategies into microservices and cloud-native systems necessitates consideration of how these
mechanisms interact. Inter-service communication protocols such as
gRPC or HTTPS should be employed to secure communications between services. Additionally, API gateways can provide a centralized

264

point to handle authentication and direct traffic accordingly while providing flexible authorization controls.

Furthermore, adopting a service mesh architecture, such as Istio or Linkerd, simplifies secure service-to-service communication. Underpinned by mutual TLS, a service mesh can enforce both authentication and authorization policies transparently, relieving individual services of this responsibility and embedding security uniformly across the ecosystem.

In practice, adapting these strategies involves deploying sidecar proxies and implementing policy configurations that align with organizational security requirements. A typical deployment might resemble the pseudocode:

Algorithm 17: Example process for inter-service communication in a service mesh

---

Result: Secure inter-service communication
1 initialization()
2 **while** *service operational* **do**
3 | authenticate request()
4 | authorize request based on policy()
5 | route request to destination()
6 | log result()
7 **end**

By meticulously integrating appropriate authentication and authorization strategies, microservices and cloud-native architectures can ensure a secure operating environment. This solid foundation not only enforces security but also facilitates compliance with various regulatory standards. The precise and systematic implementation of these security measures is a critical step towards realizing the full potential of distributed system architectures.

10.4 Securing Service-to-Service Communication

In the context of microservices and cloud-native architectures, service-to-service communication represents one of the critical facets where security must be robustly enforced. Various communication patterns, such as synchronous API calls, asynchronous messaging, and event-driven interactions, each introduce their own security risks and require tailored mitigation strategies to ensure confidentiality, integrity, and availability.

Encrypting Traffic with TLS: Transport Layer Security (TLS) is a fundamental technology used to secure communications between services. When configuring TLS, it is imperative to use strong cipher suites and up-to-date protocol versions to protect the data in transit against eavesdropping, tampering, and forgery. Consider the application of TLS as follows:

```
1   # Example configuration in Nginx to enforce the use of a strong TLS protocol
2   server {
3       listen 443 ssl;
4       server_name example.com;
5
6       ssl_certificate /etc/ssl/certs/example_com.crt;
7       ssl_certificate_key /etc/ssl/private/example_com.key;
8       ssl_protocols TLSv1.2 TLSv1.3;
9       ssl_ciphers 'EECDH+AESGCM:EDH+AESGCM';
10      ssl_prefer_server_ciphers on;
11  }
```

Implementing mTLS (Mutual TLS) further enhances this security by requiring both the client and the server to present certificates, thus ensuring mutual authentication which is particularly important in microservices environments where services frequently interact with each other.

Access Tokens for Authentication and Authorization: When securing service-to-service communication, it's crucial to correctly implement authentication and authorization mechanisms. JSON Web Tokens (JWT) are widely adopted for this purpose due to their versatility in carrying claims and being easily verifiable. To secure communications using JWT, follow these steps:

- Validate the authenticity of the JWTs using digital signatures.

- Ensure all tokens are transmitted over secure channels.

- Use scoped access tokens to limit the permissions granted to each service.

```
1   # Decoding and verifying a JWT using Python JWT library
2   import jwt
3
4   token = 'eyJ ...' # Your JWT token here
5   public_key = 'YOUR_PUBLIC_KEY'
```

```
6  decoded_token = jwt.decode(token, public_key, algorithms=['RS256'])
7  print(decoded_token)
```

Service Meshes for Enhanced Security: Service meshes such as Istio or Linkerd extend the security features inherent in modern microservices systems. They provide automated SSL/TLS encryption, in-built support for mTLS, fine-grained access control policies, and sophisticated traffic management capabilities. Configuring a service mesh can help in standardizing security practices across services without altering application code:

```
1  # Example Istio policy for enforcing mTLS in a service mesh
2  apiVersion: security.istio.io/v1beta1
3  kind: PeerAuthentication
4  metadata:
5    name: default
6    namespace: istio-system
7  spec:
8    mtls:
9      mode: STRICT
```

Rate Limiting and Anomaly Detection: In addition to traditional security mechanisms, rate limiting is essential to protect APIs from abuse and DoS attacks. Implementing rate limits can be performed at the ingress controller or by the application itself. Anomaly detection systems, either based on static rules or more advanced machine learning models, can identify and block unusual patterns in service-to-service communications which might indicate a security threat.

```
1  # Setting up a simple rate limit rule in Nginx
2  http {
3      limit_req_zone $binary_remote_addr zone=mylimit:10m rate=10r/s;
4      server {
5          location /api/ {
6              limit_req zone=mylimit burst=20;
7          }
8      }
9  }
```

Through the implementation of these techniques, organizations can significantly enhance the security posture of their microservices architectures. By encrypting all in-transit data, authenticating and authorizing service interactions carefully, utilizing service meshes, and employing additional protective mechanisms such as rate limiting and anomaly detection, the integrity and security of service-to-service communication can be effectively safeguarded. As these systems continue to evolve, staying abreast of emerging security threats and evolving mitigation strategies remains a critical activity for all stakeholders involved.

10.5 Data Encryption and Protection Techniques

When developing microservices and cloud-native systems, the protection and encryption of data is not merely an additional feature; it's an essential component of security architecture that ensures confidentiality and integrity of data, be it at rest or in transit. This section delves into the practical implementation of encryption protocols, strategies for data protection, and key management practices necessary to safeguard sensitive information effectively.

Encryption in transit is paramount to secure data as it moves between services, systems, or users and services. Transport Layer Security (TLS) is the industry standard for securing communications between clients and servers. Implementing TLS involves configuring both service and client to use SSL/TLS protocols, which ensure that data remains encrypted during its journey through networks possibly exposed to unauthorized entities.

```
1   # Configuration example in Apache server
2   SSLEngine on
3   SSLProtocol all -SSLv2 -SSLv3
4   SSLCertificateFile /path/to/your_domain_name.crt
5   SSLCertificateKeyFile /path/to/your_private.key
6   SSLCertificateChainFile /path/to/DigiCertCA.crt
```

For scenarios where TLS alone is insufficient due to advanced threat models, applying layered encryption like using IPsec for network level encryption can be considered. Each layer serves to add a barrier against potential intercepts or unauthorized access, thus providing a more robust protection model.

Data encryption at rest is key to protect against unauthorized access to data stored on physical media, in databases, file systems, or storage networks. This typically involves encrypting files on disk using symmetric encryption algorithms such as AES (Advanced Encryption Standard). Encryption can be implemented within database management systems or can be handled at the application level.

```
1   # Using PyCrypto library to encrypt data in Python
2   from Crypto.Cipher import AES
3   import base64
4
5   data = 'plaintext data to encrypt'
6   encryption_key = b'Sixteen byte key'
7
8   aes = AES.new(encryption_key, AES.MODE_CBC, 'This is an IV456')
9   encrypted_data = base64.b64encode(aes.encrypt(data))
```

```
10
11   print(encrypted_data)
```

When implementing encryption, it's essential to manage encryption keys rigorously. Keys must be protected and securely stored using a dedicated service like HashiCorp Vault, AWS Key Management Service (KMS), or Azure Key Vault. These services help automate the tasks of key creation, rotation, and revocation, thereby maintaining the security integrity over time.

- Ensure keys are rotated regularly, with old keys retired securely such that the data encrypted with older keys can still be accessed or re-encrypted.

- Employ least privilege principle whereby access to keys is strictly controlled and limited to roles that absolutely need it.

- Monitor access to keys closely, using logging and alerting to detect any unauthorized access attempts or anomalies in use.

Encryption's effectiveness hinges on the underlying algorithm's strength and the key management practices in place. Poor practices, such as reusing keys across different datasets or weak random key generation methods, can substantially weaken encryption assurances.

It is also imperative to comply with legal and regulatory standards governing data security, such as the General Data Protection Regulation (GDPR) for businesses operating in the EU, or the Health Insurance Portability and Accountability Act (HIPAA) for entities handling healthcare information in the United States. These regulations often prescribe specific encryption standards and key management practices, ensuring data protection that aligns with global security expectations.

Strategically, adopting a comprehensive protocol for data encryption and protection not only facilitates compliance but also builds trust with clients and users by demonstrating a commitment to safeguarding sensitive data from breaches and leaks. As data forms the lifeblood of many businesses, securing this critical asset must be a foundational component of any system's architecture, especially in the dynamically scaled environments of microservices and cloud-native systems.

10.6 Managing Secrets and Configuration Security

Managing secrets and configuration security is a critical aspect of maintaining the integrity and confidentiality of a microservices and cloud-native system. Secrets include credentials, tokens, keys, and other sensitive data that an application requires to interact securely with other services and resources. In a distributed architecture like microservices, the challenges of managing secrets exponentially increase due to the multiple, loosely coupled services that require secure configuration management.

The Importance of Centralized Secret Management

In traditional architectures, secrets are often dispersed across multiple locations and managed inconsistently. This practice poses significant security risks in cloud-native environments, where dynamic scaling and automated deployments are commonplace. Thus, centralizing secret management becomes imperative. Centralized secret management systems not only provide a uniform way to handle secrets but also are equipped with mechanisms to automate access control, auditing, and rotation of secrets.

Tools for Centralized Secret Management

Several tools are available to facilitate centralized secret management. HashiCorp's Vault is one of the leading tools, offering robust capabilities such as dynamic secrets, secure storage, leasing and renewal of secrets, and detailed audit logs. Similarly, AWS Secrets Manager and Azure Key Vault provide secure mechanisms to store and manage secrets used by cloud applications and services.

```
Example of using Vault to retrieve a secret:
$ vault kv get -field=my_password secret/data/myapp/config
```

Secure Transmission of Secrets

When secrets are transmitted over a network or moved between services, ensuring their secure transmission is vital. Utilizing encrypted communication channels such as HTTPS or secure RPC (Remote Procedure Call) protocols with TLS (Transport Layer Security) can mitigate the risk of interception by malicious actors.

Envelope Encryption

A recommended practice for enhancing the security of transmitted secrets is envelope encryption. In this model, a data encryption key (DEK) is used to encrypt data at rest, and this key itself is encrypted with a key encryption key (KEK), which is managed and rotated regularly by a centralized key management service.

```python
1   # Python example using envelope encryption
2   from cryptography.hazmat.backends import default_backend
3   from cryptography.hazmat.primitives.asymmetric import rsa
4   from cryptography.hazmat.primitives.asymmetric import padding
5   from cryptography.hazmat.primitives import hashes
6   from cryptography.hazmat.primitives.serialization import load_pem_public_key
7
8   # Assuming the public key is stored and retrieved securely
9   public_key = load_pem_public_key(public_key_pem, backend=default_backend())
10  encrypted_dek = public_key.encrypt(
11      data_encryption_key,
12      padding.OAEP(
13          mgf=padding.MGF1(algorithm=hashes.SHA256()),
14          algorithm=hashes.SHA256(),
15          label=None))
```

Configuration Management Practicing Least Privilege

Configuration management, which involves handling and deployment of configurations across multiple services, must adhere to the principle of least privilege. Each service should have access only to the secrets and configurations that are necessary for its operation, and no more. Oversharing of credentials and configuration data can lead to security breaches if any single component of the system is compromised.

- Audit configurations and update permissions regularly.

- Use role-based access controls to enforce minimum necessary permissions.

- Segregate environments and manage their configurations separately to avoid leaks and unintended access.

Automated Secret Rotation and Expiry

Automating the rotation of secrets is essential for minimizing the risk associated with potentially exposed credentials. Automated rotations reduce the timeframe during which an exposed secret can be exploited by a malicious entity. Furthermore, setting an expiry date on secrets forces periodic verification and renewal, thus enhancing the security posture.

Implementing Secret Rotation Policies

Using automation tools like Kubernetes' Secrets, Chef, or Ansible can help implement and manage rotation policies. Cloud services such as AWS Secrets Manager also support automated rotations, making it easier to integrate into the CI/CD pipeline of microservices architectures.

Example of an automated rotation policy in AWS Secrets Manager:

```
{
    "Version": "2012-10-17",
    "Statement": [
        {
            "Effect": "Allow",
    ...
```

As microservices and cloud-native systems continue to evolve, the strategies to manage secrets and configurations must also advance. Implementing robust centralized management, securing transmission, enforcing least privilege in configuration management, and automating the rotation and expiry of secrets are all paramount practices. These combined efforts help mitigate risks and enhance the overall security framework within a dynamic distributed system environment, contributing to the reliable and secure operation of business-critical applications.

10.7   Implementing Robust Access Control Measures

Access control is a fundamental aspect of security in any software architecture, but it takes on additional complexity in a microservices or cloud-native environment. In these distributed systems, ensuring that only authorized users can access specific services, data, or resources becomes significantly more challenging because of the sheer number of independent and often dynamically scaled services. This section discusses the implementation of robust access control measures tailored for microservices architectures, including role-based access control (RBAC), attribute-based access control (ABAC), and the importance of identity and access management (IAM) systems.

Role-Based Access Control (RBAC)

RBAC is a widely used access control mechanism that restricts system access based on the roles of individual users within an enterprise. In the context of microservices, roles are defined according to user responsibilities and the nature of the interaction with the services. Access to resources is granted based on the assigned role rather than the identity of the individual, offering a simplified, yet effective means to control the capabilities of different user types when interacting with various services.

```
1   // Example of RBAC policy
2   {
3     "Role": "Service Operator",
4     "Permissions": [
5       "startService",
6       "stopService",
7       "monitorService"
8     ]
9   }
```

In the above example, a service operator is granted permissions to start, stop, and monitor services. Each service in a microservices architecture checks these permissions before allowing operations related to service lifecycle management.

Attribute-Based Access Control (ABAC)

Unlike RBAC, ABAC provides more granular access control and offers flexibility by using policies that combine multiple attributes, rather than roles alone. Attributes can include user attributes (e.g., organization, role, clearance level), environmental attributes (e.g., time of access, location), and resource attributes (e.g., resource owner, sensitivity of the data).

A typical ABAC implementation requires a policy enforcement point (PEP) that intercepts access requests, a policy decision point (PDP) that makes decisions based on access policies, and a policy information

point (PIP) that provides additional information necessary to make the
decision.

```
1   // Example of ABAC rule
2   {
3     "Rule": "Allow access if user role is admin and resource sensitivity is low",
4     "User": {
5       "Role": "Admin"
6     },
7     "Resource": {
8       "Sensitivity": "Low"
9     },
10    "Action": "Allow"
11  }
```

Here, an access policy is defined where users with an admin role are
allowed to access only resources classified with low sensitivity. This
demonstrates how ABAC's flexibility supports complex access controls
scenarios.

Identity and Access Management (IAM)

IAM systems are crucial for managing identities and permissions
across a microservices architecture. An IAM system generally provides
the following functionalities:

- User Authentication: Confirming the identity of users by requiring credentials, such as passwords, biometrics, or other verification methods.

- User Authorization: Determining if a user is allowed to perform a
  requested action based on the established access control policies.

- Credential Management: Facilitating secure management of user
  credentials and access rights.

Integrating IAM systems with microservices architectures typically involves the use of security tokens, such as JSON Web Tokens (JWT),
that encapsulate user identity and claims information. The token is
presented to the services, enabling them to ascertain both the identity
and the associated permissions of the bearer.

```
1   // Example of JWT payload
2   {
3     "sub": "1234567890",
4     "name": "John Doe",
5     "admin": true,
6     "exp": 1516239022
7   }
```

In the payload of a JWT shown above, the subject (sub) field contains a unique identifier for the user, the name field shows the user's name, and the admin field indicates administrative privileges. The exp (expiry) field represents the expiration timestamp after which the token is no longer valid.

Managing a robust access control system in microservices involves careful planning and implementation of security practices tailored to the operational and business requirements. The practices outlined above should be adapted and extended based on specific security needs, ensuring safe and controlled inter-service communications and data interactions. These provisions, when strategically implemented, can uphold the principles of least privilege, ensuring that users and services have no more access than necessary to perform their functions. This capability is critical in minimizing potential vulnerabilities and safeguarding against both internal and external threats.

10.8 Security Testing: Best Practices and Tools

Security testing is an integral part of ensuring that a microservices and cloud-native architecture is robust against potential threats and vulnerabilities. This section delves into the best practices for security testing in these environments and discusses various tools that aid in maintaining security standards.

Best Practices for Security Testing: Security testing in microservices and cloud-native systems should be continuous, comprehensive, and integrated into the CI/CD pipeline. The following practices are essential:

- **Integrate Security Testing Early**: Security tests should be integrated into the development lifecycle as early as possible. This practice, often referred to as "shifting left," ensures that security considerations are not an afterthought but a priority from the start of software development.

- **Automate Security Tests**: Automation of security tests promotes consistency and ensures that security checks are performed regularly without manual intervention. Automated tests can be run as part of the continuous integration process each time the codebase is updated.

- **Test Separately and in Combination**: While testing individual microservices in isolation is crucial, testing how they interact is equally important. This approach helps uncover vulnerabilities that only arise during the interaction between services.

- **Include Dynamic and Static Analysis**: Utilizing both static application security testing (SAST) for examining source code for security flaws and dynamic application security testing (DAST) for testing the running application exposes different types of vulnerabilities.

- **Perform End-to-End Encryption Tests**: Since microservices often communicate over networks, it's critical to test the encryption and security protocols that protect data in transit and ensure they meet the required standards.

Tools for Security Testing: Selecting the right tools is crucial for effective security testing. Below are several types of tools that should be considered:

- **Static Application Security Testing (SAST) Tools**: Tools such as SonarQube, Checkmarx, or Fortify are used for scanning source code to detect security vulnerabilities early in the development phase. They are typically integrated into IDEs and source control systems.

- **Dynamic Application Security Testing (DAST) Tools**: Tools like OWASP ZAP and Burp Suite are used for identifying security vulnerabilities in running applications. These tools simulate attacks on the application and analyze the responses.

- **Container Security Tools**: Given the prevalent use of containers in microservices, tools like Aqua Security, Sysdig Secure, and Anchore Engine offer specialized scanning capabilities for container images to detect vulnerabilities and misconfigurations.

- **Secrets Management Tools**: Managing secrets securely is critical in microservices architectures. HashiCorp Vault, AWS Secrets Manager, and Azure Key Vault provide mechanisms to securely store and access sensitive data like passwords, tokens, and API keys.

- **Compliance and Infrastructure as Code Scanning Tools**: Tools such as Terraform Compliance and Chef InSpec allow teams to enforce security policies and compliance as part of the infrastructure provisioning process.

The establishment of an efficient security testing practice in microservices and cloud-native systems necessitates not only the right tools but also a cultural commitment to security. Teams should foster an environment where security is everyone's responsibility, continuously educated upon, and informed by the latest industry trends and insights. Additionally, leveraging these tools to their fullest potential and integrating them into the daily development process ensures that security testing becomes an integral part of the workflow, promoting the development of safer, more secure software applications.

10.9 Compliance and Auditing in a Microservices Environment

Understanding Legal Requirements and Standards

Legal and regulatory requirements in microservices and cloud-native environments are pertinent to ensuring that systems handle data securely and perennially comply with applicable laws. Regulatory bodies often enforce standards and frameworks such as the General Data Protection Regulation (GDPR), the Payment Card Industry Data Security Standard (PCI DSS), and the Health Insurance Portability and Accountability Act (HIPAA). Each of these sets mandatory requirements for managing and protecting data, particularly sensitive personal and payment information, and they necessitate specific auditing procedures to verify compliance.

Microservices architectures must be configured to flexibly adapt to these regulations, ensuring that services can isolate data and implement layers of protection appropriate to the compliance requirements. For example, ensuring encryption of personal data both at rest and in transit could be stipulated under GDPR. Developing a thorough understanding of these regulations is crucial, as non-compliance can result in hefty fines and damage to reputation.

Role of DevOps in Enabling Continuous Compliance

Using the DevOps culture to synergize development with operations
in the realm of compliance can yield numerous benefits in maintaining
continuous adherence to prescribed legal and procedural standards.
Implementing compliance as code is a progressive strategy, integrating
regulatory compliance into automated deployment processes. This
approach uses scripts and automation tools to instantiate and enforce
compliance measures throughout the development pipeline, reducing
human errors and accelerating compliance checks.

```
1   # Example: Automating compliance checks in a CI/CD pipeline
2   name: "Compliance-Check-Workflow"
3   on: [push, pull_request]
4   jobs:
5     compliance_job:
6       runs-on: ubuntu-latest
7       steps:
8       - uses: actions/checkout@v2
9       - name: Run compliance checks
10        run: compliance-check-tool --config compliance_rules.yml
```

Security Audit Mechanisms for Microservices

Conducting audits in microservices architectures involves several layers of inspection and review, targeting different aspects such as network traffic, data access, and configuration management. Implementing centralized logging is a fundamental approach. All microservices
log their actions to a central repository, enabling auditors to piece
together a comprehensive view of the activity across services.

```
2023-03-15 14:22:33 AUTHSERVICE [INFO] User authentication successful for userID: 9453
2023-03-15 14:22:35 ORDERSERVICE [NOTICE] Order 122534 placed by userID: 9453
2023-03-15 14:24:12 PAYMENTSERVICE [WARNING] Payment declined for Order 122534 by userID: 9453
```

Additional mechanisms include periodic snapshots of configurations
and dependencies, ensuring that each microservice complies with the
security baselines. Tools such as Kubernetes' built-in features, like
Pod Security Policies (PSP) or Open Policy Agent (OPA), can automate
compliance by enforcing policies at different stages of deployment.

- Ensuring dependencies are up-to-date and audited for vulnerabilities.

- Automatically applying security patches.

- Auditing changes to configurations and environments.

278

Adaptability to Evolving Compliance and Legal Landscape

The realm of regulations and standards is perpetually evolving, with amendments and additions being commonplace. Microservices architectures, with their loosely coupled and independently deployable nature, offer adaptability in responding to such changes. This adaptability allows organizations to implement updates in a targeted fashion, without the need to overhaul entire systems.

To ensure this adaptability remains efficiently manageable:

- Service versioning should be handled meticulously, preserving backward compatibility while enforcing new compliance measures as they become mandated.

- Regular training and updates for development teams on the latest regulatory changes can aid in maintaining a culture of compliance.

- Utilization of external consultants or legal experts to periodically review and update compliance practices and strategies.

Assuring compliance and facilitating comprehensive auditing in microservices architectures is challenging due to the decentralized nature of these systems. However, with careful planning and the integration of compliance and audit mechanisms into DevOps practices, organizations can build systems well-equipped to handle current and future regulatory demands. Continuous monitoring and adaptation to changes, supported by automated tools and a well-informed team, are pivotal in preserving the integrity and legality of microservices environments. Properly implemented, these strategies not only mitigate the risk of non-compliance but also fortify the security framework of the entire architecture.

10.10 Handling Security Incidents and Breach Preparedness

The effective management of security incidents and breaches is paramount in microservices and cloud-native environments due to the complex and distributed nature of these systems. A security incident can be defined as any unauthorized access, misuse, or damage to the system or data. This section delves into the structured approach to handling security incidents and maintaining preparedness for potential breaches.

Incident Response Plan: Every organization deploying microservices should develop an incident response plan. This plan outlines the procedures to follow when a security breach occurs, ensuring a quick, organized, and effective response. The key components of an incident response plan include:

- **Identification:** This involves detecting and acknowledging the breach or incident. Effective monitoring tools and logging systems are essential in identifying anomalies quickly. For example, monitoring could be set up to detect unusual patterns of requests to a microservice or unexpected data retrieval volumes that could indicate a data breach.

- **Containment:** Once an incident is identified, the immediate step is to contain it to prevent further damage. This includes temporary measures such as cutting off the affected parts of the network or the particular microservices.

- **Eradication:** After containment, the cause of the incident must be found and eradicated. This could involve patching software, closing security loopholes, or upgrading systems that were exploited by the attackers.

- **Recovery:** The next step is to safely restore and restart services that were impacted. This should be done in stages, ensuring that security measures are effective and that the system is not still vulnerable.

- **Lessons Learned:** After an incident, it's crucial to analyze what happened and why. Improving future response and preventive measures hinges on understanding every aspect of how the incident occurred and was handled.

Breach Detection Systems: Implementing advanced breach detection systems is key to identifying and mitigating threats early. Features of an effective breach detection system include:

- **Intrusion detection systems (IDS)** that monitor network traffic for suspicious activity and known threats.

- **Anomaly Detection Tools** that use machine learning to detect deviations from normal operational patterns which may be indicative of a breach.

- **Log Analysis Tools** that help in examining logs to find irregular patterns and sequences of events that suggest malpractice.

Example code for setting up a basic anomaly detection model using Python's Scikit-learn library would look like this:

```
1   from sklearn.ensemble import IsolationForest
2   import numpy as np
3
4   # Generate sample data
5   rng = np.random.RandomState(42)
6   X = 0.3 * rng.randn(100, 2)
7   X_train = np.r_[X + 2, X - 2]
8   X_test = 0.3 * rng.randn(20, 2) + 1
9
10  # Fit the model
11  clf = IsolationForest(max_samples=100, random_state=rng)
12  clf.fit(X_train)
13
14  # Predict anomalies
15  y_pred_test = clf.predict(X_test)
```

Effective training and awareness programs ensure that all individuals involved know their roles and responsibilities in the incident response process. Regular drills and simulations can prepare the team for actual incidents, making the actual response more fluent and less prone to errors.

Maintaining breach preparedness is an ongoing process. Regular audits and assessments should be performed to ensure that both the technology and the response procedures are kept up-to-date with current threats. Organizations should ensure compliance with regulations such as the General Data Protection Regulation (GDPR) for data protection and privacy.

To summarize, handling security incidents effectively in microservices and cloud-native systems requires a robust preparedness strategy, quick response mechanisms, and ongoing staff training. The sophistication of these architectures demands a dynamic and proactive approach to security and breach management. By embracing these practices, organizations can mitigate potential damages and uphold their security posture in the event of a security incident or breach.

10.11 Using AI and Machine Learning for Security Enhancements

The utilization of Artificial Intelligence (AI) and Machine Learning (ML) in enhancing the security of microservices and cloud-native systems is an evolving discipline that leverages the capabilities of AI to detect, analyze, and respond to security threats in real time. This section delineates the application of AI and ML technologies to augment security measures in these distributed environments.

AI and ML models can analyze vast quantities of data from network traffic, access logs, and other sources to detect anomalies that may indicate a security threat. By training these models with historical data, they learn to identify patterns and deviations that are indicative of malicious activities such as unauthorized access, data breaches, or distributed denial-of-service (DDoS) attacks.

Anomaly Detection Using Machine Learning

Machine learning models are particularly effective at identifying anomalies that deviate from normal operational patterns. For example, a sudden spike in traffic from a particular IP address can be flagged for further investigation. This capability is crucial in a microservices architecture where services may scale dynamically and traditional threshold-based monitoring tools might fail to adapt.

Applying ML for anomaly detection involves several steps:

- Collecting and preprocessing data: Data from logs, network traffic, and usage patterns is aggregated and preprocessed to form a suitable input for training.

- Feature selection: Selecting the most relevant features that contribute to the accuracy of the model in detecting anomalies.

- Model training: Using historical data, the model is trained to learn the normal operational baseline of the system.

- Anomaly detection: The trained model continuously evaluates new data, identifying anomalies based on learned patterns.

Predictive Security Posturing

Integrating AI into security mechanisms allows for predictive security measures, where potential threats are anticipated and mitigated before they can impact the system. By analyzing trends and evolving patterns from the data collected, AI models can predict potential security vulnerabilities and suggest actions to preemptively resolve them.

This predictive capability requires robust training of the models to accurately forecast threats based on a variety of indicators such as unusual user behavior, risky configuration changes, or signs of external threats like phishing and malware.

Automated Threat Response Systems

Once a potential threat is identified, the next step is responding to it effectively. AI-driven automated response systems can perform a variety of actions in real time to mitigate or contain the detected threat. This includes tasks like isolating affected microservices, revoking access tokens, or initiating backup protocols.

```
1   # Sample code for an automated threat response system
2   def isolate_service(service_id):
3       print(f"Isolating service {service_id}")
4       # Additional code to isolate the service
5
6   def revoke_tokens(user_id):
7       print(f"Revoking tokens for user {user_id}")
8       # Additional code to revoke user tokens
9
10  # Example usage
11  if anomaly_detected:
12      isolate_service(service_to_isolate)
13      revoke_tokens(affected_user_id)
```

```
Output example when an anomaly is detected:
Isolating service 123
Revoking tokens for user 456
```

| Alert Generation | ⟶ | Analysis | ⟶ | Automated Action |

The diagram above illustrates a simplified workflow of an automated threat response system. The process starts with alert generation, followed by analysis, and concluding with automated actions.

The integration of AI and ML in security operations of microservices and cloud-native systems represents a significant advance in tackling the complex security challenges associated with these architectures. By automating detection, analysis, and response activities, organizations can enhance their security posture more effectively and reduce the time to react to potential threats. Moreover, the continued development and improvement of AI technologies promise even greater capabilities in the future, potentially transforming how security is implemented in distributed systems.

10.12   Continuous Security in DevOps Workflows

Continuous security, or the practice of integrating security measures throughout the DevOps pipeline, is paramount in maintaining the integrity and security of microservices and cloud-native architectures. By embedding security protocols into the development, deployment, and maintenance phases, organizations can avert security pitfalls that typically arise in traditional development models where security is often an afterthought.

Embedding Security into DevOps Pipelines

To effectively embed security within the DevOps workflow, teams must undertake specific automated and manual security tasks at different phases of the CI/CD pipeline. Firstly, during the coding phase, static application security testing (SAST) tools should be integrated into the version control systems to scan the code for potential vulnerabilities as soon as it is committed.

```
1   # Example of integrating a SAST tool into a Gitlab CI pipeline
2   stages:
3     - analysis
4   sast:
5     stage: analysis
6     script:
7       - ./run-sast-tool.sh
8     tags:
9       - security
10    only:
11      - main
```

This code snippet configures a CI pipeline to execute a static analysis tool script whenever the main branch is updated, thereby facilitating immediate feedback on security vulnerabilities introduced by new changes.

Next, in the build stage, dependency scanning tools should be employed to verify both direct and transitive dependencies of your application for known security flaws. These tools can be integrated into your build system.

```
1   # Dependency scanning integration into a Jenkins build script
2   pipeline {
3       agent any
4       stages {
5           stage('Dependency Check') {
6               steps {
7                   sh 'dependency-check --project "MyProject" --out . --scan .'
8               }
9               post {
10                  always {
11                      archiveArtifacts artifacts: 'dependency-check-report.*',
                            fingerprint: true
12                  }
13              }
14          }
15      }
16  }
```

In the context of deploying microservices to a cloud-native architecture, dynamic application security testing (DAST) must be performed on the staging or pre-production environments. This step ensures that runtime conditions are evaluated, identifying vulnerabilities that only surface when the application is fully operational.

Automating Security Remediations

Automation does not stop at the detection of vulnerabilities; it extends into the realm of remediation. Once a security issue is detected, automated workflows can be designed to remediate these vulnerabilities or to escalate them based on pre-defined criteria.

- If a vulnerability is detected as critical and can be resolved by updating a dependent library, the system can trigger an automated pull request or patch to update the library to a secure version.

- For less critical vulnerabilities, the system might generate a notification or alert for manual review during non-critical operation windows.

The coupling of automated testing and automated remediation ensures that security vulnerabilities are not only identified quickly but are also addressed expeditiously, thereby reducing the window of exposure and enhancing the overall security posture.

Proactive Security Measures and DevSecOps Culture

Instilling a culture of security among the development and operations teams (DevSecOps) is as crucial as integrating technical tools and processes. This cultural shift involves training teams on the best security practices, encouraging proactive security discussions during design reviews, and fostering an environment where security considerations are viewed as important as functionality and performance.

Engaging in regular security training and maintaining awareness of new security threats and mitigation techniques are essential practices within this culture. Besides, promoting an open dialogue about security between the developers, operations staff, and security teams reduces the friction that traditionally exists and speeds up the security response times.

Monitoring and Response in Continuous Security

Continuous monitoring of applications in production is crucial to detect and respond to security incidents that may arise. Modern monitoring tools not only track the performance but also scrutinize the behavior of the application to flag anomalies that could suggest a security compromise.

```
1  # An example snippet for configuring a security monitoring tool
2  rules:
3    - alert: HighHTTPRequestRate
4      expr: rate(http_requests_total[5m]) > 100
5      for: 10m
6      labels:
7        severity: critical
8      annotations:
9        summary: High HTTP request rate detected
```

This monitoring rule triggers an alert if the rate of HTTP requests exceeds a threshold, indicative of a potential DoS attack or other suspicious activity. Such detections can be tied to automated or manual incident response procedures.

Implementing continuous security in DevOps workflows closes many of the gaps that exist in traditional security models and enhances the overall defense mechanisms within microservices and cloud-native systems. With the proactive embedding of security measures, automation of detection and remediation, and fostering a strong culture of security awareness, organizations position themselves to dramatically mitigate risks in their DevOps environments.

www.ingramcontent.com/pod-product-compliance
Lightning Source LLC
LaVergne TN
LVHW051436050326
832903LV00030BD/3116